Beginning SQL Server Modeling

Model-Driven Application Development in SQL Server 2008

Bart Weller

Apress®

Beginning SQL Server Modeling: Model-Driven Application Development in SQL Server 2008

Image copyright notices and permissions:

      Page 1: ©iStockphoto.com/tompics
      Page 13: ©iStockphoto.com/tiridifilm
      Page 33: ©iStockphoto.com/EricHood
      Page 81: ©iStockphoto.com/seamartini
      Page 115: ©iStockphoto.com/Leadinglights
      Page 137: By permission of the Master and Fellows of St John's College, Cambridge, UK, and Ned Lee
            Fielden
      Page 163: ©iStockphoto.com/pavlen

ISBN-13 (pbk): 978-1-4302-2751-9

ISBN-13 (electronic): 978-1-4302-2752-6

Printed and bound in the United States of America 9 8 7 6 5 4 3 2 1

      Publisher and President: Paul Manning
      Lead Editor: Mark Beckner
      Development Editor: Ewan Buckingham
      Technical Reviewer: Fabio Claudio Ferrachiatti
      Editorial Board: Clay Andres, Steve Anglin, Mark Beckner, Ewan Buckingham, Gary Cornell, Jonathan
            Gennick, Jonathan Hassell, Michelle Lowman, Matthew Moodie, Duncan Parkes, Jeffrey Pepper, Frank
            Pohlmann, Douglas Pundick, Ben Renow-Clarke, Dominic Shakeshaft, Matt Wade, Tom Welsh
      Coordinating Editors: Candace English and Debra Kelly
      Copy Editor: Kim Benbow
      Compositor: Bytheway Publishing Services
      Indexer: Brenda Miller
      Artist: April Milne
      Cover Designer: Anna Ishchenko

Distributed to the book trade worldwide by Springer-Verlag New York, Inc., 233 Spring Street, 6th Floor, New York, NY 10013. Phone 1-800-SPRINGER, fax 201-348-4505, e-mail **orders-ny@springer-sbm.com**, or visit **www.springeronline.com**.

For information on translations, please e-mail **rights@apress.com**, or visit **www.apress.com**.

Apress and friends of ED books may be purchased in bulk for academic, corporate, or promotional use. eBook versions and licenses are also available for most titles. For more information, reference our Special Bulk Sales–eBook Licensing web page at **www.apress.com/info/bulksales**.

The source code for this book is available to readers at **www.apress.com**. You will need to answer questions pertaining to this book in order to successfully download the code.

To: Kathie—wife and companion
Riley, Grady, Sallie, and Brook—the future
Future generations, with sincere apologies from the present
Willy—a great llama and herd jester; may he rest in peace

Contents at a Glance

Contents

About the Author

■ **Bart Weller** is a software developer and consultant specializing in object-oriented software development. Over the years he has worked on a system simulation of a satellite command and control system, a laser remote sensing system for measuring trace amounts of atmospheric pollutants, and scientific instrumentation systems for NASA's Apollo Skylab. Enterprise business applications he has worked on include an online commodities trading system, several insurance applications, and a telecommunications network. He currently divides his time between working part-time at Colorado Mountain College and writing. He lives in the central Rockies of Colorado with his wife, his dog Duffey (named in honor of the late John Duffey, former lead tenor and mandolin player with The Seldom Scene), two country cats, and seven llamas, some of whom are happy to hike with him. He is a volunteer DJ at the local community radio station, and his hobbies are clearing deadfall and fixing things. Among the people he admires are Albert Einstein, Abraham Lincoln, Alan Kay, Patch Adams, and J.J. Cale.

About the Technical Reviewer

■ **Fabio Claudio Ferrachiatti** is a senior consultant and a senior analyst/developer of Microsoft technologies. He works for Brain Force at its Italian branch (www.brainforce.it). He is a Microsoft Certified Solution Developer for .NET, a Microsoft Certified Application Developer for .NET, and a Microsoft Certified Professional, as well as a prolific author and technical reviewer. Over the past ten years, he's written articles for Italian and international magazines and coauthored more than ten books on a variety of computer topics.

Acknowledgments

I would like to acknowledge the patience, hard work, and great advice of my coordinating editors, Candace English and Debra Kelly. Mark Beckner, member of the Apress editorial board, served as Lead Editor on this project, and first suggested the book, lo so many months ago, back in the days when the project was still known by the code name "Oslo." Both Mark and Ewan Buckingham, Development Editor with Apress and also a member of the editorial board, provided technical comments and suggestions on how to improve the drafts. Fabio Ferracchiati and Roy Brandt provided technical reviews of the early chapter drafts.

Kraig Brockschmidt and David Matson with the Microsoft SQL Server Modeling team provided outstanding technical help when the need arose. Lars Corneliussen also provided helpful feedback. Thank you all, gentlemen.

I would also like to thank my wife, Kathie, for her constant support and for enduring long hours with me closeted in a dim and cluttered office, sipping old coffee and glowering at my laptop.

And finally, many thanks to Dr. Meeta Goel and my co-workers at Colorado Mountain College— Barb Johnson, Ashiyana Regmi, Vee Kinion, Jonathan Hansen, and Melissa DeHaan—for their unflagging patience with bad moods and long absences from the office.

The making of a book always involves a surprising number of people, most of whose names remain unknown to the author. I hope at least some of them might see these words and accept my appreciation.

Bart Weller

Introduction

SQL Server Modeling is Microsoft's new model-driven .NET framework for rapidly designing and building software applications. In the past, software has traditionally been developed from static models or requirements—the data (e.g., inventory, customer data, or financial) can change over time, but the model structure and logic remain fixed in code that may have been developed and compiled years ago.

Model-driven development, as reflected in the SQL Server Modeling .NET framework, supports the design and creation of more dynamic applications where the model can change over time. This form of agile development, with much shorter release cycles, is ideal for businesses operating in rapidly changing technological, regulatory, and competitive environments: The list covers a broad gamut of IT-intensive enterprises. Examples might include financial services, insurance, telephony, and high-tech manufacturing. Shorter release cycles enabled by model-driven development can significantly enhance the competitiveness and agility of these kinds of enterprises.

Another advantage of SQL Server Modeling is that it enables stakeholders not trained as programmers to create a business or process model using a modeling tool (called Quadrant), and immediately generate executable code based on their model. This enables business owners, managers, and others to become involved in a quick, iterative refinement process for designing and testing the model and application over a much shorter release cycle than would be possible with more traditional approaches.

As Bob Muglia, President of Microsoft Server & Tools Business, said,

> *"The benefits of modeling have always been clear, but traditionally only large enterprises have been able to take advantage of it and on a limited scale. We are making great strides in extending these benefits to a broader audience by focusing on three areas. First, we are deeply integrating modeling into our core .NET platform; second, on top of the platform, we then build a very rich set of perspectives that help specific personas in the lifecycle get involved; and finally, we are collaborating with partners and organizations like OMG [Object Management Group] to ensure we are offering customers the level of choice and flexibility they need."*

SQL Server Modeling includes the following components, all of which are covered in this book:

- **SQL Server Modeling Services**—Where the specifics of the model entities and relationships all reside, and which provides the Base Domain Library consisting of pre-built patterns and services ready to be leveraged to your modeling needs.
- **Quadrant**—A modeling tool for creating and modifying the model.
- **Intellipad**—Short for Intellisense Workpad , this is a text-based code editor incorporating Microsoft's implementation of code-autocompletion. It also the basis of the code-editing part of Quadrant.

- **The M Programming Language**—Microsoft's new modeling language for quickly defining and managing the metadata inherent in a specific model, and for developing domain-specific languages (DSLs).

■ ■ ■

CHAPTER 1

Installing and Setting Up SQL Server Modeling

This chapter will walk you through the procedures of downloading, installing, repairing, and uninstalling SQL Server Modeling, as well as what's required for getting software pre-requisites in place. These pre-requisite applications should, of course, be up and running before you install SQL Server Modeling. I will take this step by step, and if you follow the procedures outlined in this chapter, you should have a working installation of SQL Server Modeling by the time you finish.

But before downloading or installing anything, take a look at the current version of the SQL Server Modeling release notes. As of this writing, these can be found at the following MSDN URL:

```
http://msdn.microsoft.com/en-us/data/dd823315.aspx
```

The release notes provide links for downloading the SQL Server Modeling setup file as well as links for downloading the software pre-requisites listed in the next section. They also provide important information affecting how you should go about installing SQL Server Modeling and what needs to be in place for a successful setup. Once you have run the setup file, there should be a Readme file installed under Program Files/Microsoft Oslo/1.0 /Readme.htm. (This is the installation path for the CTP R3 release. The path may be different for subsequent releases.) The Readme file provides much of the same information as that provided in the release notes and can be viewed by loading it in your web browser using the browser's File → Open menu.

The procedures that follow are based on the November, 2009 CTP Release 3. (CTP is the acronym for Community Technology Preview.)

Software Pre-Requisites

Several software systems must be in place before you begin the actual installation of SQL Server Modeling:

- Windows Installer 4.5 or later (search for "Windows Installer 4.5 Redistributable" on www.Micorosoft.com]

    - To run setup, Windows Installer 4.5 is required.

    - If Windows Installer is not installed, a system restart will be requested after its installation completes.

- .NET Framework 4

- SQL Server 2008 SP1 Express (or higher edition)

- Visual Studio 2010 (any edition): Visual Studio is not required for SQL Server Modeling CTP Release 3, but for full functionality with Visual Studio and M Tools integration, Visual Studio 2010, Visual C#, and Visual Web Developer are required.

Hardware and Operating System Requirements

SQL Server Modeling must be installed on a computer with any combination of the following CPU architecture and operating systems. Note the SP (Service Pack) for some of the listed operating systems. If the Service Pack listed is not installed, it should be downloaded and installed before proceeding.

Supported CPU Architectures:

- X86

- X64 (Windows-on-Windows)

Hardware Requirements:

- Minimum: 1.6 GHz CPU, 1GB RAM

- Recommended: 2.2 GHz CPU, 2GB RAM

Supported Operating Systems:

- Windows XP SP3 or later

- Windows Vista (SP1, SP2, or later)

- Windows Server 2003 R2 (SP2 or later)

- Windows Server 2008 SP2

- Windows 7

Configuring SQL Server

Before running the installation executable, be sure SQL Server is running. Bring up the SQL Server Configuration Manager as shown in Figure 1-1. Here's the sequence for bringing up this tool:

1. Click the Start button on your Windows Taskbar.

2. Click All Programs.

3. Go to Microsoft SQL Server 2008 (if, for example, you are running the 2008 SKU).

4. Click Configuration Tools.

5.   Click SQL Server Configuration Manager.

Figure 1-1. *Opening the SQL Server Configuration Manager*

Once you have the Configuration Manager running, navigate to Configuration Tools, then to SQL Native Client XX.X Configuration/Client Protocols, (where XX.X will correspond to the version number of your SQL Server installation, such as 10.0), as shown in Figure 1-2. Which client protocols are enabled will depend on whether the database is running on the same computer on which you're installing SQL Server Modeling, or remotely. If it's running on your local machine, all you should need is the Shared Memory protocol. If it's running on a server on your network, Named Pipes and/or TCP/IP should be enabled.

It doesn't hurt to have Shared Memory, Named Pipes, and TCP/IP all enabled, but their specified order may affect performance. If SQL Server is running on a local server, your network administrator should be able to tell you whether TCP/IP or Named Pipes will provide better performance. On most large networks, TCP/IP would be the preferred protocol.

VIA (Virtual Interface Adapter) would normally be disabled unless your hardware environment supports this protocol, in which case the other protocols can be disabled. The order can be changed in the Configuration Manager by right-clicking in the right frame on any of the enabled protocols. You will see a popup menu where Order will be one of the possible selections.

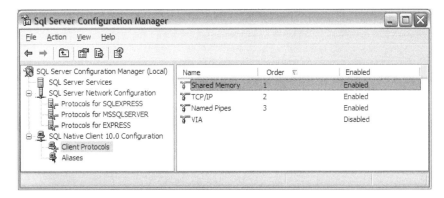

Figure 1-2. *Setting the SQL native client protocols*

Downloading and Installing

Once the software pre-requisites previously listed are in place, you're ready to download the SQL Server Modeling installation file from the SQL Server Modeling download website. The file size is around 40 MB, so it can take a few minutes if you have a slow Internet connection. After it has downloaded, you should be able to open it in your browser's download facility. Another option would be to open Windows Explorer and navigate to the folder where you have saved the downloaded file. Open the file by right-clicking on the filename and then clicking the Open option. You may see a security warning like the one shown in Figure 1-3.

Figure 1-3. Open File – Security Warning dialog when running the installation file

Click the Run button to start the installation process. The next dialog window to appear (shown in Figure 1-4) will be the initial SQL Server Modeling installation window. This gives you two choices: Install Now or Customize. If you are running the SQL Server Modeling install for the first time, click the Install Now option.

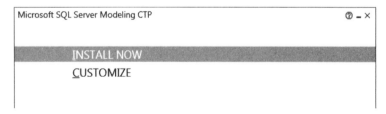

Figure 1-4. SQL Server Modeling initial installation window

After clicking Install Now, you should next see the Usage Reporting window, as shown in Figure 1-5.

Figure 1-5. Usage Reporting window

Check or uncheck the box, according to whether you would like to participate in the Customer Experience Improvement Program, then click the Continue button.

The next step is to accept the End User License Agreement (shown in Figure 1-6). Read the agreement and (if you agree) click the I Accept button.

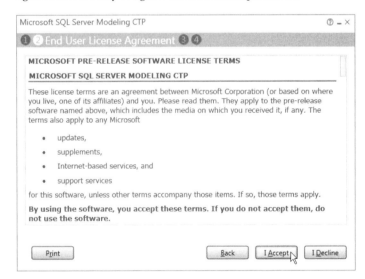

Figure 1-6. Accepting the End User License Agreement

This will start the third step in the installation process, which should present the Installation Progress window similar to the one shown in Figure 1-7.

Figure 1-7. Step 3: Installing SQL Server Modeling Services, Quadrant, and other components

This portion of the installation process can take ten minutes or more, depending on your computer's speed. Once this part of the installation has completed, the process will move on to the fourth and final step, which configures and deploys the Repository to SQL Server (see Figure 1-8). Again, this may take several minutes to complete.

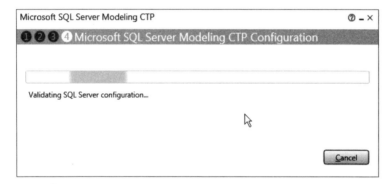

Figure 1-8. Step 4: Configuration and deployment

Once step 4 has completed, you should see a window similar to that shown in Figure 1-9, notifying you that setup has completed successfully.

Figure 1-9. Successful setup completion

At this point, simply click on the close button to finish the installation.

Checking the Installation

After the installation is completed, click the Start button on the Windows Taskbar, then click All Programs to see if the Microsoft SQL Server Modeling CTP program group appears in the All Programs list. If you click on this program group, you should see Intellipad, Quadrant, and other options listed, as shown in Figure 1-10. The order of the items may not be the same as shown in the figure, but you can rearrange the items by clicking and dragging each to the position you want.

Figure 1-10. The SQL Server Modeling CTP program group

If you don't see the Microsoft SQL Server Modeling CTP group in the All Programs list, go to the Windows Control Panel, bring up Add or Remove Programs, and check to see if it appears in the list of installed programs. Make sure the list is sorted by name, then scroll down in the list to the Microsoft programs. You should see the SQL Server Modeling CTP application listed, as shown in Figure 1-11.

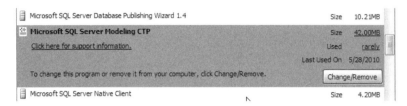

Figure 1-11. *SQL Server Modeling CTP listed in Add or Remove Programs*

In the Start button All Programs list, double-click on Intellipad. As it is loading, the Intellipad "splash screen" should display more or less as it appears in Figure 1-12.

Figure 1-12. *Intellipad splash screen*

Bring up Quadrant and each of the other three options in turn, just to familiarize yourself with them. I recommend taking a close look at the Readme file, which has some tips on troubleshooting in case you run into problems, as well as links to other resources, including release notes and the online Help page. It's good to keep these resources in mind as you start working with the software, in case any issues or questions should come up.

If Something Goes Wrong…

If you run into problems with the installation, there are several things you can do:

1. The Readme file includes a troubleshooting section that discusses what to do if you run into several different kinds of problems.

2. The release notes list a number of breaking changes and known issues in detail. If you don't find what you need in the Readme file, you may find some useful tips in the release notes. The Readme file provides a link to online release notes.

3. You can run the Repair option by clicking the Change/Remove button in the Add or Remove Programs section of the Control Panel (refer to Figure 1-11). This option is discussed briefly in the following section.

4. You can uninstall and then re-install with the hope of resolving the problem on the second go-around.

The Repair Option

Clicking the Change/Remove option for Microsoft SQL Server Modeling CTP in the Add or Remove Programs list (refer to Figure 1-11) will present a window with three selections (shown in Figure 1-13):

1. Add or Remove Features

2. Repair

3. Uninstall

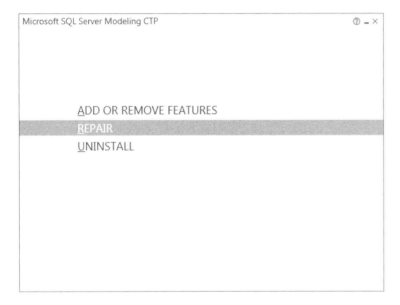

Figure 1-13. Selections after clicking the Change/Remove button

I won't cover Add or Remove Features here, since that option isn't relevant to what I will be discussing in the rest of the book, nor is it relevant to recovering from a faulty installation.

To invoke the Repair option, simply click on the option or cursor down one line and press Enter. The repair process will display a progress bar as it's executing (similar to the window shown in Figure 1-7). After the process is finished, you should see a completion window similar to what was shown in Figure 1-9. Click the Close button and re-test the installation to see if running the Repair process has resolved the problem.

If the problem persists, the next step would be to uninstall and then re-install, as described in the next section.

The Uninstall Option

To uninstall SQL Server Modeling, bring up the Control Panel, click on Add or Remove Programs, and scroll down to Microsoft SQL Server Modeling CTP (refer once again to Figure 1-11). Click on SQL Server

Modeling CTP, and then click on the Change/Remove button. Leave Add or Remove Programs window open so you can later check that the uninstall ran successfully.

You should see the Uninstall window, as was shown in Figure 1-13. Click on Uninstall. Next, you should see an Uninstall confirmation window (shown in Figure 1-14).

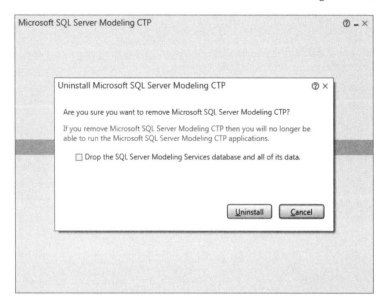

Figure 1-14. Uninstall confirmation window

Note that this window includes a checkbox to drop the SQL Server Modeling Services database and all its data. If you want to perform a complete uninstall, check this box, but understand that all data in the Repository will be lost. If you are uninstalling with the intent of re-installing because of problems with your current installation, and you know there is data in the Repository you would like to retain (say from going through one or more of the exercises later in the book), then leave this box unchecked. If on the other hand, there is no data you want to keep, there would be no reason to leave this box unchecked.

If you are uninstalling because you believe you have a damaged or corrupt installation, you may want to try the Repair option first. There is always a chance that the Repair option will take care of certain issues without having to go through a complete uninstall and re-install.

To proceed with the uninstall, click the Uninstall button. Once it starts, you should see a progress window similar to that shown in Figure 1-15.

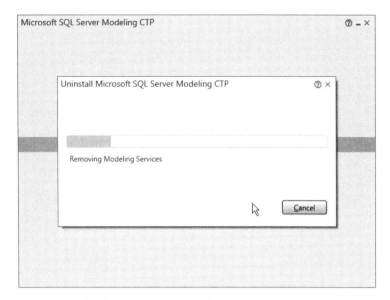

Figure 1-15. *Uninstall progress window*

After the process finishes, you will see a successful completion notification window like that shown in Figure 1-16.

Figure 1-16. *Successful completion of the uninstall*

Click the close button to complete the process. If you would like to confirm that the uninstall was successful, go back to the Add or Remove Programs window, and hit the F5 function key to refresh the list of installed applications, and scroll down to where SQL Server Modeling CTP previously appeared in the list. If the uninstall was successful, it should no longer be show in the list.

Summary

In this chapter, I've covered the procedures for installing, repairing, and uninstalling SQL Server Modeling. The last part of the installation process should be invoking all items in the SQL Server Modeling CTP program group, not only to check that they are working properly, but also to see what happens and what the interface looks like when you invoke each one. The Readme file and release notes are important resources; it's a good idea to take a look at these, especially if you run into problems with the installation or with running any of the development tools.

In the next chapter, I'll cover the ins and outs of using Intellipad, one of the development tools provided with SQL Server Modeling.

CHAPTER 2

Introduction to Intellipad

We've used text editors to write code from the beginning—at least as far back as assembler and COBOL. Everything from Notepad to Emacs to Eclipse, and all flavors in between.

This chapter introduces Intellipad, SQL Server Modeling's code editor. Intellipad is a lightweight but talented text editor for building and editing models and domain-specific languages (DSLs) in M code. It can be used for coding or editing a wide range of programming languages, like the editor included with Visual Studio. In fact, the Intellipad core is a close relative to Microsoft's Visual Studio code editor. It contains a built-in Python interpreter, and can be configured and enhanced using Python scripts. Most of its functionality is implemented through named components that can be modified or removed. Some developers have taken to calling it "Emacs.NET" because of its flexibility and configurability.

Getting Started with Intellipad

Intellipad is the text editing tool used for editing M. It can also be used to write and edit other kinds of languages, such as Python and T-SQL. Like Emacs, it can be extended and configured to support development in a wide array of languages. It has even been configured to behave as an IM chat or Twitter client. In its most basic incarnation, it is a small and simple application kernel, but is easily enhanced with plug-ins or add-ons that enable it to support syntactic colorizing, indenting, or "Intellisense," similar to that provided in the Visual Studio text editor.

There is one exercise at the end of this chapter, but you can use what follows as one big exercise. Bring up Intellipad and see if you can invoke each feature more or less in the same way as it's discussed in what follows. The interface may appear a little differently on your computer, depending on which version of Windows and Intellipad you are running. But if you follow along by invoking each feature as it's discussed, you should have a much better feel for the capabilities of this tool by the time you finish this chapter.

So let's start up Intellipad and have a look. Click on the Start button on the Taskbar, then click on All Programs and find Microsoft SQL Server Modeling → Intellipad, as shown in Figure 2-1.

Figure 2-1. *Starting Intellipad from Start/All Programs*

This should bring up an empty Intellipad window with a default text buffer named "untitled1," similar to what is shown in Figure 2-2. As soon as you type anything in the pane (more properly called *buffer view*), an asterisk will appear next to the buffer name to indicate that the contents of the buffer have changed but have not yet been saved to a file.

Figure 2-2. *Initial Intellipad window with some sample text*

Look at the top banner of the window, and you'll see four top-level menus:

- File

- Edit

- View

- Help

I'll talk about each of these in turn, but I won't go through the entire menu tree in every detail. I'll also cover the remaining parts of the text buffer view interface appearing below the menu banner—what you see displayed as "untitled1*," "100%," and "Standard mode."

The File Menu

To start with, it helps to keep in mind that Intellipad works with one or more buffers. A buffer is simply an area of memory where the text being created or edited is stored. The buffer being edited in the single Intellipad buffer view shown in Figure 2-2 is named untitled1*, with the asterisk indicating that the buffer has been changed from its original state. When a new buffer view is opened, it will automatically be named untitledX, where X will be an integer between 1 and some arbitrary number, according to how many previous untitled buffers have been opened during the Intellipad session. As you get a little farther into the chapter, you'll see how multiple buffers are displayed in the Intellipad interface. Only one buffer, or *pane*, will be active at a time, and this is the pane where the editing cursor will appear. When menu actions are invoked, the target of the action will be the active pane. The one exception to this is the

Find in Buffers command under the Edit menu, which applies to all buffers. As with most Windows-based text editors, you can open multiple instances of Intellipad.

Figure 2-3 shows the Intellipad File menu. As you can see, most of the options have keyboard shortcuts, and this is also the case with the other top-level menus in Intellipad.

The New option, of course, opens a new, empty buffer, ready for typing in new code. New M Project opens a new M project and changes the buffer view to Project mode. This mode provides a display of errors in the error list if the content is not a syntactically valid MSBuild file. (This is a more advanced subject and is beyond the scope of this book.)

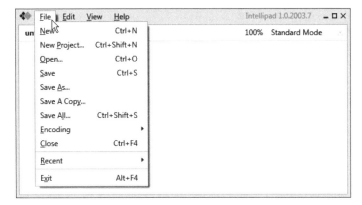

Figure 2-3. The Intellipad File menu

Save, Save As, and Save a Copy are all self-explanatory. (As usual in the Windows environment, the underlined character of a menu option indicates the single-character keyboard shortcut for invoking that option.)

The Encoding option allows you to save the current buffer in three encoding standards: ASCII, Unicode, or UTF8, which is the default. If you change the encoding, it changes the setting only for the active buffer view, leaving the encoding unchanged for files saved from other buffers. If a file with an encoding other than ASCII, Unicode or UTF8 is opened, no item is checked in the encoding submenu. If you mistakenly check one of these, close the file without saving, or choose Save As and save the buffer to a different filename to avoid changing the encoding of the original file.

Close closes the active buffer view pane. If there is only one active buffer view, this option is disabled.

Recent displays a list of the most recently used (MRU) files you've worked with in Intellipad, whether these were used in the current session or past sessions.

Exit will close the current Intellipad session. If one or more buffers haven't been saved, you'll be prompted whether you want to save any unsaved buffers, as shown in Figure 2-4. You have the option to Save All (the default if you press the Enter key), Discard All, or Cancel, which will return you to the Intellipad window with no action taken.

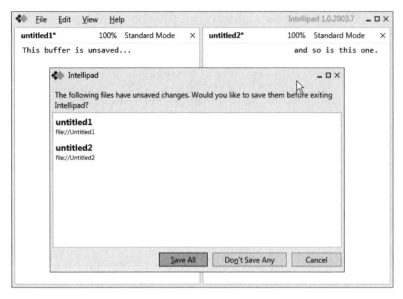

Figure 2-4. Prompt to save unsaved buffers on exit

The Edit Menu

Figure 2-5 shows the Intellipad Edit Menu. As you can see, some of the options (Undo, Redo, Cut, and Copy) are disabled (grayed out) because, in the current state of the buffer view, there's nothing these options can do. These options are self-explanatory, and behave as one might expect. The same goes for the next two options: Paste and Delete.

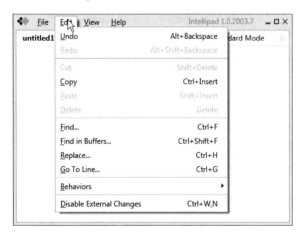

Figure 2-5. The Intellipad Edit menu

The Find Commands

When you try the Find option, however, you see some new behavior. Here Intellipad shows its colors more as a code editor rather than a simple Notepad-like text editor. Let's try doing a Find with two different buffers, as shown in Figure 2-6. I've written some sample text in both buffers, with the word "amazing" in both views.

Figure 2-6. The Intellipad Find command

Clicking on Find (or using the Ctrl-F keyboard shortcut) brings up something called the *mini-buffer* as a third buffer view, with a command prompt, indicated by the three angle brackets (>>>) followed by Find('|'). The mini-buffer is a special buffer that allows you to execute Intellipad command functions directly. I'll discuss use of the mini-buffer at more length in the section called "The View Menu" later in the chapter.

But for now, let's see what happens when you enter the word "amazing" between the single quotes. In Figure 2-7 the untitled1* buffer view shows what happens after you've done this: The word "amazing" is highlighted in the first (active) buffer view, but not in the second (inactive) one. Also note that the bottom (mini-buffer) buffer view is not in Standard mode, but in MiniBuffer Interactive mode.

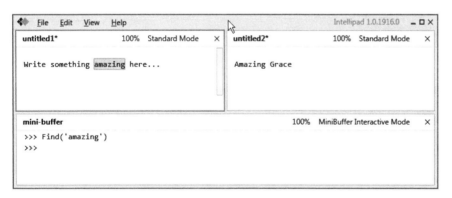

Figure 2-7. Find function highlighting the target word

Figure 2-8 shows the Find in Buffers (Ctrl-Shift-F) function. This will find the target string in all of the displayed panes or buffers. This option invokes the FindInBuffers() function in the mini-buffer, and when the string "amazing" is entered as the target pattern, you get an additional findresults buffer with the line/column location of each found pattern location in each buffer where it occurs—including previous strings already in the mini-buffer.

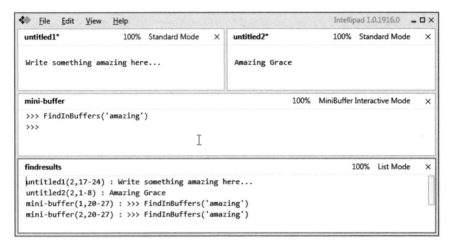

***Figure 2-8.** Find in Buffers command*

The Replace Command

The next option under the Edit menu, Replace (Ctrl-H), uses the mini-buffer facility in the same way, except that the Replace('<searchPattern>','<replacePattern>') function, with two arguments, is used. Figure 2-9 shows an example, with two different buffers containing the same target word, after the replacement function has been invoked from the first (untitled1) buffer view. This example makes it clear that the function works only in the context of the active buffer view. The replaced string remains highlighted.

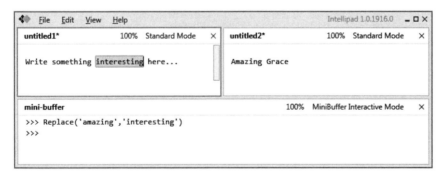

***Figure 2-9.** Replace command example*

The Go to Line Command

The Go to Line option again uses the mini-buffer to enter the target line number and execute the command, using the Goto(<line number>) function, where line number is an integer.

Behaviors

The Behaviors option allows you to control some specific behaviors of any particular buffer view, as shown in Figure 2-10. Enabled behaviors are indicated with a check mark after the name.

Selection Highlight is useful for highlighting strings with the Find and Replace functions. Error squiggles will flag syntax errors or other errors when working with the various programming modes (e.g., M or MGrammar, or Python) where Intellipad has built-in syntax awareness.

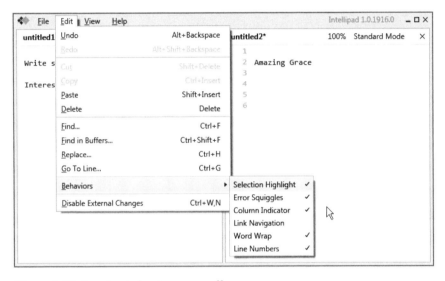

Figure 2-10. Turning behaviors on or off

Turning the column indicator on demarcates columns higher than column 80 with a grayed background, enabling you to see when a line exceeds 80 characters. This can be useful in some coding or data contexts, and is illustrated in Figure 2-11.

Link Navigation, turned on by default, supports the use of hyperlinks in modes supporting this functionality. However, enabling this feature to work requires adding some configuration data that defines a NavigationSource and other settings, which is beyond the scope of this book.

Figure 2-11. Line numbers and the column indicator turned on

Turning Word Wrap on will wrap a line too long to otherwise display within the buffer view. Figure 2-12 shows two buffer views addressing the same buffer (that is, displaying exactly the same data). Line numbering has been turned on in both buffer views, but Word Wrap is turned off in the left one and turned on in the right.

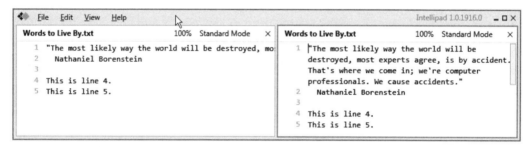

Figure 2-12. Word Wrap off (left pane) vs. Word Wrap on (right pane)

Disable External Changes

This behavior, if enabled, will disable external changes to all buffers belonging to the Intellipad session. For example, if you are editing metadata in the M Graph mode that has been persisted in the Repository, and this metadata is changed through an external interface, changes to the buffer will not occur. If multiple Intellipad sessions are running, each session has its own setting for this behavior.

The View Menu

The View menu provides options for switching to the Full Screen view, zooming, splitting the current pane horizontally or vertically, or viewing special buffers such as the mini-buffer, errors, and notifications. The View menu options are shown in Figure 2-13.

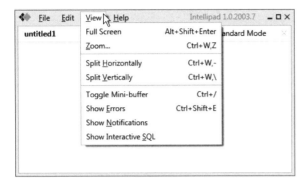

Figure 2-13. Intellipad View menu

Full Screen

The Full Screen option switches to a view where the current Intellipad window fills the entire display, and the title/menu bar at the top is removed. This provides as much real estate as possible on the display for reading, editing, or typing new content in the window. Besides dispensing with the menu bar, the buffer name (normally displayed under the menu bar in the upper left) and the zoom level and mode in the upper right disappear.

Figure 2-14 shows a three-pane Intellipad window before being put into the Full Screen format, while Figure 2-15 shows the same window in Full Screen format, but at a reduced scale, in order to fit on the page.

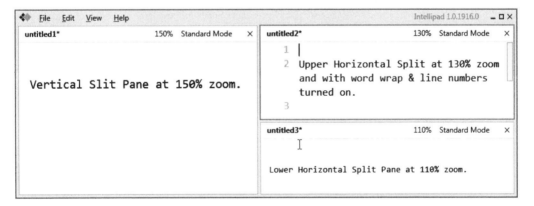

Figure 2-14. Sample three-pane window before being put in Full Screen mode

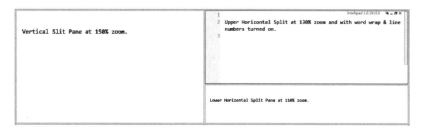

Figure 2-15. *Window from Figure 2-14, but in Full Screen mode (reduced scale)*

Figures 2-16 and 2-17 show a closeup view of the window control icons for full-screen and restored size windows in this view mode.

While the text and upper right of the window in Figure 2-15 are difficult to read because of the reduced scale, you can see that the display behaviors of each pane remain the same. The primary difference is that the menu bar, zoom setting display, and mode display are gone. If you click on the icon to the left of the Close icon ⧉, this will restore the window to its previous size, but will retain the Full Screen format without the menu bar and other items.

Intellipad 1.0.2003.7   ⧉ _ ⧉ ✕ ⃒⃒

Figure 2-16. *Detail of Intellipad Full Screen icons: Full Screen view*

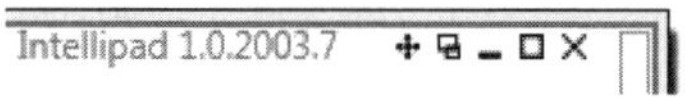

Intellipad 1.0.2003.7   ✛ ⧉ _ ⧉ ✕ ⃒⃒

Figure 2-17. *Detail of Intellipad Full Screen icons: restored size and position*

Here's a description of the action performed by clicking each of these control icons:

- ⊞ Latches and drags the window to a new position. This icon is displayed only when the Intellipad window is restored to its previous (not full display) size, but disappears when the window is actually at full-screen size. Cursoring over it will cause the cursor to change to a "grab and drag" cursor ⊕ . Left-clicking while this cursor is displayed allows you to grab and drag the window to a different position on the screen.

- ⧉ Restores the default Intellipad view format, with menu bar and pane titles.

- ⊟ Minimizes the window.

- ⧉ Restores window to its previous size and position (prior to setting to Full Screen view). After this function is executed, this icon will change to a Full Screen icon: ⧉.

- ⊠ Closes the Intellipad window. If any buffers are unsaved, you will be prompted whether you want to save them.

Zoom

Any Intellipad pane can be zoomed in or out. There are several ways to do this, but the easiest way is to press the Ctrl key while moving the scroll wheel on your mouse. Pressing the Ctrl key while scrolling forward will zoom the active pane in (increasing the scale, or effective size of the font), while scrolling back will have the opposite effect. (This also works in Quadrant, which I'll be talking about in the next chapter.) The zoom level, which defaults to 100%, is displayed on the right of the title line of the pane. The location is to the left of the mode name on the pane's title line, indicated by the cursor in Figure 2-18.

Executing the Zoom function under the View menu causes the mini-buffer pane to appear at the bottom of the Intellipad window. (I wrote about this feature in the earlier section titled "The Find Commands") The Zoom() function is automatically invoked in the mini-buffer, with the argument set to the active pane's current zoom setting. The current zoom setting is highlighted, as shown in Figure 2-18, so that you can easily change it to a different level by typing the new value. Note that you can also zoom by clicking the Zoom setting, displayed as a percentage. Clicking this will invoke the mini-buffer with the Zoom function in exactly the same way as zoom can be invoked from the View menu.

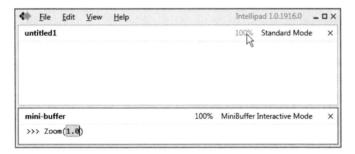

Figure 2-18. Intellipad Zoom function

Split Windows

You've already seen examples of how the Intellipad window can be split horizontally and/or vertically into multiple panes, addressing the same or different buffers. Splitting the current pane (the pane with focus) is accomplished using the View → Split Horizontally (Ctrl-W,-) or View → Split Vertically (Ctrl-W,\) menu options. Initially, the new pane created by the split action will address the same buffer as the active pane in which the split action was invoked, so you should see exactly the same content in the new pane as you did in the original, and at the same zoom level. However, other behaviors set in the original pane, such as line numbers or Word Wrap will be defaulted.

You can set the new pane to a new or different buffer, and whatever other properties you want. In Figure 2-19, there are two views of the same unsaved buffer, the left one at 100% zoom with no line wrap and no line numbers, and the right one at 80% zoom with line wrap on and line numbers displayed.

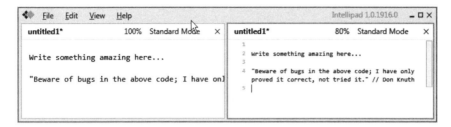

Figure 2-19. Vertical split views addressing the same buffer (unsaved)

In Figure 2-20, the untitled1 buffer shown in Figure 2-19 has been saved to the file My First Buffer.txt, and a horizontal split pane has been created (using the Split Horizontally menu option or the Ctrl-W,- key combination) at the bottom of the window with a new unsaved buffer. The name of this new buffer defaults to the name untitled2, since the default1 name was used in creating the first new buffer and then renamed to My First Buffer.txt when it was saved to a file. As soon as you type a single character in the untitled2 pane/buffer, the buffer has new content, and an asterisk is appended to the name to indicate the buffer has changed. The zoom level in this buffer has been increased to 120%.

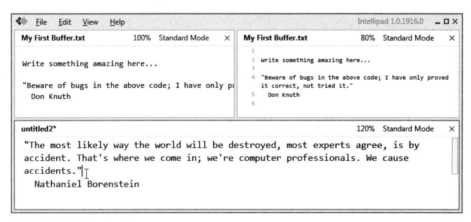

Figure 2-20. Vertical and horizontal split buffer views with different saved and unsaved buffers

The Mini-Buffer

The mini-buffer is a special-purpose, interactive buffer enabling you to invoke a wide range of functions or behaviors in Intellipad. Think of it as a way of interacting or controlling your editor in command-line mode. I touched on it briefly in the sections titled "The Find Commands" and "The Replace Command."

You can see some of the available mini-buffer commands in Figure 2-22 below, and the entire set of mini-buffer commands is provided in Appendix B at the end of the book. You can also see this list by pressing the F1 key in any buffer view or clicking on the Help menu at the top of the window, then selecting the Commands option.

The Help Menu

The Help menu, shown in Figure 2-21, provides two options: Commands and Intellipad Primer. The latter option can also be invoked with the F1 function key.

Figure 2-21. *Intellipad Help menu*

Commands List

Invoking the Commands option will display a list of functions in the current active pane in Rich Text mode. These functions must be executed in the mini-buffer (previously discussed), but also can be used in a script file. Figure 2-22 shows some of the functions listed in the Commands view.

Figure 2-22. *Intellipad MiniBuffer Commands list (note the Rich Text mode, upper right)*

Intellipad Primer

Invoking the Intellipad Primer option of the Help menu displays a useful overview of the Intellipad interface and features, including a discussion of what is involved in customizing and configuring the editor. Like the Commands list, this is displayed in the currently active pane in Rich Text mode. Figure 2-23 shows the top part of the Primer text.

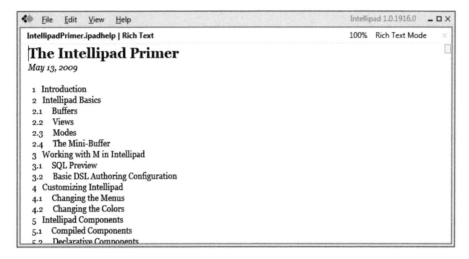

Figure 2-23. The Intellipad Primer

View Title Banner Functions

You've probably noticed each pane has a title banner with the name of the view or buffer on the left and the zoom level and mode on the right. Each of these three parts provides some functionality if you click on it. Clicking on the title, as shown in Figure 2-24, reveals a drop-down menu allowing you to select any of the currently active buffers. Clicking on one of these will switch the view to the selected buffer.

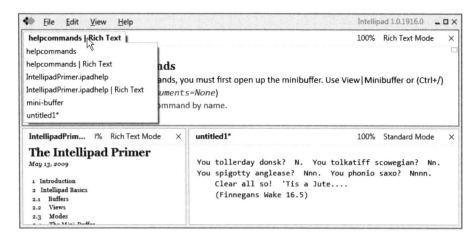

Figure 2-24. Current buffers drop-down menu

Clicking the zoom level, as discussed in the upcoming "Zoom" section, will bring up the mini-buffer with the Zoom(<zoomLevel>) function, allowing you to enter a different zoom level setting.

View Modes

Clicking the current mode setting at the right of the title banner (see the cursor position in Figure 2-25) will display a drop-down of available modes. I'll give a brief overview of these in this section. Some of this will be covered in more detail in later chapters, since I'll be using them to show how domain-specific languages and models are developed.

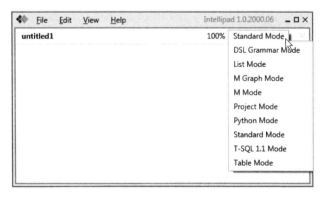

Figure 2-25. Intellipad view modes

Some of the extended modes, such as DSL Grammar and M Graph, will add an additional menu option to provide additional functionality specific to that mode.

Standard mode is the basis on which the other modes are developed. It provides straight-ahead text editing functionality, more or less along the lines of any simple text editor, like Notepad. The other modes are provided by components that build functionality on top of the Standard mode.

27

DSL Grammar mode provides the functionality for writing domain-specific languages, or DSL grammars. This includes features such as syntax colorization, error marking (if this behavior is enabled), and the ability to see the parsing output for your grammar with DSL input. In this mode, a fifth menu option, DSL, is added to the Standard mode menu items. One of the choices under this menu option, Split New Input and Output Views, will split the window into three views, as shown in Figure 2-26. In this figure, you can see that the titles of the left and right panes both start with untitled2. This doesn't mean that the left and right panes are the same buffer, however. The left view displays the text of the DSL input, while the right view, which is read-only, displays the resulting M Graph output generated by the DSL grammar (contained in the center view).

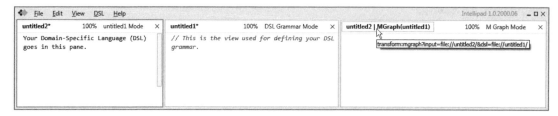

Figure 2-26. DSL Grammar mode with DSL input and M Graph output views

List mode is used internally by some Intellipad features to display a buffer showing a list whose items can be clicked to navigate to the selected destination buffer.

I have already briefly touched on the M Graph mode, used in conjunction with the DSL Grammar mode.

M mode is used for developing M code. As with the DSL Grammar mode, M mode provides syntax colorization, error marking of syntax errors, and the T-SQL preview mode.

Project mode provides support for developing projects. These projects will normally consist of multiple M or DSL grammar (.mg) files and can be managed and edited in Visual Studio with the Visual Studio M language plug-in.

Python mode supports development of Python code. As with M mode, Python mode provides syntax colorization and error flagging for syntactically incorrect Python. For test metric purposes, code coverage is provided if you launch Intellipad from the command line with the /coverage option.

Table mode is used primarily in the Errors pane (when the Errors pane is enabled) to display a list of errors. Using this mode to display errors enables the errors to be sorted on any column.

T-SQL 1.1 mode provides a view of the T-SQL code generated by M code. To show how this works, let's try a small exercise.

Demonstrating the Intellipad T-SQL Preview Mode

In this exercise, you will create some very simple M code to demonstrate how the SQL Server Modeling framework is able to generate T-SQL output code from M input code. The exercise involves creating an *extent* of entities I will call SandwichOrders. An extent is a concept in M that maps to data storage (a table) in SQL Server. For the time being, I would recommend not being concerned about the syntax of the M code used in this example. I will get into this in future chapters. The primary objective here is to demonstrate how T-SQL code can be generated from M code.

Here is the procedure:

1. Open Intellipad and save the empty buffer as a file with the name LunchCounter.m. Do this from the File → Save As menu option. This will switch the mode to M mode. Create an empty module called LunchCounter, as shown in Figure 2-27.

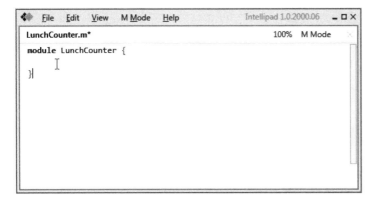

Figure 2-27. Creating an empty LunchCounter module in M

2. Click on the M Mode menu and select T-SQL Preview (shown in Figure 2-28).

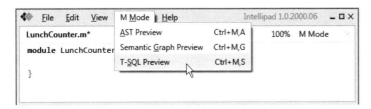

Figure 2-28. Selecting the T-SQL Preview for the M code

3. This will present a split screen view, with the generated T-SQL code shown in the right pane. The reason you don't see any code generated yet is that there is nothing to generate until you define an extent in your M code. Defining an extent will cause a table to be created in SQL Server.

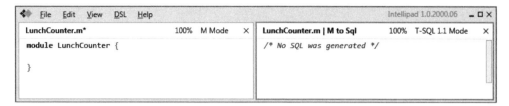

Figure 2-29. *No code is generated yet because you only have an empty module with no extent (SQL Server table) defined.*

4. Now let's add the following line within the scope of the LunchCounter module to create a SandwichOrders extent:

```
SandwichOrders : {Text*};
```

This simple line of code can be interpreted to say that the SandwichOrders extent (table) is defined as a collection of text strings. This is enough to cause the T-SQL code generator to spring into action and generate the code shown in the right pane of Figure 2-30. This pane is intended as a preview pane for the generated code, and as such, is read-only. However, you can do a File → Save As to save this code to a text file.

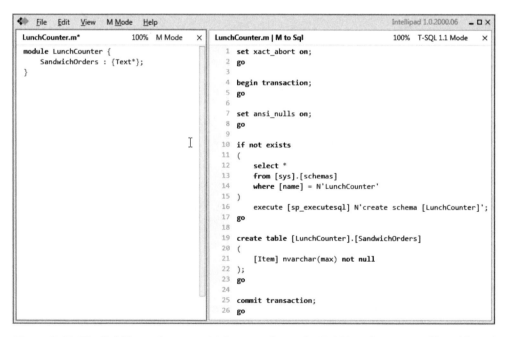

Figure 2-30. *The T-SQL preview pane (right) now shows the T-SQL code generated by adding the extent definition.*

5. To carry the example a little further, you can add a couple of sample
    SandwichOrders instances to the M code and see how this affects the generated
    T-SQL code. Lets add a "Pastrami on Rye" order and a "Ham on Sourdough"
    order. You can do this by simply adding the collection of the two text strings,
    represented between braces and with the two items of the collection separated by
    a comma:

```
{"Pastrami on Rye", "Ham on Sourdough"}
```

You place this code for the collection immediately after the extent definition
(Figure 2-31). Note that carriage returns and new lines are regarded as white
space by the compiler, which is what is generating the T-SQL code in the preview
pane on the right.

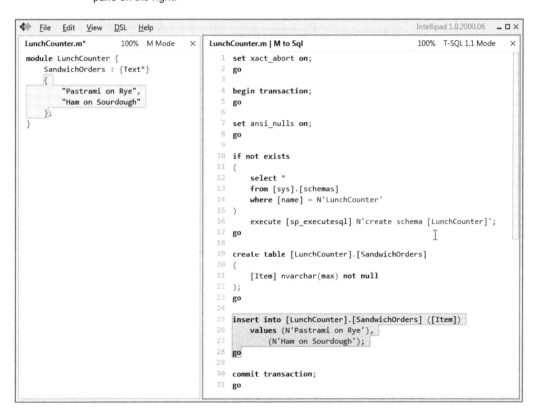

Figure 2-31. *Adding two SandwichOrders instances to the extent*

Let's walk through the generated T-SQL code in the right pane of Figure 2-31 to see what's happening:

Lines 1-8: This does some initial configuration stuff and begins a transaction for code sequence
to follow. This transaction will be committed at the end of the sequence.

Lines 10-17: This tests whether a `LunchCounter` (the name of the module) schema already exists in the database. If it doesn't, the schema is created.

Lines 19-23: This section creates the `SandwichOrders` table with a single text field to contain the text of the order.

Lines 25-28: This inserts the two sample `SandwichOrders` instances into the table.

Lines 30-31: This commits the transaction that was initiated at the top of the code.

And all of this from just a few lines of M code! It looks like the advantage provided by the SQL Server Modeling framework—in terms of enabling a developer to create, refine, and maintain a domain model—is significant.

In the next chapter, I will walk you through a much more extended exercise showing how to use Intellipad to create and refine a domain-specific language.

CHAPTER 3

■ ■ ■

Domain-Specific Languages 101: Lola's Lunch Counter

 In this chapter, I'll talk about domain-specific languages (DSLs), and you'll build a very simple DSL using Intellipad. As one might guess, the descriptive term *domain-specific* means using the language to define a model or do something useful in a specific area of activity or knowledge. In the context of software development, the term *domain* normally applies to a business operation, process, or workflow, such as micro-brewing or creating insurance products. The term could apply to areas as diverse as risk management, modeling traffic flows, or creating a just-in-time inventory system. Most DSLs, however, are not so ambitious and address more narrowly constrained domains.

Not unlike a map (the kind on paper showing highways and towns), a DSL is a way of abstracting away the conceptual "chaff" of a domain or process so that you have a cleaner and simpler way of representing and analyzing the problem at hand. The benefit is greater ease of analysis and development; the risk is that some of the conceptual chaff that's removed might include a few grains that you really could use later on. Usually (but not always), it's easy to add these kinds of things back in if you need them.

Martin Fowler's definition of a DSL is, "a computer programming language of limited expressiveness focused on a particular domain" (DSLDevCon 2009 talk: http://msdn.microsoft.com/en-us/data/dd727707.aspx). The phrase "limited expressiveness" is key here, and it is what differentiates a DSL from a general programming language like C# or Java. But why would you want limited expressiveness? Isn't expressiveness a good thing in a programming language? Well. . .yes and no. Usually, there's a strong correlation of expressiveness with complexity, and if you can remove some of the complexity to gain clarity and ease of use in a domain, that could be a good thing.

DSLs are especially useful as a means of communication between the technical people and stakeholders. If the stakeholders have a relatively simple tool, like a clear and well-designed DSL, it makes it that much easier to communicate their intent to the software architect, designer, or developer.

In this chapter, you'll develop a very simple example of a DSL, the code to process the language (sometimes called Mgrammar, or DSL Grammar, in the context of SQL Server Modeling), and deploy the resulting model with instances to SQL Server. If all goes according to plan, you should see a direct mapping from the DSL model and the structure of the data model reflected in the database.

Some Caveats

Before I get into the details of the example, however, I should say a few words about the development approach used in the LunchCounter example in the next section. The approach used could be

33

characterized as a rudimentary form of test-driven development. What I mean by this is that I start with some very simple sample data (e.g., some simple sandwich order expressions for the DSL); then you build some code with this sample data, and see if it works. If it does, you move to the next level of refinement in terms of the DSL syntax, and modify the sample DSL statements to reflect this new level of complexity. This will nearly always break the existing grammar definition used for parsing the DSL, so you modify the grammar to correct the errors. This turns into an iterative process where you can go through many of these refinement cycles and build up a reasonably sophisticated system. I don't want to call the end product in this example sophisticated, by any means. The point is that some readers may find this approach frustrating at times because things keep breaking as the example unfolds. If you haven't done test-driven development before, it may take a little getting used to. If you have, it shouldn't be an issue.

On a separate note, I will be introducing some new and possibly unfamiliar terms (like *extent*, which you will see shortly) that have a very specific meaning within the M language and the SQL Server Modeling framework. If you haven't run across some of these terms before in your travels or reading, they may take some getting used to. I know they sometimes caused me a little uncertainty in the course of getting up to speed with this new framework. I have found the best approach is to forge ahead through the code samples and the explanations, and things will usually become clear in due course. Often things will become even clearer on a second or third reading and as you become more conversant in the language.

And one more thing—please don't feel that, once you've finished this chapter, you will walk away knowing how to construct a DSL or write a grammar in M to process DSLs. My intent here is to unpack a very simple use case, but at a somewhat higher level than the coding basics: what a DSL and a grammar look like and some of the thinking that goes into building these things from the ground up. That's why I decided to use a narrative-based approach in the exercise—to show how the thinking and analysis might unfold, as well as provide a taste of how working with a nontechnical (but intelligent) stakeholder might happen. If you don't like storytelling in computer books, be patient. It's the only place in the book where I try it.

The bottom line: Don't be too concerned when reading the code if you don't understand every nuance of what you're seeing. That's not the intended purpose of this chapter. Otherwise, it would have been called "Domain-Specific Languages 201."

A Simple Exercise: The Sandwich Language

So—let's pick a simple domain to work with. As domains go, the sandwich is as simple as you can get. Let's say you're the owner of <Your Name Here>'s Lunch Counter. Perhaps your name is Lola, but if not, feel free to substitute your name for Lola anytime Lola occurs in what follows.

The name of your business is, naturally, Lola's Lunch Counter. Your specialty is pretty good sandwiches (apologies to Garrison Keillor), and the business has grown to the point you're thinking about automating your order and kitchen workflow, maybe with an eye to franchising the business. Your nephew is a hotshot .NET developer, and says he will help. So let's follow along as you, Lola <or your name here>, and your nephew (whose name shall be Norm) work together in the process of developing a model for tracking and processing sandwich orders. Norm says the problem is amenable to developing a DSL, and (not knowing any better) you say this sounds like a good plan.

Where You Want to End Up

You'll want to have an idea of where this is heading so that you might have a better sense of how things are falling into place as you watch over Lola's and Norm's shoulders. You want to end up with a working

DSL and grammar that allows Lola's business to track and record sandwich orders, and which supports the representation of sandwich order data in a database.

A sandwich order is pretty much what you might think. It describes the sandwich a customer wants for lunch, consisting of three types of ingredients:

- Some kind of stuff (lunchmeat or some other non-meat stuff, like portabella)

- Some kind of bread (rye, French, etc.)

- Some combination of condiments (lettuce, tomato, mayo, etc.)

There are no constraints as to how these three kinds of ingredients might make up a sandwich, except that a sandwich can have one and only one kind of bread. You may add some business rules down the road, like you can't have more than two kinds of stuff (main ingredient) in a sandwich or more than five condiments. (Let's be reasonable folks—no Dagwoods allowed.)

Figure 3-1 is a preview of where you'd like to end up. It shows some sample DSL sandwich orders in the left pane, the grammar that processes and parses the DSL statements in the center pane, and the output M Graph that results in the right pane.

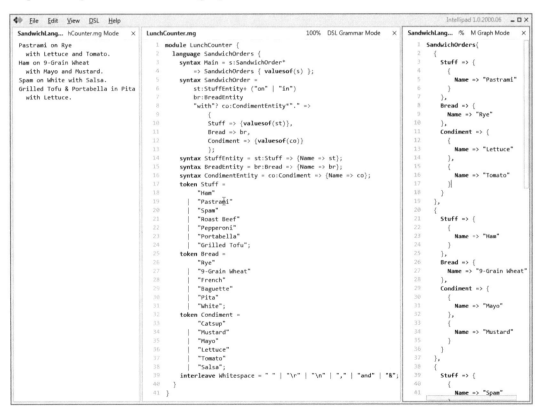

Figure 3-1. *Where you're headed: the final Intellipad view of the SandwichOrders DSL (left pane), DSL Grammar (center pane), and M Graph of the orders data (right pane)*

The SandwichOrders DSL in the left pane is very easy to understand and requires no explanation. The DSL Grammar code in the center pane is not easy to understand, unless you've been working with M for a while. Some of what appears in this pane will become clearer as you work through this exercise. The text in the right pane is what is called an M Graph, which is an M code representation of the DSL, generated through the DSL Grammar.

The M Graph is essentially a big named collection. The name of the collection is SandwichOrders (line 1). Collections are represented in M within curly braces,

```
{"this", "is", "a", "collection", "of", "words"}
```

and collections can have other collections as members, which is what you are seeing in the right pane. (This is why there are so many curly braces in this pane.) The first SandwichOrder in the graph, generated by the first order in the DSL (Pastrami on Rye with Lettuce and Tomato.) is a collection of three entities (lines 2 – 19). An *entity* is simply a collection of named values, so the first entity is a Stuff entity with the name "Pastrami", the second entity is a Bread entity with the name "Rye", and the third entity is a two-element collection of Condiment entities with the names "Lettuce" and "Tomato". You could read on down the M Graph and parse out the entities for the other orders.

With those preliminaries in mind, let's get on with Lola and Norm's conversation.

Getting Started with the Intellipad DSL Grammar Mode Interface

You'll watch over Norm's shoulder, along with Lola, as he brings up Intellipad to start developing what you might call the LunchCounter DSL. The first thing you see, of course, is an empty and untitled view in the Standard mode (see Figure 3-2).

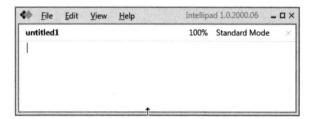

Figure 3-2. The initial view of Intellipad after opening

Norm clicks on the Mode selection menu (see Figure 3-3), and selects DSL Grammar Mode, since you're going to be developing the DSL grammar for your new language.

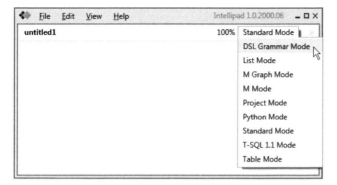

Figure 3-3. *Changing to the DSL Grammar mode*

Once you're in the DSL Grammar mode, you see a new DSL menu on the main title bar (between View and Help), as shown in Figure 3-4. Norm clicks the DSL menu and selects Split New Input and Output Views. (Another way to invoke this mode is the Ctrl-Shift-T key combo.)

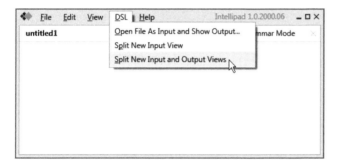

Figure 3-4. *Selecting the three-way Split view from the DSL menu*

Now you see three views (shown in Figure 3-5), but they only address two new buffers: untitled1 and untitled2. (See Chapter 2 for an explanation of buffers.) The left pane is where you will start entering your DSL statements. The view in this pane is essentially in Standard mode, but it shows untitled1 Mode in the pane title banner. This means that the input DSL statements in the left pane will be processed using the DSL Grammar module you'll be creating in the untitled1 (center pane) buffer. The right pane, in M Graph mode, is read-only and will show the M code generated by the DSL Grammar module you will be creating in the untitled1 pane. Going from left to right in this Intellipad window then, the left pane contains the input DSL statements, the center pane contains your DSL Grammar definition for processing these DSL statements, and the right pane shows the resulting (read-only) output M Graph.

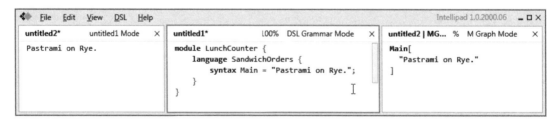

Figure 3-5. *Initial Intellipad window after selecting Split New Input and Output Views*

Norm: "Let's start by writing an order for your most popular sandwich in the left pane."
Lola: "Okay—that would be pastrami on rye."
And she enters the order `Pastrami on Rye.` in the left untitled2 pane. (Intellipad appends an asterisk to the buffer name as soon as she types the first character, since the buffer has been changed but not saved.) Figure 3-6 shows the results of Lola's typing.

Figure 3-6. *The first line of the SandwichOrders DSL*

Nothing happens in the other two panes, since you haven't defined any grammar to process Lola's sample order. To get started, Norm sets up a bare-bones DSL Grammar definition in the center pane to see if it will generate some M language output in the right pane (see Figure 3-7).

```
module LunchCounter {
    language SandwichOrders {
        syntax Main = "Pastrami on Rye.";
    }
}
```

```
Main[
    "Pastrami on Rye."
]
```

Figure 3-7. *The simplest possible DSL Grammar definition that works…*

Let's review what you are seeing in the center (grammar definition) and right (M graph output) panes. The center pain contains a complete (if impractical) DSL Grammar definition. All DSL Grammar definitions—in fact all M language programs—must be contained in one or more modules. In M, a module is a namespace or unit of compilation. (In reality, an M file is the unit of compilation. But I will try to follow the convention of defining only one module per file.)

I'll name this module LunchCounter to correspond with the domain you're addressing. Within this module, you have defined a DSL language called SandwichOrders, containing one simple rule. A requirement in DSL grammar definitions is that there must always be a Main syntax rule. A DSL module can contain any number of syntax rules, but the required `Main` rule is the top-level rule to which all input statements or documents must conform in order to be valid within the grammar definition of the language.

So far, you've set up a language that will accept only the statement `"Pastrami on Rye."` If this is your system, then as long as a customer orders only pastrami on rye, you're good. Anything else will generate an error.

Norm has made sure that Lola's sample order includes a period at the end, and he's included the period as part of his `Main` syntax rule definition. In the present context, this isn't important because the system will be well defined, even if it is nonsense to a human reader, as long as the input DSL sequence of characters (string) matches the string expected by the grammar definition. But later on, Norm expects to use a period to tell the system it has reached the end of a `SandwichOrders` statement.

In the right pane of Figure 3-7, you see that the input DSL and the simple-minded DSL Grammar definition have generated an M language program (termed an M Graph).

Broadening the Choices

Lola: "This is all well and good, but what if someone is tired of pastrami on rye and orders pastrami on wheat?"

Norm: "Well. . .let's see what happens." He changes Rye to Wheat in the left pane DSL view. After this change, the red squiggles will underline the entire order statement. These indicate an error, and the generated M code in the right pane is `null`, indicating the system is no longer well-defined and is unable to generate code for the given DSL statement or order.

To see the errors generated, Norm clicks on the View menu and selects Show Errors. Figure 3-8 shows the Error List pane at the bottom of the window.

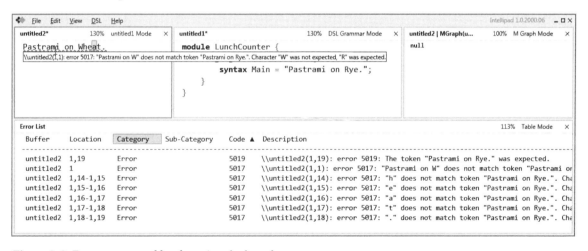

Figure 3-8. Errors generated by changing the bread

That the entire string `Pastrami on Wheat.` (and not just the word `Wheat`) is underlined with red squiggles, indicating the error is generated by the entire string. Reviewing the error list makes this clearer. The first error in the list indicates the processor accepts the presented string up to the character "W" in Wheat, but after that, it keeps checking for the first character of a valid string, which is the first character of the only acceptable statement.

Interleaving (Ignoring) Whitespace

Norm: "Let's break the syntax rule in the grammar definition into its component words: "Pastrami" "on" "Rye.""

Lola says: "Fine—go for it."

Figure 3-9 shows the result. You see errors (again, the red squiggles) at the two spaces, but the processor, based on the new grammar definition in the center pane, generates the new M Graph code anyway—so at least it's not a fatal error this time. It looks as though "PastramionRye." would have been acceptable, but nothing with spaces in it. The first definition had the two spaces between the three words included, but the new one doesn't.

Note that when you click on one of the two error descriptions in the Error List pane, the associated place in the DSL where the error occurs is highlighted. This is a handy troubleshooting aid when you need to track down exactly where a specific error is occurring.

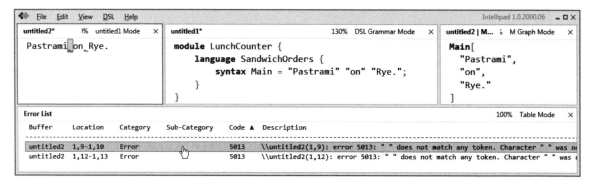

Figure 3-9. *Breaking the syntax rule definition into separate words*

Norm: "Aha! I haven't allowed for whitespace in the grammar definition code."

Lola: "What's whitespace?"

Norm: "*Whitespace* is mostly spaces and formatting characters like tabs, carriage returns, and line feeds. These don't have any meaning as far as what the processor needs to do, so I need to tell the grammar definition to ignore, or *interleave*, these characters."

Norm adds an `interleave` rule in the grammar definition. An `interleave` rule tells the processor what kind of content, such as comments, can be interleaved, and ignored, with the main content, which must be processed.

Figure 3-10 shows how adding a single space as an ignorable character resolves the problem: No error squiggles occur.

Figure 3-10. *Interleaving whitespace*

Lola: "So, you're pretty much back to where you started. I need something that's going to work with more than pastrami on rye! How are you going to get there from here?"

Norm: "Right. So how do you define a sandwich, anyway? At the simplest level, it's some kind of lunchmeat on some kind of bread. So let's change the main syntax definition to something like that."

Norm changes the DSL Grammar code to reflect his thinking, along the lines shown in Figure 3-11. Of course, the grammar processor (center pane) has no idea what the terms Lunchmeat and Bread are because they are undefined.

Defining Tokens

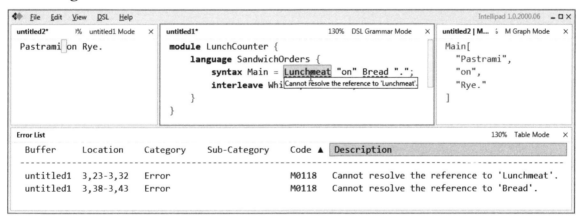

Figure 3-11. *First cut at making the SandwichOrders syntax rule more general*

Norm has redefined the Main syntax, but now he needs to define Lunchmeat and Bread as *tokens*. To get started, he'd like the processor to accept any string for Lunchmeat, followed by the preposition "on", and any string for Bread, with a period at the end. Right now, anything from "foo on bar" to "Brecht on Brecht" would mean some progress in Lola's eyes. So Norm adds a couple of token statements to the grammar definition to define Lunchmeat and Bread as tokens within the grammar that can contain any sequence of characters.

Figure 3-12 shows the result. Again, the grammar works with this and shows no error. The two token statements define Lunchmeat and Bread in exactly the same way: They can be a single contiguous string of one or more characters, a through z or A through Z. But I've introduced a number of new M language forms:

"a".."z"" means a single alpha character anywhere in the range from a to z. Similarly, "A".."Z" means a single capitalized alpha character anywhere in the range from A to Z.

A pipe character (|) is the logical OR operator.

A plus sign (+) is a postfix *Kleene operator*, meaning "one or more of this entity."

So given this syntax, ("a".."z" | "A".."Z")+ means "any sequence of one or more alpha characters, upper- or lowercase." So Rye and rAzzLeDaZZle both qualify, and rAzzLeDaZZle on Rye would be a valid sandwich order, according to the newly defined DSL Grammar code. This removes one of the constraints of the extremely limited Pastrami on Rye straight jacket, but you're still a long way from anything resembling a useful sandwich order system.

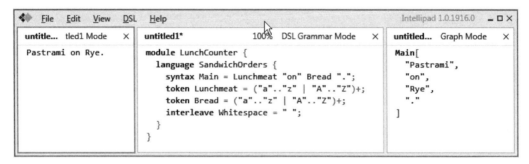

Figure 3-12. Defining the Lunchmeat and Bread tokens as arbitrary strings

Enabling Multiple DSL Statements

Lola: "Okay, say I just had another customer order a ham on 9-grain wheat sandwich. Will your system handle that?"

Norm: "I don't think so, but let's try it and see where it breaks."

Figure 3-13 shows the results of adding the ham on 9-grain order.

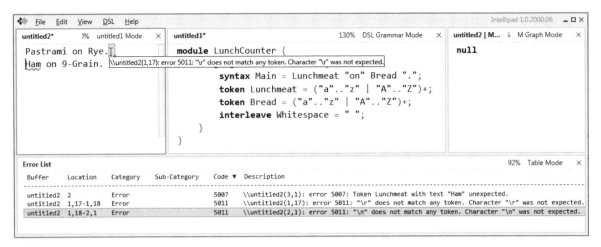

Figure 3-13. Errors generated by adding a second sandwich order in the DSL

The Error List pane indicates that a carriage return and line feed were unexpected, so you need to add these to the Whitespace rule.

Lola: "But why the first error in the list? Doesn't that order conform to the syntax you've defined?"

Norm: "In a sense, yes. The new statement itself conforms to the grammar, but the syntax really is valid for only one statement."

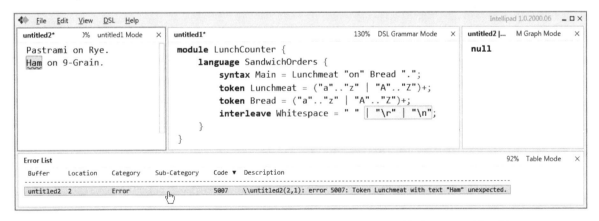

Figure 3-14. One remaining error after carriage return, and new-line are added to ignorable whitespace

In Figure 3-14, Norm has added the carriage return (the UTF8 encoding for this is written as "\r") and new line (written as "\n") to the interleave rule. After this, the only remaining error is the unexpected Lunchmeat token, which is really caused by the unexpected second order statement. To fix this problem, Norm encloses the Main syntax phrase on the right side of the equals sign (=) in parentheses and adds a postfix + to indicate that one or more instances of the conforming statement are expected (Figure 3-15). [Similar operators, called *Kleene operators*, are an asterisk (*) to indicate zero or more occurrences, and question mark (?) to indicate zero or one occurrence.]

43

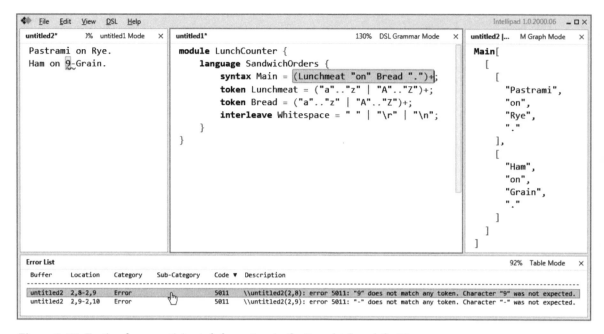

Figure 3-15. *Testing for unanticipated characters in the Bread token definition*

Modifying the Main rule to allow for multiple orders still leaves you with two errors in the Error List pane: the 9 and hyphen (-)characters are unexpected. So for the time being, Norm adds the numeric characters 0 through 9 and the hyphen character to the Bread token definition, as shown in Figure 3-16.

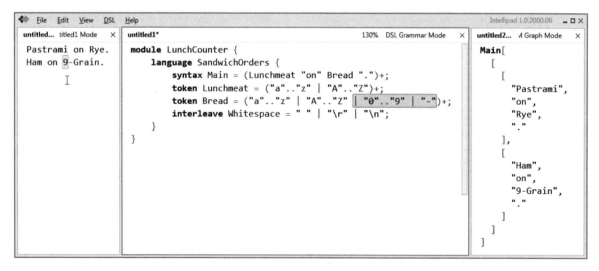

Figure 3-16. *Multiple orders now valid after modifying the Main syntax rule*

Tightening Up the Syntax

No errors here, so you're good so far. It looks like the processor will accept, generally speaking, any kind of sandwich order that conforms to the pattern `<some alpha string>` `"on"` `<some alpha string>`. The two strings can even be the same, like

`Blue on Blue.`

This would be valid under the current syntax definition.

Lola: "So, Norm, let's cut to the chase here. I'm not impressed with this system so far. Some wing nut could walk in and order "blue on blue," and the server wouldn't know whether to go to the jukebox or the order screen.

Lola types in "Blue on Blue." as a new sandwich order (Figure 3-17).

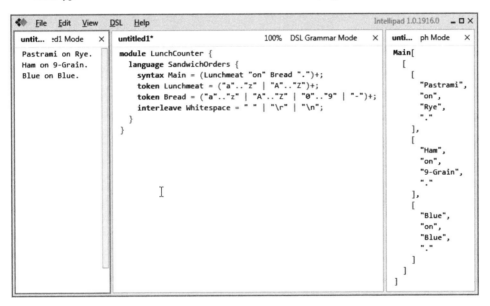

Figure 3-17. A syntax too ill-defined

Norm: "Exactly right, Lola—you catch on fast. Let's see if I can tighten up the language definition to do two things: 1) Provide a way of syntactically identifying which is the `Lunchmeat` and which is the `Bread` in a `SandwichOrders` statement, and 2) Provide a mapping of the components of a `SandwichOrders` statement to a database table. You want the system to allow an order for pastrami on rye, but reject an order for rye on pastrami. And, of course, the Blue on Blue problem should no longer happen.

Lola: "Fine."

Moving Toward Structured Data

The first thing Norm does is to change the `Main` syntax rule to define it as a collection of one or more `SandwichOrders`. This will result in creating a collection in the M Graph code, which would map to what is called an *extent*. Extents correspond to tables within the database, once the model is deployed to SQL

Server. When the image file generated by the M compiler is installed in the Repository database, this would result in a table of SandwichOrders. (For now, think of *repository* as a fancy word for database.)

Figure 3-18 shows the results of the first of these changes.

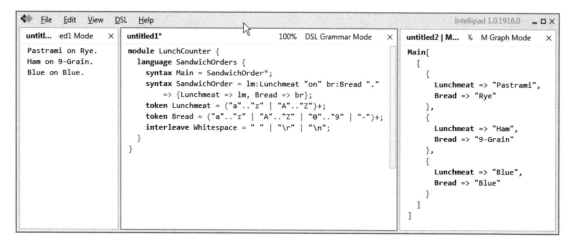

Figure 3-18. *Changing the Main syntax role and adding the SandwichOrder syntax rule*

You still have the Blue on Blue problem, but in the generated M Graph you are identifying the Lunchmeat and Bread data components, even if there are no semantic constraints on these.

Let's walk through the structure of the code of the DSL Grammar definition (center panel). At the highest level (outermost curly braces), you have the LunchCounter module, which defines your namespace. Within the module, you have a single language definition, named SandwichOrders. The language definition (contained within the next set of curly braces) consists of a collection of syntax rules, token rules, and an interleave rule (discussed in the section titled "Defining Tokens").

The Main syntax rule:

```
syntax Main = SandwichOrder*
```

sets the Main syntax rule to be a collection of zero or more SandwichOrders. (Recall that the asterisk * is a multiplicity operator designating a collection of zero or more instances.)

The SandwichOrder syntax rule:

```
syntax SandwichOrder = lm:Lunchmeat "on" br:Bread "."
        => {Lunchmeat => lm, Bread => br}
```

is really the heart of the SandwichOrders language definition. This construction says two things. A SandwichOrder consists of a Lunchmeat token, given the identifier lm, followed by the literal "on", followed by a Bread token given the identifier br, followed by the period character ".". => is the binding operator, so the second line of the preceding code syntax rule statement means that the construction results in an entity with two members: a Lunchmeat token with the value lm and a Bread token with the value br. Entities are simply collections with named values, so here you're defining an entity with two values: a Lunchmeat value (bound to the identifier lm) and a Bread value (bound to the identifier br).

Next, Norm again refines the Main syntax rule to store the collection of SandwichOrders in an extent named SandwichOrders. You see the results in Figure 3-19. What you see in the M Graph pane shows that you're getting a little closer to what you might call structured data.

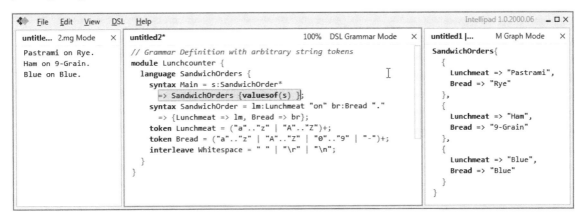

Figure 3-19. Generating the SandwichOrders collection with restructured syntax rules

Lola: "Okay Norm—one step forward, and one back. I can see you're making some progress in getting to where the system knows its lunchmeat from its bread. Not to complicate things too much, but do you think you could add in condiments, like mayo or mustard?"

Norm: "Sure thing. As usual, I'll add an order with a condiment and see how this breaks the DSL grammar definition. Type an order with a condiment, and I'll see what kind of error you get."

Lola types: "Ham on Baguette with Mayo." Figure 3-20 shows the results.

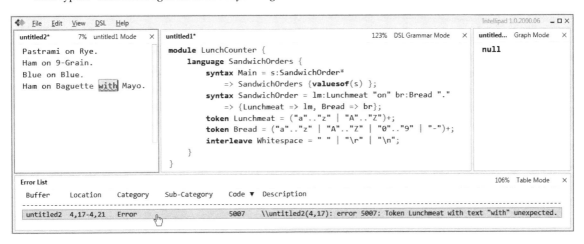

Figure 3-20. Testing a condiment addition

Norm has clicked on the single error description in the Error List pane, and this has highlighted the DSL segment "with" after the Bread token, the cause of this particular error.

Norm: "Well, clearly you've broken the grammar definition in at least a couple of ways, since it is no longer generating M Graph output in the right pane. From what you see in the error list, it thinks the word "with" is a Lunchmeat token. Here's what I'd suggest. Let's not add condiments into the system for the time being, and instead focus on refining the Lunchmeat and Bread syntax so that you get rid of the Blue on Blue problem, and the system is smart enough to exclude nonsense orders like ham on pastrami, even though ham and pastrami are both valid token values."

Lola: "Makes sense. One thing at a time."

Norm changes the token definitions for Lunchmeat and Bread to be collections of a few of the sandwich makings that comprise some sandwiches on Lola's menu. And he removes the condiment fragment from the last order to keep things simple. Figure 3-21 shows the result.

Figure 3-21. Redefining the Lunchmeat and Bread tokens

Redefining the syntax in this way, where only valid names are given for the Lunchmeat and Bread tokens in the grammar definition, has trapped nonsense orders like Blue on Blue.

Testing the Syntax

Lola: "Good—this is looking much more specific now. But let's check something. What will it do with an order like ham on pastrami?"

Norm: "Okay, here it is."

Norm enters the order "Ham on Pastrami." in the DSL pane, with the resulting error shown in Figure 3-22.

Figure 3-22. Testing a syntactically nonconforming sandwich order

Norm: "Clearly, that's not accepted. It breaks the syntax rules of the grammar definition. And look at the error description: the processor knows Pastrami is a Lunchmeat token, but it occurs in an unexpected part of the order. See what happens when I highlight the error list line in the Error List pane? It highlights the offending word in the DSL view, along with underlining the word with red squiggles."

Lola: "Great, it seems to be getting a little smarter, and you've clearly gotten rid of the Blue on Blue issue. Let's do a different test. I have a good Wall Street customer who loves Spam on white bread. He always comes in with big take-out orders, so even though it offends my sense of nutritional aesthetics, I'm going to have to stock some Spam and white bread. I'll just have to keep it off-menu. I know you don't have this in your test orders, but let's see what the system does with a Spam on white order."

Norm: "You got it. As usual, let's try the new order statement before I change the grammar and see what kind of error is generated."

He types in the order "Spam on White." raising the errors shown in the Error List pane at the bottom of Figure 3-23.

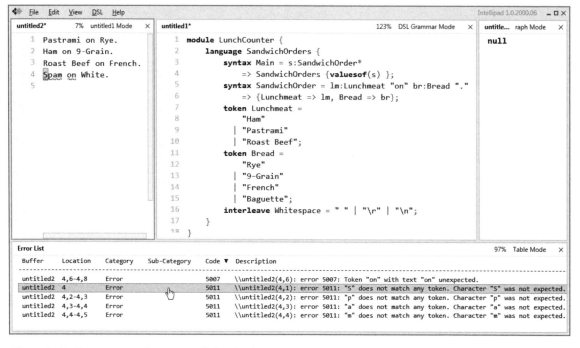

Figure 3-23. *Error output from an undefined token*

Norm: "So as soon as I type the first character S of the word Spam, the processor recognizes that there's no Lunchmeat token starting with S, and indicates an error. The next character, a lowercase p, doesn't occur as the first of a Lunchmeat token either, and so on. The prepositional word "on" is a required part of an order statement, but it still results in an error because it's not occurring after a valid Lunchmeat token.

Lola: "And what happens if you change the lowercase p to an uppercase P? The Pa matches the first two characters in Pastrami."

Norm: "Excellent! I'll try it."

He changes the word "Spam" to "Spam" in the last order, raising the error shown in Figure 3-24.

Figure 3-24. *More syntax testing*

Norm: "It takes the Pa fragment with no problem. It's looking for an s next, since that's the only character that matches with a valid Lunchmeat token. But when you type the m, it throws an error because it's looking for an s. Let's go ahead and add Spam as a lunchmeat and White as one of your breads, even though they'll be off-menu."

Lola: "Right."

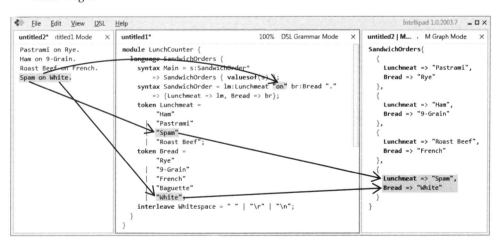

Figure 3-25. *Adding the "Spam" Lunchmeat and "White" Bread tokens*

Norm adds "Spam" to the Lunchmeat token list, and "White" to the Bread token list. Figure 3-25 shows the result, with the callout arrows tracing how the grammar processes each token to produce the last node shown in the M Graph pane at the right of the figure.

Making the Syntax More Flexible

Norm: "So it looks like you're back on firm ground."

Lola: "Affirmative. So let's add Portobello and grilled tofu as lunchmeat ingredients, and pita as a bread choice. And I want the system to accept an order for grilled tofu *in* pita, not *on* pita.

Norm: "Easily done. I'll simply redefine the SandwichOrder to accept either ""on" or "in" as the prepositional connector between the Lunchmeat and Bread tokens."

In terms of the grammar, this is written as ("on" | "in") in the syntax rule, as shown in Figure 3-26. This code segment means either "on" or "in" is valid.

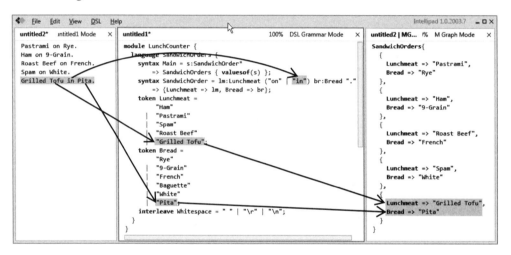

Figure 3-26. Providing options in the syntax definition

Norm: "But notice you've added a couple of main ingredients that aren't considered to be in the Lunchmeat category. Maybe you should broaden the name to something like Stuff for lack of something more scientific. Pastrami and Spam and grilled tofu could all be considered the primary stuff of a sandwich, right? The grammar definition doesn't really care about these kinds of lexical or naming questions, but it affects human readability. And that's one of the important benefits of DSLs."

Lola: "Makes sense to me."

Norm: "And now that you have things tightened up in terms of separating the lunchmeats. . .er, stuffs. . .from the breads, maybe it's time to get back to including the condiments. Unlike the stuff and the bread, which are the essential components, the condiments are optional, and you could possibly have more than one condiment, like mustard and relish together.

Lola: "Can you do that?"

Norm: "Piece of cake."

Norm adds a new token definition for Condiment, not unlike the previous definitions for Stuff and Bread. And he modifies the SandwichOrder syntax rule to include an optional "with" preposition and zero or more condiments. The "with"? in the modified rule definition means that "with" can occur at the place in the SandwichOrder zero or one times, and the asterisk in co:Condiment* means you can have zero or any number of condiments. Finally, he adds the conjunctions "and" and "&" as ignorable tokens in the Whitespace interleave definition so that these can be used in the condiments fragment of an order statement without affecting the syntax validity of the order.

Lola takes the keyboard and adds a condiment or two to each of the sample sandwich orders she previously entered in the left pane. Figure 3-27 shows the results.

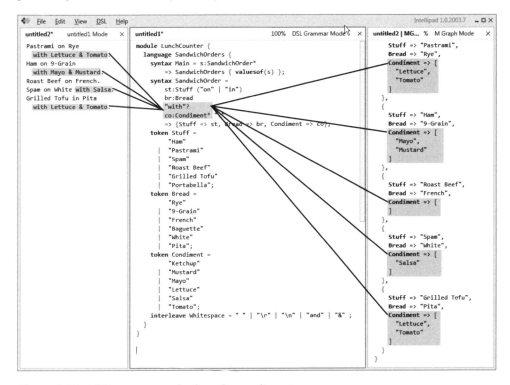

Figure 3-27. Adding syntax and tokens for condiments

The SandwichLanguage DSL MGraph

The right pane in Figure 3-27 shows what is called an M Graph. This is similar to what is usually called an abstract syntax tree (AST), but not quite the same, and is a representation of the DSL statements in the left pane after being processed through the grammar defined in the center pane. The trace lines show how the condiment components of the DSL statements in the left pane result in one value of the nodes in the M Graph on the right. If you look at the bottom SandwichOrder node of the M Graph shown in this figure, the expression within the innermost curly braces is an entity with three named values:

- A Stuff value bound to "Grilled Tofu". (Remember that => is the binding operator.)

- A Bread value bound to "Pita".

- A Condiment value bound to an *ordered* collection, or list, (indicated by the square brackets) with two members: "Lettuce" and "Tomato". If this were an *unordered* collection, the square brackets [ ] would be replaced with curly braces { }.

So, looking again at the M Graph in the right pane of Figure 3-27, you can view it simply as a named collection, with the name SandwichOrders (first line) of SandwichOrder entities, and with each entity of the collection having three named values: Stuff, Bread, and Condiment. According to the way the grammar has been defined, the Condiment value can be null (as with the Roast Beef on French SandwichOrder), have a single value (as with Spam on White with Salsa), or have a list of values (as with Grilled Tofu in Pita with Lettuce & Tomato).

In the next section, you'll see how you can modify the grammar to support more than one main ingredient, or Stuff.

Extending SandwichOrders to More Than One Main Ingredient

Lola: "This is starting to look a little more realistic now, Norm. But I have one more request: I need a way of adding an additional main ingredient. For instance, someone might order grilled tofu and Portabella in pita, or ham and pepperoni on French. What would it take to do that?"

Norm: "One character."

Lola: "Surely you jest, mon neveu."

Norm: "No, I'm serious. Let's add Portabella to the grilled tofu in the last order, and see if it breaks as you expect it to.

Figure 3-28 shows the resulting error.

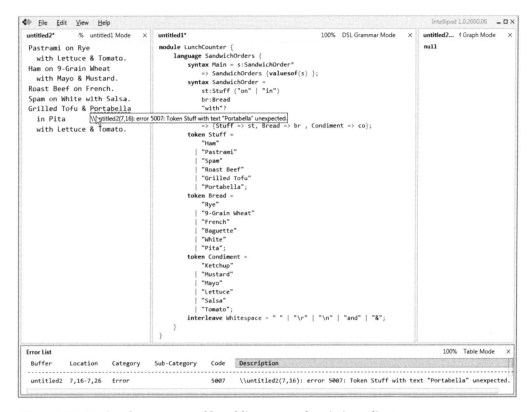

Figure 3-28. Testing the error caused by adding a second main ingredient

Norm: "Just as I thought: The processor complains about the second Stuff component added in the order. But if you add a + operator after st:Stuff fragment of the SandwichOrder syntax definition, this fixes the grammar to handle one or more primary ingredients. This is exactly what the + operator means: one or more. And it's the single character I said you would need. Without it, the st:Stuff fragment in the rule is interpreted to mean one and only one Stuff token."

Figure 3-29 shows the results after adding the + postfix operator after the Stuff token in the SandwichOrder syntax rule.

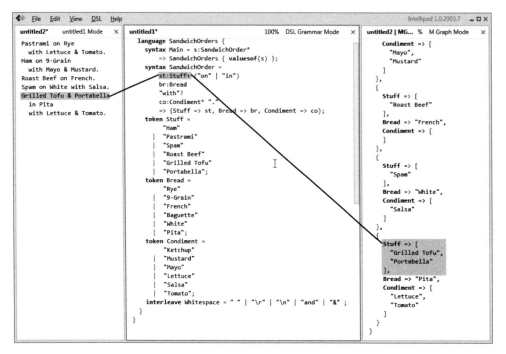

Figure 3-29. Changing the syntax to allow additional ingredients

Deployment

Now you will take your leave Lola and Norm and their lively investigations of the LunchCounter domain because it's time to think about how to deploy this model to SQL Server. Lola and Norm have developed a reasonable sandwich model here, but as you shall find shortly, it's not yet in a configuration that can be deployed to the database. The problem has to do with one-to-many relationships in the model; how to represent these relationships in a way that enables deployment remains an issue.

Looking back at Figure 3-29, you have the following:

- A DSL representation of four sandwich orders, represented in a language about as close to natural English as you can get (left pane).

- A DSL Grammar program for processing these DSL statements in the middle pane.

- An M Graph parse of the DSL statements in the right pane, created by processing the DSL through the DSL Grammar machinery.

Your mission (should you wish to accept it) is to compile the DSL Grammar code into an image (.mx) file and use it to deploy the model (schema), with SandwichOrder instances represented by the DSL into SQL Server.

Schema vs. Model

Think of the word *schema* as meaning a complete description of a database in a formal language supported by the database management system. A schema will include a formal description of all tables included in the database, their relationships and constraints, and other information needed for creating or reconstructing the database. A schema should be a complete description of the structure of the database, but will say nothing about the actual data contained in it. I introduce the term here because, in the context of SQL Server Modeling, it can often be used more or less synonymously with the word *model*. *Schema* is more appropriately used in the database context, whereas *model* is used in the modeling context. But the two terms are closely linked in the context of the SQL Server Modeling framework.

Getting back to the exercise, before you go any further, you should save your code. Save the DSL Grammar code by clicking in the center pane so that it has focus, then click the File → Save As menu option. Click the Create New Folder icon in the Save As dialog box and rename New Folder to LunchCounter, as shown in Figure 3-30. Save the code in the untitled1* DSL Grammar Mode pane as LunchCounter.mg in the new LunchCounter folder. (The "mg" file extension is short for Mgrammar, another term for DSL Grammar.)

Click in the left pane, then follow a similar procedure (except for creating the new folder), and save the DSL sandwich code as SandwichLanguage.dsl in the LunchCounter folder.

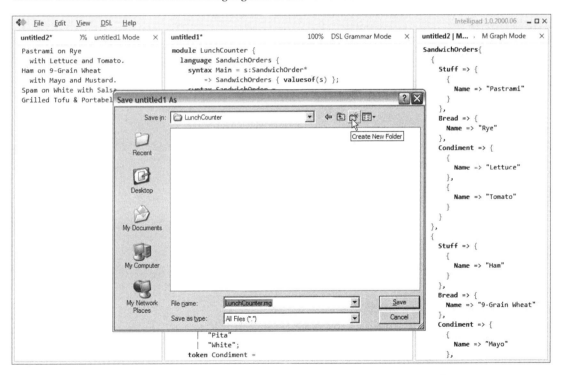

Figure 3-30. *Creating the C:\LunchCounter folder and saving the DSL Grammar code as LunchCounter.mg*

You should now have the DSL file (SandwichLanguage.dsl), and the DSL Grammar definition file (LunchCounter.mg) in your new working folder (C:\LunchCounter). But you can't yet deploy this code. The problem is with the generated M Graph tree, displayed in the right pane of Intellipad. This is not yet in a form that can be used by the command-line tools to build the SQL Server tables.

Since this is an introductory level book, I will avoid going through all of the diagnostics necessary to arrive at a version of the DSL Grammar code that allows you to deploy the model, with instances, to the database. (Pay no attention to the man behind the curtain.) The primary fix is to reset the Stuff, Bread, and Condiment types to named entities rather than text types. The Bread component will be set as a collection, even though it will always be a collection of one for a particular instance of SandwichOrder. This will also require three new syntax definitions for the new entity types: BreadEntity, CondimentEntity, and StuffEntity. These changes appear in the gray portion of Figure 3-31, and the right pane shows the new M Graph.

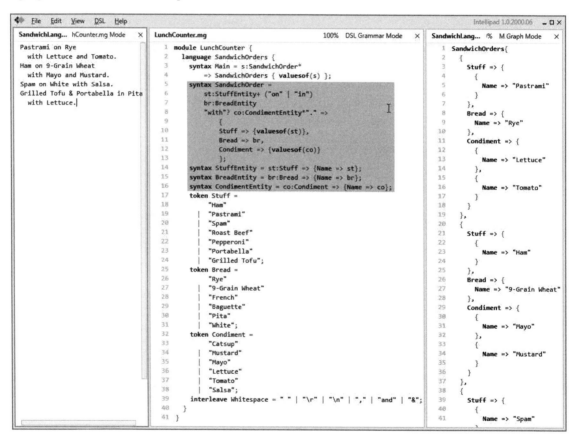

Figure 3-31. *The final LunchCounter DSL Grammar definition (center pane) and generated M Graph (right pane)*

The other component you need for a successful deployment to the database is a schema definition. Here again, I won't get into the details of how this is constructed, but the code, which is shown in Figure

3-32, should be reasonably self-evident, based on what you've already seen in this exercise. I've added some constraints to show how business rules might be expressed directly within the code in terms of the allowed number of Stuff and Condiments values in a sandwich and the fact that only one kind of bread can be used in a sandwich.

The grayed area shows the important part of the schema code, particularly in terms of creating the database. This expresses the relationship constraints in the schema. Remember that && is the logical AND operator, and the <= operator means that the left operand collection is constrained to be a subcollection of the right operand collection. This where constraint is the core logic that determines how the tables are built in the database.

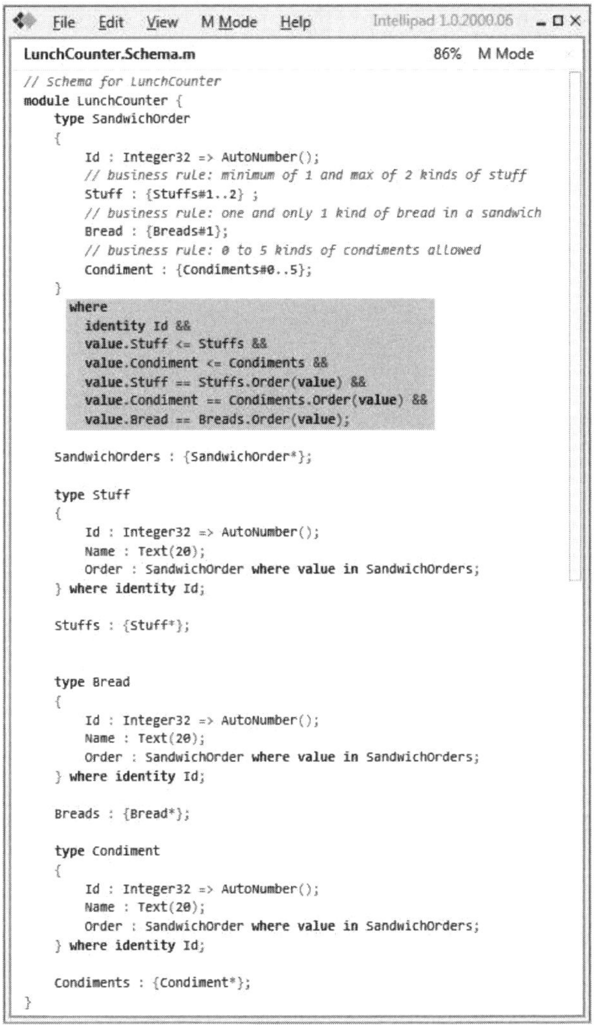

```
File    Edit    View    M Mode    Help        Intellipad 1.0.2000.06    _ □ ×

LunchCounter.Schema.m                        86%    M Mode

// Schema for LunchCounter
module LunchCounter {
    type SandwichOrder
    {
        Id : Integer32 => AutoNumber();
        // business rule: minimum of 1 and max of 2 kinds of stuff
        Stuff : {Stuffs#1..2} ;
        // business rule: one and only 1 kind of bread in a sandwich
        Bread : {Breads#1};
        // business rule: 0 to 5 kinds of condiments allowed
        Condiment : {Condiments#0..5};
    }
    where
        identity Id &&
        value.Stuff <= Stuffs &&
        value.Condiment <= Condiments &&
        value.Stuff == Stuffs.Order(value) &&
        value.Condiment == Condiments.Order(value) &&
        value.Bread == Breads.Order(value);

    SandwichOrders : {SandwichOrder*};

    type Stuff
    {
        Id : Integer32 => AutoNumber();
        Name : Text(20);
        Order : SandwichOrder where value in SandwichOrders;
    } where identity Id;

    Stuffs : {Stuff*};

    type Bread
    {
        Id : Integer32 => AutoNumber();
        Name : Text(20);
        Order : SandwichOrder where value in SandwichOrders;
    } where identity Id;

    Breads : {Bread*};

    type Condiment
    {
        Id : Integer32 => AutoNumber();
        Name : Text(20);
        Order : SandwichOrder where value in SandwichOrders;
    } where identity Id;

    Condiments : {Condiment*};
}
```

Figure 3-32. The LunchCounter MSchema definition

If you're following along with this example on your computer, open a new M file in Intellipad, change the Standard mode to M mode, key in the schema code or download it from the Apress website, and save it as LunchCounter.Schema.m in your new working directory, C:\LunchCounter.

Now that you have the DSL, DSL Grammar, and schema code saved, you can begin to work with the SQL Server Modeling command-line tools to attempt to deploy the model to SQL Server. *Deployment* means that you have a representation of the model in SQL Server in terms of a schema and tables, constraints on the data derived from any business rules, and sample data in the tables.

Bring up the SQL Server Modeling command prompt by clicking on the Start button → All Programs and navigating to Microsoft SQL Server Modeling CTP → Microsoft SQL Server Modeling CTP Command Prompt. The verbiage might be a little different on your machine, depending on when you are reading this and whether you are running the CTP, Beta, or commercial release. Figure 3-33 shows a screen capture of this step.

Figure 3-33. *Invoking the Microsoft SQL Server Modeling Command Prompt*

This will bring up the command prompt window, as shown in Figure 3-34.

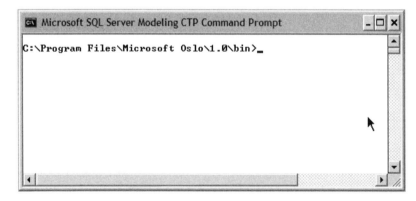

Figure 3-34. *SQL Server Modeling Command Prompt in its default directory*

Change the current directory to C:\LunchCounter by entering the following command:

```
cd  \LunchCounter
```

Execute the `dir` command to verify that your DSL Grammar, DSL, and schema files exist in this directory, and then compile the DSL Grammar code by entering the following command:

```
m.exe  LunchCounter.mg
```

and execute another dir command to be sure the compiler created the LunchCounter.mx image file (see Figure 3-35).

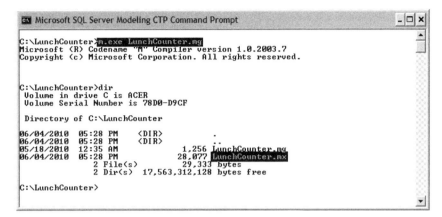

Figure 3-35. *SQL compiling the LunchCounter.mg file to create the LuncCounter.mx image file*

Next, you want to use the DSL Grammar executor command-line tool to generate an M code version of the SandwichLanguage.dsl file. (The executable was formerly called the Mgrammar executor, which is where it got its mgx.exe name.) With any executable command-line tool, you can normally enter the name of the command followed by /? to get a listing of the parameters that can be used to pass information to the tool when it executes. Figure 3-36 shows a list of these parameters. The two you're interested in are reference and MModuleName. (Note that most, but not all, have shorthand aliases, like /r: for /reference:, to save you time when you're using the tool frequently.)

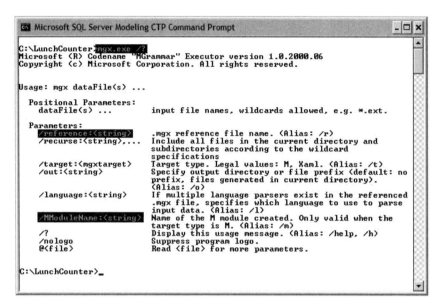

Figure 3-36. Displaying the MGX tool parameters

At the command prompt, enter and execute the command as follows:

```
Mgx.exe SandwichLanguage.dsl /reference:LunchCounter.mx /MModuleName: LunchCounter
```

Figure 3-37 shows this, except that I've used aliases for setting the parameters to keep the command from wrapping in the command window. You can try it either way. If you do a dir directory listing, you can see that this command created the SandwichLanguage.m file.

Figure 3-37. Running the MGX MGrammar executor tool to generate the SandwichLanguage.m file

Loading this file into Intellipad (see Figure 3-38), you can see that it is an M Graph almost exactly the same as the one generated earlier when you made the final revisions to the DSL Grammar code prior to setting up for the deployment phase. The one difference is that the graph is now defined within the LunchCounter module.

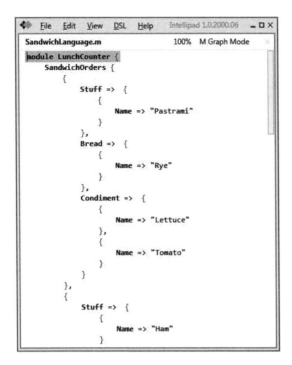

Figure 3-38. Displaying SandwichLanguage.m in Intellipad M Graph mode

You should be ready for the last step of installing the schema and instances to the database. You can do this with the mx.exe executor tool.

The MSchema file, LunchCounter.Schema.m, defines the four types and extents that the M Graph uses: SandwichOrders, Breads, Stuff, and Condiments. The MSchema file tells the SQL Server Modeling framework how to store the instances of the data represented in the M Graph in a data store. With your MSchema defined, you can use both the M Graph created by the MExecutor (mgx.exe) and the MSchema (LunchCounter.Schema.m, as shown in Figure 3-32) to compile your M files for use in a SQL Server data store by using the M compiler:

```
m.exe SandwichLanguage.m LunchCounter.Schema.m /t:TSql10
```

The /t: target flag specifies that the output will be used for deploying the schema and instances. The result of executing this command is the image file SandwichLanguage.mx. (See the listing generated by the dir command in Figure 3-39.)

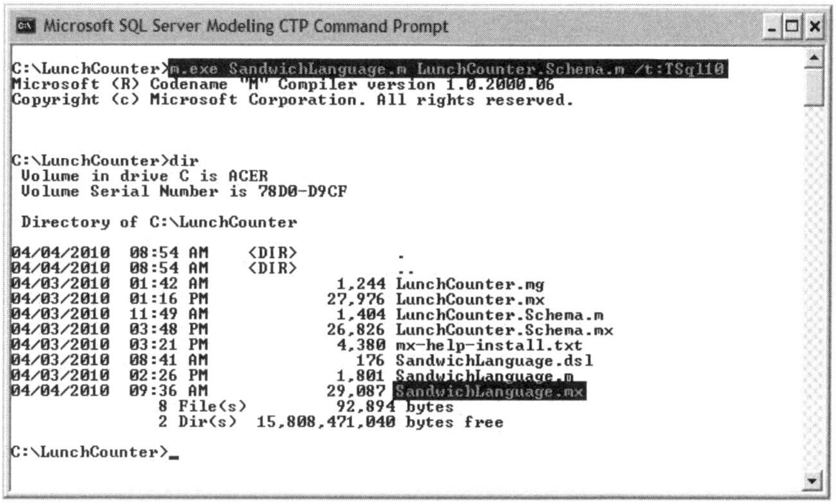

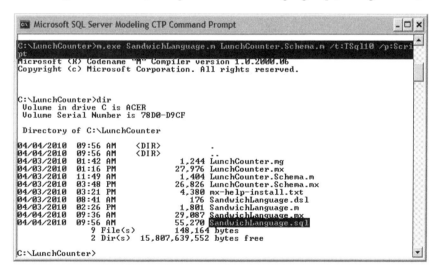

Figure 3-39. Generating the SandwichLanguage.mx image file

You can also add a package flag (/p) to specify that instead of an image file, you want a SQL script:

```
m.exe SandwichLanguage.m LunchCounter.Schema.m /t:TSql10 /p:Script
```

This generates the SQL script file SandwichLanguage.sql (see Figure 3-40).

Figure 3-40. Generating the SandwichLanguage.sql script file with the m.exe compiler

You can run this script as a query in SQL Server Management Studio (SSMS) to load the database. Bring up SSMS, click on the File menu, then Open → File (see Figure 3-41).

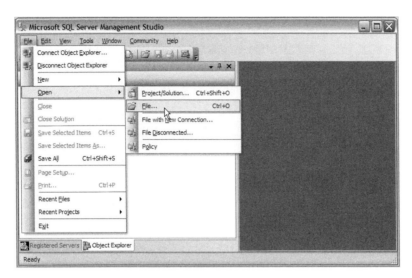

Figure 3-41. Opening the generated SQL script file in SQL Server Management Studio

When the Open File dialog box appears, browse to the C:\LunchCounter folder and select the SandwichLanguage.sql. To open it, either double-click the file or click the Open button. This will display the contents of the T-SQL script file. Click the Execute button on the SSMS toolbar, as shown in Figure 3-42.

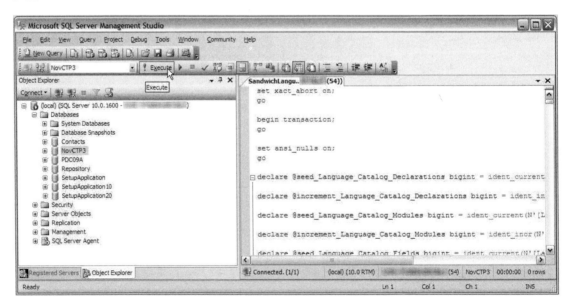

Figure 3-42. SQL Server Management Studio after opening the SandwichLanguage.sql T-SQL script file

An alternative approach to deploying the database is to use the `mx.exe` command-line utility. Figure 3-43 displays the syntax for using the `mx.exe` tool to deploy to the database, along with the output generated.

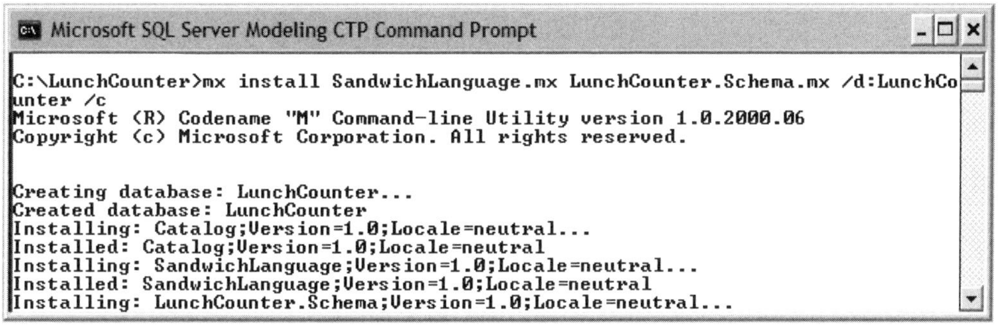

```
Microsoft SQL Server Modeling CTP Command Prompt                    _ □ ×

C:\LunchCounter>mx install SandwichLanguage.mx LunchCounter.Schema.mx /d:LunchCo
unter /c
Microsoft (R) Codename "M" Command-line Utility version 1.0.2000.06
Copyright (c) Microsoft Corporation. All rights reserved.


Creating database: LunchCounter...
Created database: LunchCounter
Installing: Catalog;Version=1.0;Locale=neutral...
Installed: Catalog;Version=1.0;Locale=neutral
Installing: SandwichLanguage;Version=1.0;Locale=neutral...
Installed: SandwichLanguage;Version=1.0;Locale=neutral
Installing: LunchCounter.Schema;Version=1.0;Locale=neutral...
```

Figure 3-43. SQL installing the LunchCounter database using the MX executor

Regardless of which way you decide to deploy the LunchCounter module, you can check the installation by bringing up SQL Server Management Studio. If it is already up, simply click the server connection and press the F5 key to refresh the display. You should now see LunchCounter displayed as one of the databases under the Databases list. Expand LunchCounter, then click on Tables. (Figure 3-44 shows a partial view of the LunchCounter database Tables list.) Scroll down the list until you get to where the LunchCounter tables should appear. You should see four tables listed:

- LunchCounter.Breads
- LunchCounter.Condiments
- LunchCounter.SandwichOrders
- LunchCounter.Stuffs

You can examine the data in each of these tables by right-clicking on the table name and selecting Edit Top 200 Rows.

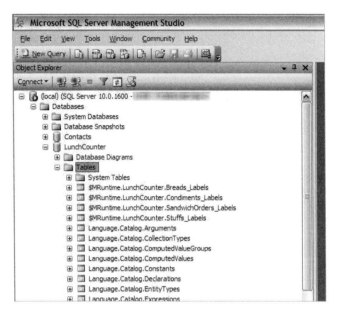

Figure 3-44. Checking the LunchCounter database Tables list in SSMS

Before reviewing the data in the tables, let's recall the four sample orders you set up in your SandwichLanguage.dsl file. The final Intellipad split-pane view (refer to Figure 3-31) shows these. They consisted of the following:

- Order 1: Pastrami on Rye with Lettuce & Tomato.

- Order 2: Ham on 9-Grain Wheat with Mayo and Mustard.

- Order 3: Spam on White with Salsa.

- Order 4: Grilled Tofu & Portabella in Pita with Lettuce.

These should be reflected in the four LunchCounter database tables. Note that there are three many-to-one relationships in these orders: two condiments in Orders 1 and 2, and two stuffs in Order 4. The tables should reflect these.

Figure 3-45 shows the four instances of SandwichOrder in the SandwichOrders table. This table contains the order keys only, since all the remaining data of an order (the Bread, Stuffs, and Condiments values) are reflected in the three other tables. If Lola and Norm get into further design iterations and refinements, the SandwichOrders table might contain other data, such as an Order timestamp. But for now, each instance in the table has only a key, reflected as a foreign key in each of the Breads, Condiments, and Stuffs tables.

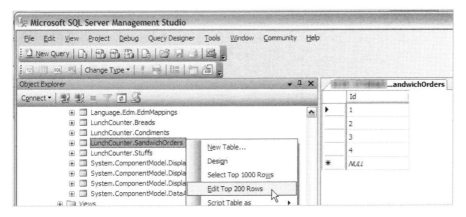

Figure 3-45. The SandwichOrders table, which contains only the order key

Figure 3-46 shows the Breads table. Note that there is only one `Bread` value for each order, which is what you would expect, since this is how the orders were set up in the sample DSL file. Besides, one `Bread` per `SandwichOrder` is a business rule that was reflected in the LunchCounter.Schema.m file.

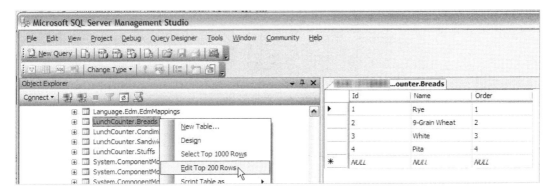

Figure 3-46. The Breads table

Figure 3-47 shows the Condiments table, and you can see there are two one-to-many relationships: Order1 has two condiments (Lettuce and Tomato) and Order 2 also has two condiments (Mayo and Mustard). This is as you would expect, given the sample orders in the DSL file.

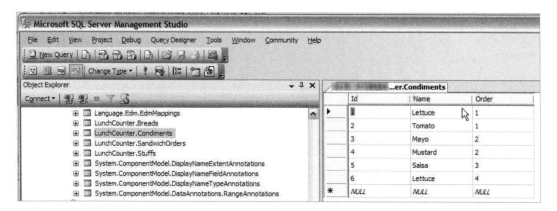

Figure 3-47. The Condiments table

Finally, Figure 3-48 shows the values in the Stuffs table, which includes a single many-to-one relationship: Order 4 has two Stuff values (Grilled Tofu and Portabella). Again, this is confirmed by the expression of the fourth order in the list: Grilled Tofu & Portabella in Pita with Lettuce. So the database instances appear to be entirely consistent with the model.

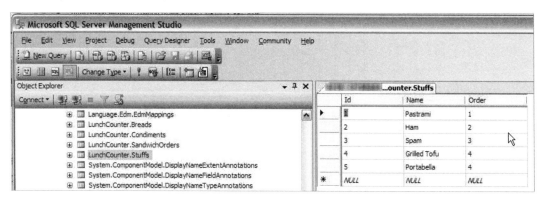

Figure 3-48. The Stuffs table

You may have notice that under the LunchCounter database item in the Object Explorer pane of SSMS is an item called Database Diagrams. Let's see if you can generate a diagram of the five tables. Click on the Database Diagrams item, and you will more than likely get a message window like that shown in Figure 3-49, asking if you would like to generate the support objects required to use database diagramming. Click the Yes button to generate the support objects.

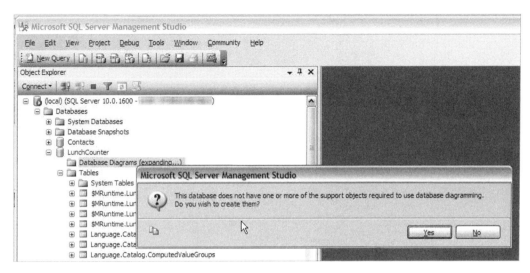

Figure 3-49. Setting up to generate a database diagram

Once this happens, you can right-click on Database Diagrams and select New Database Diagram (see Figure 3-50).

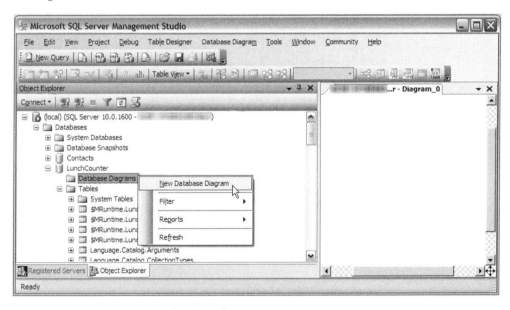

Figure 3-50. Creating a new a database diagram

A multi-select Add Table dialog box will pop up to allow you to select the database tables you want to appear in the diagram. Use the Ctrl key to multi-select the Breads, Condiments, SandwichOrders, and Stuffs tables, click the Add button, and then the Close button.

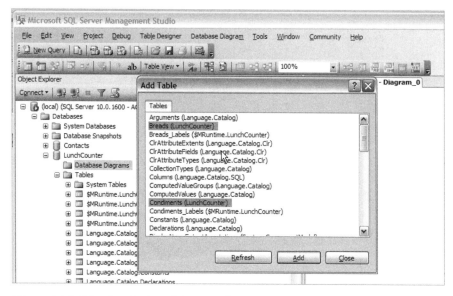

***Figure 3-51.** Selecting the LunchCounter database tables to display in the diagram*

Figure 3-52 shows the diagram of the four tables and their relationships. Diagramming is a powerful tool in SQL Server, and there is a lot of functionality provided in the diagramming tools. Covering these features is beyond the scope of this book, but I hope I've provided at least a taste of how the SQL Server Modeling tools can be used in conjunction with the traditional SQL Server tools (such as SSMS and Visual Studio) to create and deploy your own data models and model-based applications.

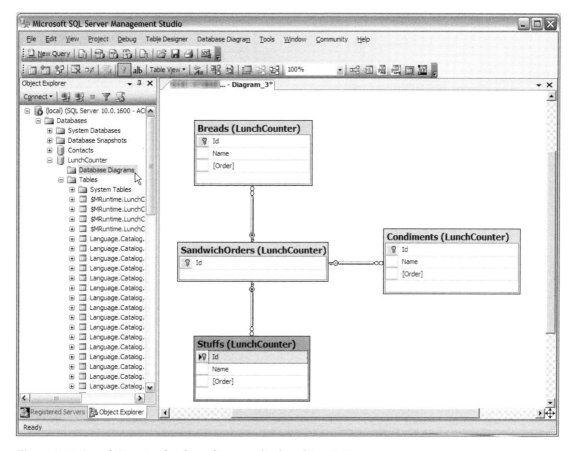

Figure 3-52. LunchCounter database diagram displayed in SSMS

You could also use a JOIN select statement to create a consolidated view of the sandwich orders. To do this, close the Object Explorer pane by clicking the X in the upper-right corner of the Object Explorer pane. Click "New Query" on the tool ribbon (Figure 3-53). Click the Query menu item, then choose the Design Query in Editor option (see Figure 3-53).

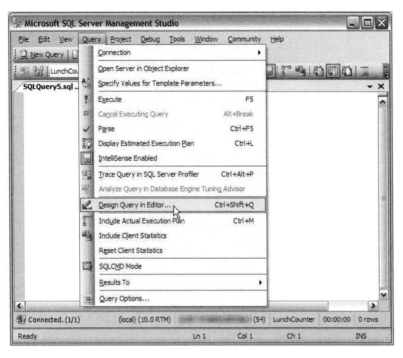

Figure 3-53. *Setting up to design the query in the Query editor*

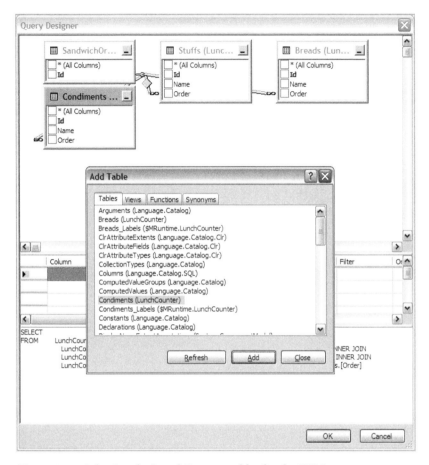

Figure 3-54. *Selecting the LunchCounter tables for the JOIN query*

This will bring up an empty Query Designer window, with an Add Table dialog box (Figure 3-54). Select the four LunchCounter tables in the following order, clicking the Add button after each selection:

- SandwichOrders (LunchCounter)

- Stuffs (LunchCounter)

- Breads (LunchCounter)

- Condiments (LunchCounter)

This should result in a table diagram similar to that shown in the upper pane of the Query Designer (see Figure 3-55). Click the Close button on the Add Table dialog box and rearrange the tables to make the diagram more readable.

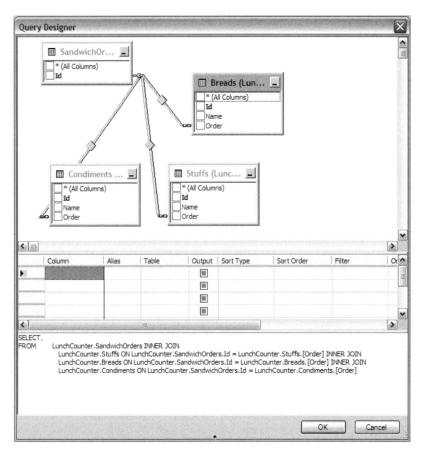

Figure 3-55. After rearranging the table diagram and preparing to select the display columns

Now you're ready to select the display columns for the query. Click in the topmost cell of the left column, and you should see a drop-down menu from which you can select the first display column (see Figure 3-56, which shows the drop-down menu for the fourth column after setting up the first three column definitions).

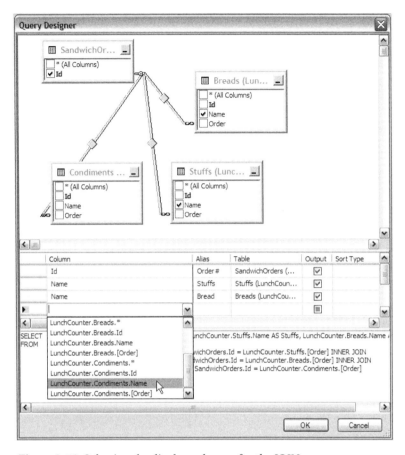

Figure 3-56. Selecting the display columns for the JOIN query

Set up the display columns according to the column, aliases, and table names shown in Table 3-1.

Table 3-1. *Display Column Configuration for the Query*

Column	Alias	Table
Id	Order#	SandwichOrders (LunchCounter)
Name	Stuffs	Stuffs (LunchCounter)
Name	Bread	Breads (LunchCounter)
Name	Condiments	Condiments (LunchCounter)

After completing the display column configuration for the query, click the OK button of the Query Designer window. The generated query text is shown in the upper pane of Figure 3-57. Press F5 or click the [! Execute] button on the toolbar to run the query.

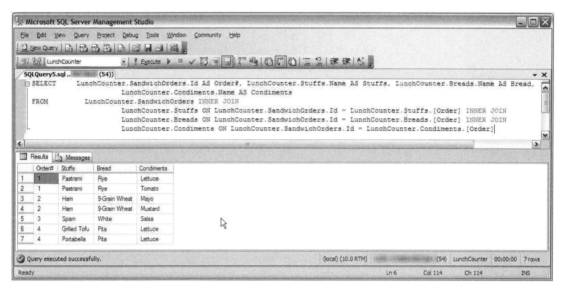

Figure 3-57. *Displaying the view of the query results*

The results of the query are shown in the table displayed in the lower pane. As you can see, you have four sandwich orders: Pastrami on Rye with Lettuce and Tomato, Ham on 9-Grain Wheat with Mayo and Mustard, Spam on White with Salsa, and Grilled Tofu and Portabella in Pita with Lettuce. This corresponds exactly with the original DSL sample.

Thinking Ahead

You could continue refining your model for SandwichOrders, and more generally the functionality of your system. Here are a few possibilities:

- Tag each order with a timestamp, the server's name, and the table number.

- Track inventory effects by decrementing the respective quantities in inventory for each order served.

- Extend the DSL to a broader range of orders, like drinks, salads, and soups.

- Have the system compute the total price of each order.

- Track whether an order is for take-out or not.

- Provide nutritional data to each customer based on his or her order. (Some restaurants provide this kind of information on their menus.)

Concluding Thoughts

This concludes your excursion through the domain of the LunchCounter. The chapter provides only a cursory overview of how one might go about creating a DSL to model a single process or workflow.

How might you sum up what you've learned from this LunchCounter exercise? This fictional exchange between a user (i.e., domain expert) and a developer (i.e., technology expert) illustrates the kind of collaboration that can begin with a rudimentary and hypothetical single line in the DSL. Over time, the DSL and its DSL Grammar definition can be gradually refined and extended until it approaches the fundamentals of a useful system.

The style used by Norm in working with Lola, the user, is a somewhat simplified version of test-driven development. Working with Lola, extensions and refinements to the DSL are written first, then he codes against the errors raised because of the fact that the grammar doesn't support these extensions. As the developer refines the grammar, these errors are removed, and the DSL and grammar definitions are validated by seeing the resulting M Graph code generated in a way that makes sense.

Knowledge of the M language specification is important to the developer, but not to the user. This knowledge can only be gained by a careful reading of the Microsoft M Language Specification, or of some other source, that provides this information in all its detail. Because this book approaches the subject at the beginner's level, I've skirted over some of the more technical aspects of developing a DSL using MGrammar and the M language tools. If you're determined to get up to speed with this technology, time invested in becoming familiar with these important sources is time well spent.

DSLs have at least three important attributes:

- Readability: This is perhaps the most important, because a well-designed DSL provides the context and the platform for communication between the domain expert and the technology expert. The clarity and ease of this communication is crucial in developing a system that provides real value to the user.

- Write-ability: This means statements written in the Domain-Specific Language are easily written, in an intuitive way, by both the domain expert and the technology expert. There is a minimum of, if any, arcane rules of syntax to learn and remember.

- Simplicity (remember the lack of expressiveness I mentioned at the beginning?): This goes hand-in-hand with the first two attributes. Readability and write-ability won't be attained without simplicity.

CHAPTER 4

■■■

Introduction to Quadrant

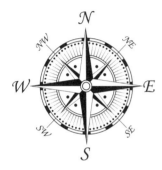

In Chapter 3, you saw how to create a domain-specific language (DSL) for a very simple domain using Intellipad, the M-aware text editor. In this chapter, you'll look at Quadrant, a modeling tool that addresses a wide range of tasks, including creating, maintaining, and editing models and data in the Repository or in other SQL database tables, as well as writing and editing M code.

Quadrant is a powerful tool in terms of its functionality, and it has an extensive feature set. I could begin with a walkthrough each of the features in its menu tree, but that may not be the most interesting or productive way of getting the first-time user up to speed. A tool with an extensive feature set can be a bit overwhelming for the new user, so this chapter will approach its subject at a somewhat higher level. The intent here is to give you an overview of Quadrant without immersing you in too many of the details.

Appendix D shows the Quadrant menu tree, so feel free to refer to that any time you would like to see where a particular feature fits.

My Car: Creating a Simple Model in Quadrant

You'll start putting Quadrant through its paces by creating a simple systems model of a car. As you know, you can analyze many complex systems (like planes, trains, and automobiles) as a composition of different levels of subsystems and components. In addition, the subsystems themselves can be further analyzed into lower level subsystems. This is a partitioning design pattern usually referred to as the *composite pattern*.

To open Quadrant, click on the Windows Start button, then All Programs, then Microsoft SQL Server Modeling CTP → Quadrant, as shown in Figure 4-1.

Figure 4-1. Opening Quadrant from the Windows Start button → All Programs menu

Building the Car Model in Quadrant

The initial Quadrant window, after opening, appears as shown in Figure 4-2, with much of the same look and feel as Intellipad. The lower-right corner of the status bar shows the current database name and zoom level.

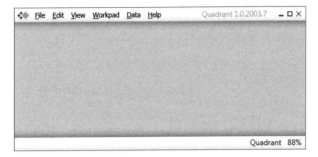

Figure 4-2. The empty Quadrant window after opening

To build the code for the car model, you'll start by opening a text pane for writing the M code for the model. Click File → New, and then select M File, as shown in Figure 4-3.

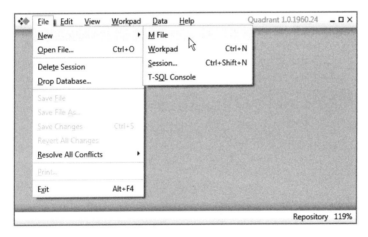

Figure 4-3. Opening a new M file

Figure 4-4 shows the M code (in its entirety) for the composition-based car model. Note that the double slashes (//) at the start of any line denotes a comment; comments are ignored by the M compiler, as they are with other programming languages. Block (multi-line) comments can also be embedded in the code by starting the first line of the comment with a slash and asterisk (/*) and ending the last line of the comment with the opposite (*/), as shown on lines 16 and 17 in Figure 4-4.

```
1  module Car.Model
2  {
3     export CarComponent, CarComponents;
4
5  // define the CarComponent type:
6     type CarComponent
7     {
8         Id : Integer64 => AutoNumber(); // used for the Id, or key for each component
9         Name : Text;
10        Level : Integer32;     // the system level of the component
11        Description : Text?;   // "?" is a "Kleene operator" meaning 0 or 1 occurrences
12        PartOfComponent : CarComponent? where value in CarComponents;
13        Quantity : Integer32 => 1; // how many needed for top-level system; default to 1
14    } where identity (Id);
15
16 /* declare "CarComponents" as the collection,
17 or extent, of all CarComponents:  */
18    CarComponents: {CarComponent*};
19 }
```

Figure 4-4. *M code for a simple car model*

Let's walk through the code line by line:

Line 1: `module Car.Model`—All M code must be contained within a named module, which is the top-level namespace in the M language. It helps to give a meaningful name to the module that more or less conveys its intent.

Line 3: `export CarComponent, CarComponents`—This makes the `CarComponent` and `CarComponents` entities visible and available to other modules. These are the only two declarations in this particular module: the type `CarComponent` and the extent (or table, in SQL-speak) `CarComponents`, which is a collection of the `CarComponent` entities. You could also import declarations from other modules, but this isn't necessary in this particular example, since the module stands by itself.

Line 6: `type CarComponent`—Here you are declaring that the type definition for `CarComponent` follows inside the braces. A `CarComponent` type is defined with the following named structure:

- Id: An `Integer64` (64-bit integer) that is set by the `AutoNumber()` function. `AutoNumber()` is normally used for defining the Id (or key) of a new entity. It is a system-provided function that automatically assigns a unique incremental number to the Id, or key, each time a new entity is instantiated.
- **Name:** Defined as unrestricted text. Name is an important attribute when defining a new type or entity, since it is, by convention, used as the tag for the entity.
- **Level:** An `Integer32`. This is the system level of the component. The top system level is 1 and defines the level of the entire system, named "My Car."

Level 2 corresponds to the highest level subsystems of the car, such as the drive train or suspension or body. Level 3 corresponds to subsystems of the Level 2 systems, and so on down the tree, until you reach the atomic level (in the system perspective) of nuts, bolts, washers, and other things that can't be deconstructed any further.

- **Description:** Text indicates unrestricted text, as with the name, and the appended Kleene operator (?) indicates either 0 or 1 occurrence. In other words, the Description text is optional, or in database parlance, nullable.

- **PartOfComponent:** `CarComponent? where value in CarComponents` means that the type instance can be null (the Kleene operator ? again), or can be part of another `CarComponent` instance. If a component is part of another subsystem, the parent system must be in the `CarComponents` collection. In fewer words, the parent component must exist in the extent. This illuminates a "self-referential" aspect to the model: One entity in the model can be a parent or child entity of another entity in themodel, and the `PartOfComponent` Id will be a foreign key referring to another entity existing in the scope of the same model and (in the database perspective) table.

- **Quantity:** This indicates the number of components needed to complete the system or parent subsystem. For example, eight pistons are required for a V-8 engine, and four wheels are required for a car.

Note that the terminating semicolon (;) after the ending right brace in the code indicates the end of the type definition.

Line 14: `Where identity (Id);`—This line of code assigns the identity (primary key in the context of the database) to the value of Id.

Line 17: `CarComponents: {CarComponent*};`—This declares the `CarComponents` extent (which results in creating a table of the same name in the database). Think of an extent in the model context as mapping directly to a table in the database context, with each entity within the extent corresponding to a record in the database table. In the present context, the extent is declared to be the collection of all `CarComponents`. The curly braces indicate a collection, and the asterisk is a Kleene operator indicating 0 or more occurrences of `CarComponent` instances within the collection.

Kleene *operators are also called repetition operators* in the M language specification, and there are three of these:

- * means zero or more occurrences of an item (as previously described).

- + means one or more occurrences of an item.

- ? means zero or one occurrence of an item. This essentially means the item is nullable, or optional.

This is the complete code for the simple car model. It allows you to model the car as a composite of subsystems and components in any number of different system levels. You could, if you wanted to, take this down to the level of nuts, bolts, O-rings, grommets, and gaskets, with thousands of records for these subsystems and components in the table.

To save this code as an M file, click File → Save File As in the Quadrant menu bar (see Figure 4-5), and save the file as CarModel.m.

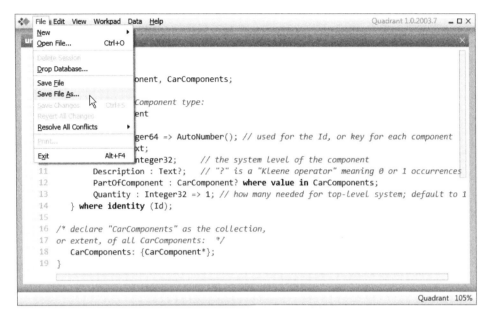

Figure 4-5. Saving the Car.Model code as Car.Model.m

Deploying the Model to SQL Server

Once the M file is saved, you're ready to deploy the model as a schema to SQL Server. In Quadrant, you are able to deploy the model directly to the SQL Server database without having to use the command-line tool set as you did in the last chapter. To use this procedure for deploying the model, click Data → Deploy in the menu bar (see Figure 4-6). (As the menu indicates, Ctrl+F5 will also work.)

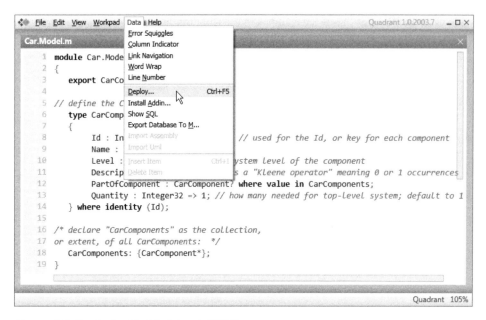

Figure 4-6. Deploying CarModel.m to SQL Server

A dialog box will pop up, as shown in Figure 4-7, giving you the option to deploy to the existing database session, to replace an existing database (this would replace the database, including schema and data), or create a new database.

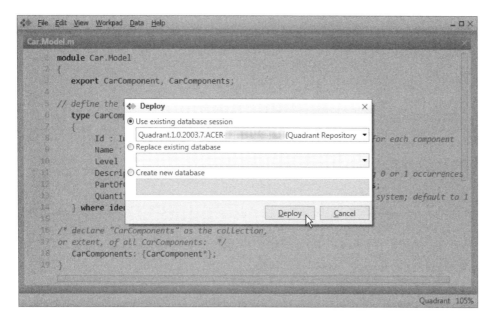

Figure 4-7. *Designating the database for deployment*

Select the Create New Database option, and name the new database "CarModel." Once the model is deployed, you can use the Quadrant Explorer to view, add, and edit data (see Figure 4-8).

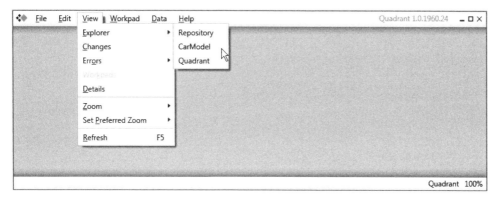

Figure 4-8. *Bringing up the CarModel Explorer*

Viewing the Model and Adding Data in the Explorer

Click View → Explorer in the menu bar, and select CarModel. This should display an Explorer pane, as shown in Figure 4-9.

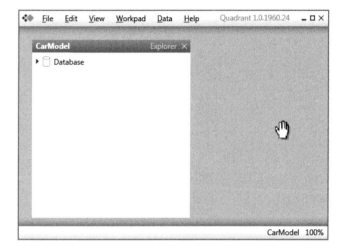

Figure 4-9. *Initial CarModel database Explorer pane*

Note that the session name in the Quadrant status bar (lower-right corner of the window) has changed to the name of the current database session: CarModel. Click on the Database arrowhead icon to expand the schemas. Car.Model should be the first item displayed, as shown in Figure 4-10. Click on the CarComponents table icon and drag this to the right onto the Quadrant canvas. Double-clicking the square icon will have the same effect.

Figure 4-10. *Double-clicking on the CarComponents icon to bring up its Explorer*

At this point, you should see an Explorer window showing the CarComponents table (shown in Figure 4-11). The table is empty, of course, because you haven't yet created any data.

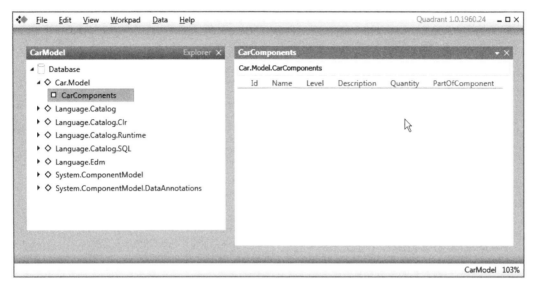

Figure 4-11. *Empty CarComponents Explorer (right window)*

Close the CarModel Explorer window. To add your first item to the model, click Data → Insert Item in the menu bar (see Figure 4-12).

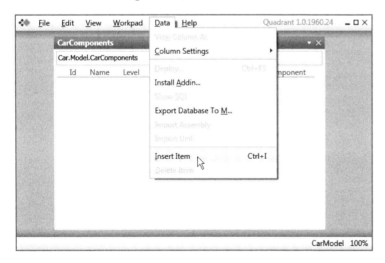

Figure 4-12. *Inserting the first item into the CarComponents table*

This will result in a detail pane for adding a new CarComponent entity, as shown in Figure 4-13. The red squiggles indicate the parts of the record that can't be null, so these must have values entered before the item can be saved. The values without squiggles are nullable (except for Id), and entering these values is optional.

The first record entered for the model should be the top-level item, which is My Car.

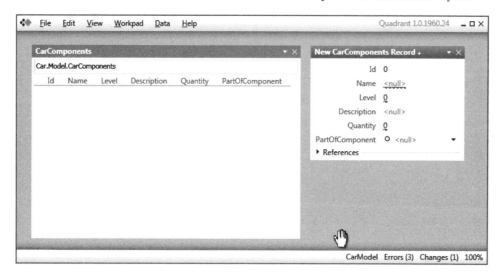

Figure 4-13. *Detail window (right) for creating the first item*

Enter the following data for the top-level record:

- *Name*: My Car

- *Level*: 1 (This is the highest system level, so it will have the lowest possible number; zero is equivalent to a null and would not be accepted.)

- *Description*: 1954 Buick Wildcat II

- *Quantity*: 1

- *PartOfComponent*: Leave this as null, since this is the top-level system.

Save the item by pressing Ctrl+S or select the File → Save Changes menu. The result is shown in Figure 4-14.

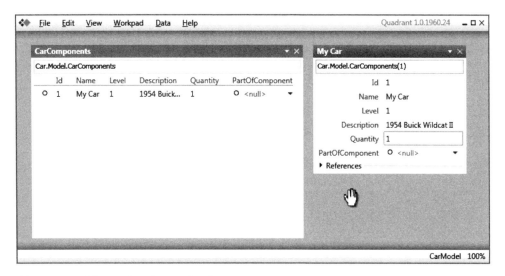

Figure 4-14. *After saving the top-level component*

If you click between the Description and Quantity column headings, you will be able to drag the right border for the Description column to the right until the entire description shows. You can also double-click the right column divider to resize the column automatically. As you work with Explorer panes in Quadrant, you will find that views are very amenable to reformatting and other UI customization.

Next, you will insert the Drive Train subsystem as a new item by pressing Ctrl+I. Enter the data shown in the new detail pane shown in Figure 4-15. This figure shows that I have added and saved the Drive Train item, and then clicked the drop-down arrow in the PartOfComponent column to set this value to My Car. Note that the asterisk in the Drive Train* title of the detail window indicates that the data has been changed but not saved. The asterisk at the far left of the corresponding line in the CarComponents pane indicates the same thing. You can also see that the Quadrant window is displaying Changes(1) in the status bar. Save the pending changes with Ctrl+S, and all indications that changes are pending should disappear.

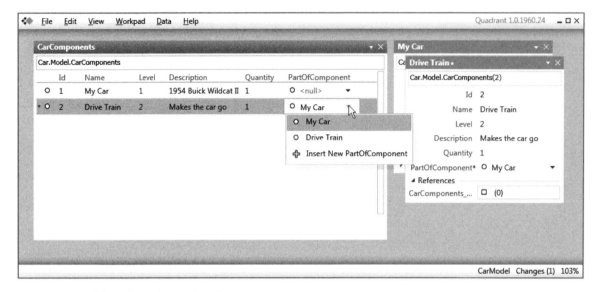

Figure 4-15. *Adding the Drive Train subsystem*

Next, you'll add the Suspension subsystem. Click the title bar of the CarComponents table pane to make sure it is active , and then press Ctrl+I to bring up a new detail window. (In Quadrant, the active window will have a colored title bar, as shown in Figure 4-16, while the others will have grayed out title bars.) Enter the data for the new item, and press Ctrl+S to save the item. You can readjust the column widths in the table pane as you go along so that the descriptions and other items are always readable.

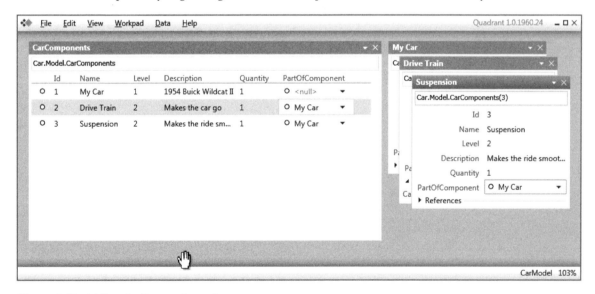

Figure 4-16. *Adding the Suspension subsystem*

Continue to use this procedure to build the CarComponents table, adding each item or subsystem in a separate detail pane until you have all nine items shown in the table in Figure 4-17. Remember to press Ctrl+S to save each item. If you prefer, you can accumulate changes as you continue to add or edit data and save the changes less frequently, or you can save the changes after you've finished entering all items. Figure 4-17 shows all but the last component (Shock Absorbers) saved, as indicated by the asterisk to the left of the Id in the CarComponents table and to the right of PartOfComponent in the Shock Absorbers detail pane.

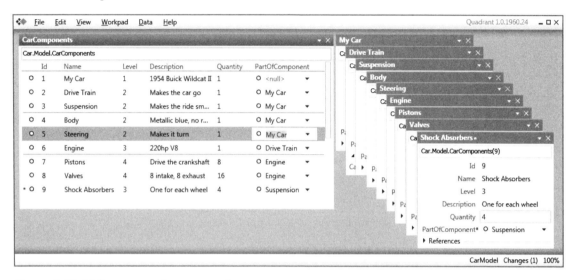

Figure 4-17. Adding more subsystems and components

Customizing Column Views in Quadrant

You can customize views in Quadrant in a number of ways. You can choose which columns or properties will or won't be displayed in the Explorer view of an extent/table, which is the most useful way of displaying the data in each column. Figure 4-18 shows the options available for displaying values in the PartOfComponent column. Usually, one of these options will make more sense than the others, but you can try each one to see which displays the data in the most informative way.

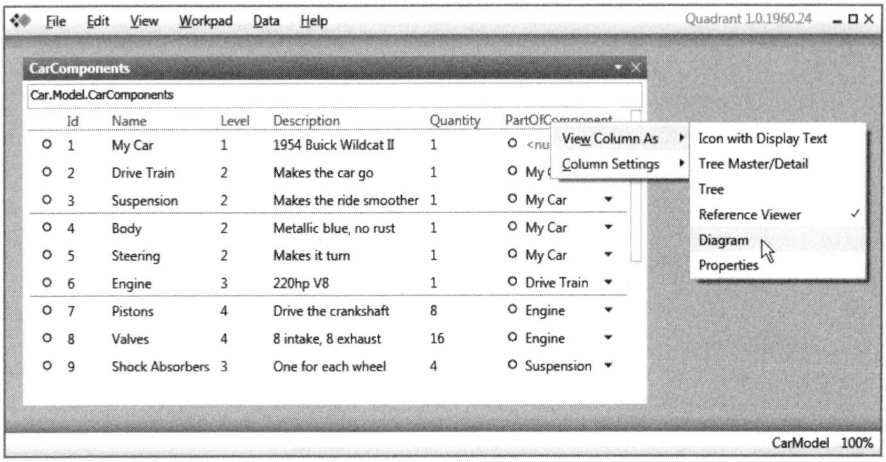

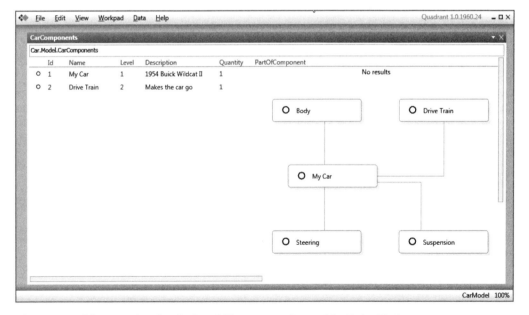

Figure 4-18. Options for displaying the PartOfComponent data

As an example, Figure 4-19 shows how the last column is displayed when you choose the diagram view. The options available for displaying a column's data depend on the type of data included for that particular field or column. Hence the PartOfComponent field has the diagram option available, since components have parent/child relationships to other components or subsystems. Using the diagram option for, say, the Description field wouldn't be a good choice, and, in fact, isn't available in the context menu for this column.

Figure 4-19. Diagram view for the PartOfComponent item of the Drive Train

Viewing and Editing the Model in SQL Server

Now that you've deployed the model to SQL Server and added some data, you should be able to view your work in the database. Before doing this, you need to determine which instance of SQL Server the model was deployed to. You can see the properties of the SQL Server connection for the Quadrant session you have been working in by going to the Quadrant Help → Quadrant Repository Connection menu. Figure 4-20 shows an example of the properties displayed for the connection to the database. In this case, you can see that the connection is to a SQLEXPRESS instance of the database.

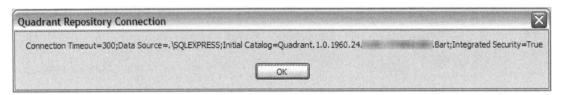

Figure 4-20. Quadrant Repository connection properties display from the help menu

To open SQL Server Management Studio, bring up All Programs from the Windows Start button, select the Microsoft SQL Server 2008 (or whatever the current release for SQL Server might be on your computer), and click the SQL Server Management Studio option, as shown in Figure 4-21.

Figure 4-21. Starting SQL Server Management Studio

Once SQL Server Management Studio is open, be sure you are connected to the proper instance of the database corresponding to the connection properties you just brought up. Under Databases, expand the CarModel → Tables group and right-click the Car.Model.CarComponents table, as shown in Figure 4-22. Click the Edit Top 200 Rows option.

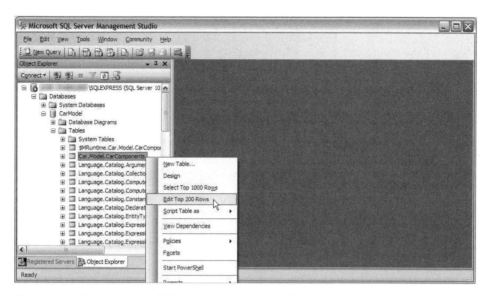

Figure 4-22. *Setting up to edit the CarComponents table in SQL Server*

Figure 4-23 shows how SQL Server Management Studio presents the Car.Model.CarComponents table in editing mode. You are able to edit data (at least the top 200 rows) in this mode.

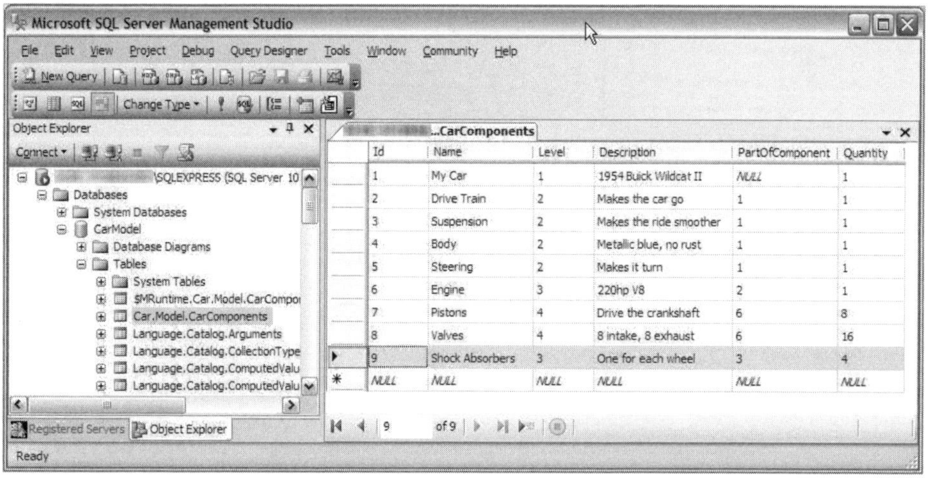

Figure 4-23. *View of the CarComponents table in SQL Server Management Studio*

If you compare this table with what you see in the Quadrant Explorer from Figure 4-17, you see an important difference. In the database table, the PartOfComponent column shows the integer Id (or foreign key) for a component's PartOf relationship, whereas in the Explorer you see the actual name of the PartOfComponent. You didn't do any coding or modifications to make Quadrant display its view of the model this way, but you know it's easier to interpret, rather than having to look up the

PartOfComponent name by the key value. It turns out that Quadrant defaults to displaying the name of an item rather than the key, as long as a Name field exists. This is usually more informative, as compared to seeing only the numeric key.

Managing Changes to the Data in Quadrant

As you've seen, Quadrant flags changes to the data (additions or edits) with an asterisk and by displaying a count of changes at the right of the status bar. Figure 4-24 shows that I've mistakenly changed the PartOfComponent value for the Valves item from Engine to Steering, but I haven't yet committed this change. This, of course, would be an error, so I would like to reverse this change without saving it. I've brought up the detail window for the Valves item, and it shows that only the PartOfComponent value has been altered (as indicated by the asterisk next to this property name), and nothing else. Note also that the title of the detail window also has an asterisk indicator.

If you cursor over an asterisk (edited), exclamation point (conflict), or question mark (stale) indicator, the cursor will change momentarily to an annotation that states the meaning of the indicator. (The next several figures show this feature.)

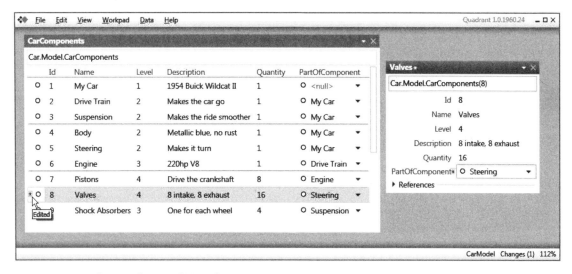

Figure 4-24. *Indicators for an editing change (*)*

There are four ways to revert changes:

- Click the View → Changes menu in the Quadrant menu bar to bring up a Changes view window, as shown in Figure 4-25. (See the name in the right side of the window's title bar.)

- Double-click Changes (1) displayed on the status bar. This will bring up the same Changes view invoked through the menu. The number of changes (in parentheses) shown in the status bar will, of course, vary according to the number of changes pending.

- Select the File → Revert All Changes menu option in the Quadrant menu bar. This is the easiest way of reverting a batch of changes if you're not interested in saving any.

- Change the value of the item back to its original value, and then save the change.

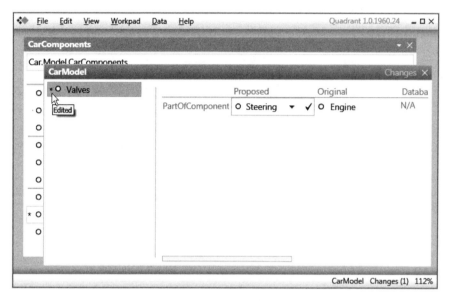

Figure 4-25. Reverting the change to the Valves PartOfComponent

I've selected the Valves item in this Changes view in order to display the nature of the change. This shows you the pending (Proposed) change to the PartOfComponent value (Steering), which is in error (for the purposes of this discussion), and the original value (Engine), which I'd like to revert back to. Right-click in the right frame of the window (shown in Figure 4-26), then select Revert Changes in the resulting context menu.

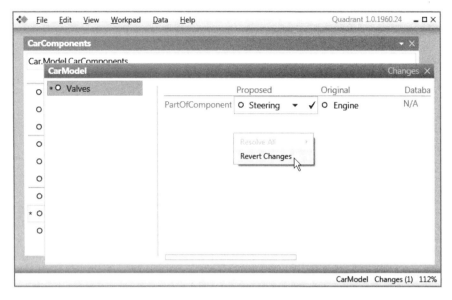

Figure 4-26. Reverting the change after right-clicking in the right frame of the Changes view

Managing Conflicts in Quadrant

As you know by now, SQL Server Modeling uses SQL Server as the Repository for persisting models. It can be used in a multi-user or team environment, as can the Repository. This means it is possible for more than one user to post conflicting changes to an entity or record in the database. Quadrant has a facility for resolving such conflicts. In this section, I'll show an example of how such a conflict can occur, and then how it can be resolved.

Say, for example, User A changes the description for the Shock Absorbers entity from One for Each Wheel to Two for Each Wheel, and User B changes this to Three for Each Wheel by editing the table in SQL Server Management Studio. By doing this, the different users have introduced a discrepancy, or conflict, between the change made in Quadrant and the change made in SQL Server Management Studio. This could also happen if two are more team members are working with Quadrant on the same data but on two different computers. It could even happen if you have a second Quadrant session open to the same database.

Figure 4-27 shows how such a conflict is indicated in Quadrant. Here again, the cursor shows an annotation as you hover over the indicator.

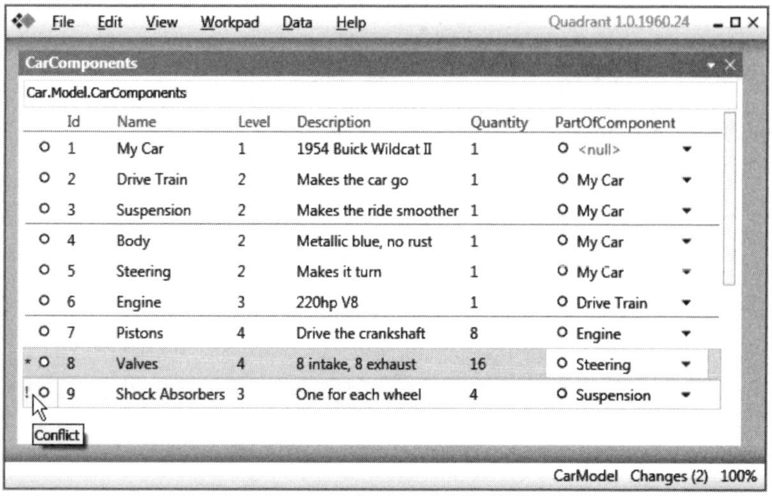

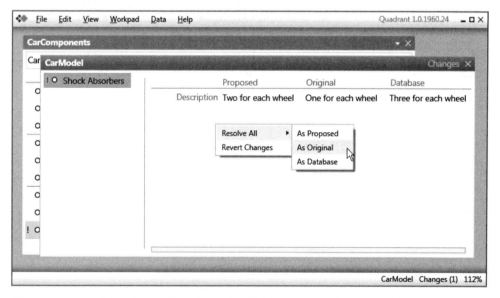

Figure 4-27. A red exclamation point (!) indicates a concurrency conflict in the data.

To resolve the conflict, bring up the Changes view (as shown in Figure 4-28) by double-clicking on Changes (1) in the status bar (or by using one of the other procedures described in the previous section). Right-click in the right frame of the window, and you will see you have three options: 1) saving the value of the description as proposed (in Quadrant), 2) saving the original value, or 3) saving the value as it is in the database.

Figure 4-28. Resolving the conflict after right-clicking in the right frame of the Changes view

In this case, I'll click the As Original option, and a check mark will appear next to the value in the Original column, indicating this is the selected value for resolving the conflict (see Figure 4-29).

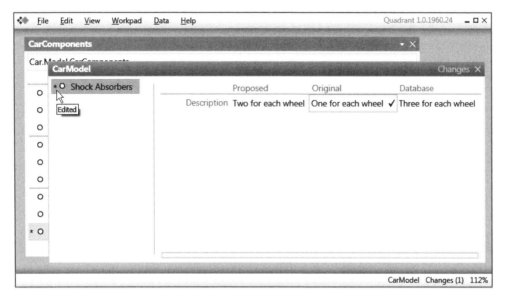

Figure 4-29. After selecting As Original to resolve the conflict

The exclamation point (!) next to the Shock Absorbers entity has now changed to an asterisk (*), and if you close the Changes view, you will see the same indication in the CarComponents Explorer. The data conflict has been resolved, but the change has not yet been committed. You can take this last step of committing this change by using Ctrl+S or the File → Save Changes menu option, which will make the data consistent again.

Finally, there can be situations where the local copy of the data can become stale because something has changed in the database, but the local copy of the data hasn't refreshed since the database change. Suppose the suspension engineering team has decided to go with two shock absorbers per wheel rather than one, and they have just changed the Description value for Shock Absorbers to Two for Each Wheel and the corresponding Quantity value from 4 to 8 in the database. This would mean the local copy of the data displayed by Quadrant is stale and no longer matches what is in the database. Figure 4-30 shows the resulting Quadrant view.

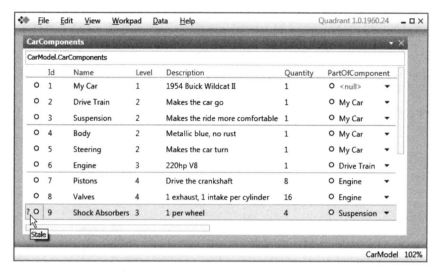

Figure 4-30. *Stale data in Quadrant after a recent change in the database*

This situation is resolved by simply refreshing the data from the data store using the F5 refresh key. Figure 4-31 shows the result.

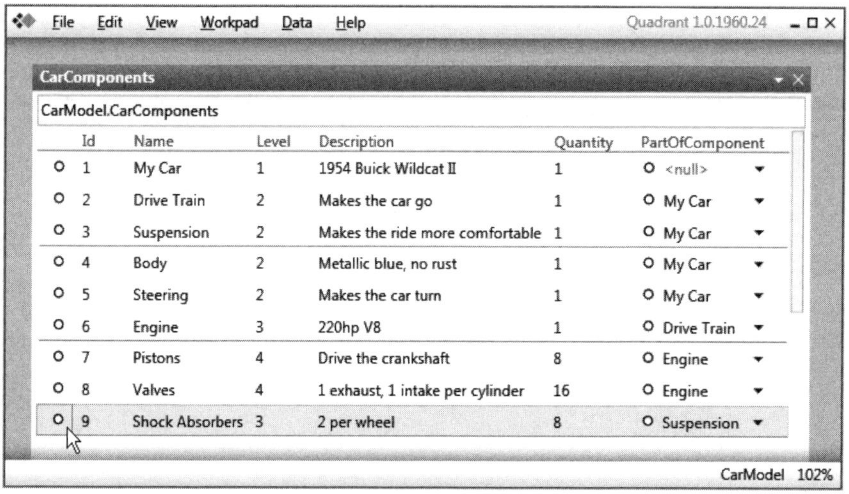

Figure 4-31. After using F5 to refresh stale data

Using the Quadrant Explorer Query Bar

The area immediately above the column titles and below the menu bar in the Explorer window is called the Query Bar. The default entry normally displayed in the Query Bar is the name of the extent, or table, that is displayed in the Explorer window; in the case of this example, it is Car.Model.CarComponents.

You can enter any SQL query in this bar to filter what is being displayed in the Explorer pane. For instance, if you wanted to see the top-level subsystem in the model, you could enter the following query in the Query Bar:

```
Car.Model.CarComponents where value.PartOfComponent.Name == "My Car"
```

The query is executed by pressing the Enter key with the cursor in the Query Bar. Figure 4-32 shows the result of this query, which is exactly what you would expect: The query returns all of the top-level subsystems. SQL keywords such as where and value are automatically bolded as the query is entered.

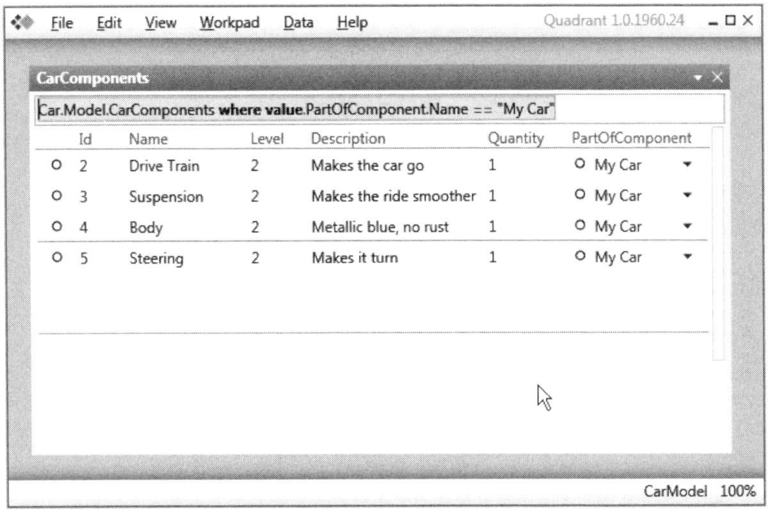

Figure 4-32. Using the Query Bar to find the top-level subsystems

Another example of a query you could perform would be to find all subsystems that have a quantity greater than 1. Figure 4-33 shows the results of such a query. To make the display more useful, you can click the Quantity column label to sort by ascending or descending quantities, as indicated by an up or down arrow to the right of the column label.

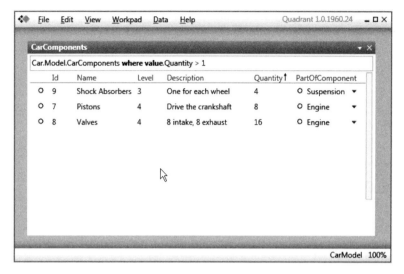

Figure 4-33. Using the Query Bar to find the components with a quantity greater than 1

As a last example, you can add .Count to any query to return the number of records found by the query. This is useful with very large tables with hundreds or thousands of records. Figures 4-34 and 4-35 show two examples.

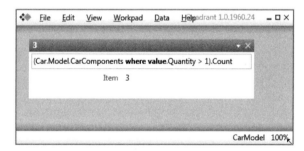

Figure 4-34. Getting a count of records for a query

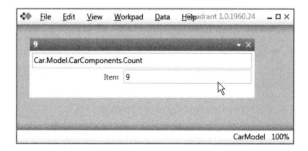

Figure 4-35. Getting a count of all items in the extent

To return to the normal table display after executing a query, click on the title bar of the Query pane to make sure the pane is active, press the Esc key to restore the default query, and then press the Enter key.

If you are not using the Query Bar in an Explorer workpad, you can remove it by right-clicking the title bar of the workpad, and clicking the Query Bar option in the context menu.

More on Customizing the View

"Know Your Audience" is an important credo in designing user interfaces, and it is just as important when designing a simple table view as it is for developing an entire application interface. A database administrator or a power user (one who is experienced in SQL and generating ad hoc queries) is usually going to want to see the data in a different format than a manager or an end user who is not conversant in SQL.

You can customize Explorer workpad views in a number of ways to give the user a more productive and convenient viewing experience. Here are a number of ways you could improve the table view of the car model for a user who is primarily interested in the domain data rather than running queries or other more technical aspects:

- Remove the Id column, since this is typically not meaningful information to the user.

- Move the PartOfComponent column to the right of the Name column, since this is probably the most significant data after the Name.

- Change the PartOfComponent label to Part Of, since this is a little more user friendly.

- Move the Level column to the right of the Description column.

- Remove the Query Bar, since this is a feature only power users would need.

Based on these requirements, the sequence of visible columns would be as follows:

- Name
- Part Of
- Description
- Level
- Quantity

To remove the Id column, right-click on any column heading, select the Column Settings option, and uncheck the Id column by clicking that menu item (see Figure 4-36). (You could also make this column visible by modifying the generated source for the view, as you will see shortly.)

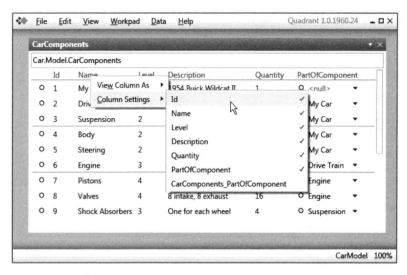

Figure 4-36. Hiding the Id column

Making the other changes you've decided on will require some simple modifications to the generated M source code for the view. To do this, bring up the source by invoking the context-sensitive menu: Right-click in the title bar of the Explorer window, and click the View Source option, as shown in Figure 4-37.

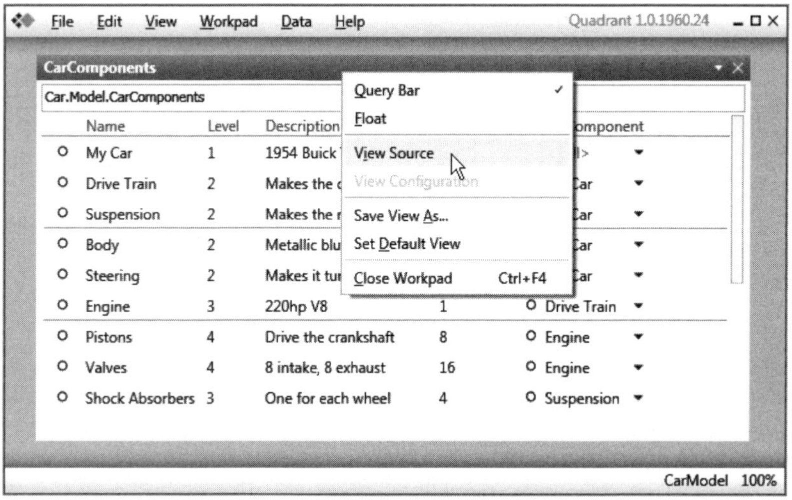

Figure 4-37. Setting up to view the source code for the table view

Figure 4-38 shows the portion of the source code you're interested in—the part where the positions and other properties of the data columns are defined. Note that you are in a Quadrant session now (as shown in the lower-right corner of the window), rather than the CarModel session, because you are changing the source code for several Quadrant modules. Once the modified source for the workpad view is deployed, you will be back in the CarModel session.

```
source                                                          ×
40  module Microsoft.Quadrant.Viewers
41  {
42      import Microsoft.Quadrant.Templates;
43
44      TableConfigurations
45      {
46          Table_2
47          {
48              Invocation => Invocations.Table_2_Root,
49              TableColumns =>
50              {
51                  {
52                      PropertyName => "Id",
53                      Position => 0,
54                      IsVisible => false,
55                      DisplayName => "Id",
56                  },
57                  {
58                      PropertyName => "Name",
59                      Position => 1,
60                      IsVisible => true,
61                      DisplayName => "Name",
62                  },
63                  {
64                      PropertyName => "Level",
65                      Position => 2,
66                      IsVisible => true,
67                      DisplayName => "Level",
68                  },
69                  {
70                      PropertyName => "Description",
71                      Position => 3,
72                      IsVisible => true,
73                      DisplayName => "Description",
74                  },
75                  {
76                      PropertyName => "Quantity",
```

Figure 4-38. Viewing the source code for the Table view

Looking at this code, you can see there is a collection named TableColumns. Each item in this collection corresponds to the properties of a column in the table and has the following four attributes: DisplayName, IsVisible, Position, and PropertyName. It's a simple matter to modify these four attributes to provide the view you're after. The IsVisible property of the Id column is set to false because of the earlier Column Settings change, as you would expect.

To get the table as you would like it to appear, you will need to change the column positions for each of the column properties, as well as the DisplayName property for two of the columns: PartOfComponent and Quantity. The code fragment in Listing 4-1 reflects the code changes:

Listing 4-1. Modified Column Properties to Customize the Table View

```
M

TableColumns =>
          {
            {
                DisplayName => "Id",
                IsVisible => false,
                Position => 0,
                PropertyName => "Id",
            },
            {
                DisplayName => "Name",
                IsVisible => true,
                Position => 1,
                PropertyName => "Name",
            },
            {
                DisplayName => "Level",
                IsVisible => true,
                Position => 5,
                PropertyName => "Level",
            },
            {
                DisplayName => "Description",
                IsVisible => true,
                Position => 3,
                PropertyName => "Description",
            },
            {
                DisplayName => "Quantity",
                IsVisible => true,
                Position => 4,
                PropertyName => "No.",
            },
            {
                DisplayName => "CarComponents_PartOfComponent",
                IsVisible => false,
                Position => 5,
                PropertyName => "CarComponents_PartOfComponent",
            },
            {
                DisplayName => "PartOfComponent",
                IsVisible => true,
                Position => 2,
                PropertyName => "PartOf",
            },
          }
```

To change the name of the view, locate the portion of the code in the `Microsoft.Quadrant` module where the table is defined, and change the `DisplayName` property from "Table" to "System Designer Table", as Figure 4-39 illustrates. If you are doing this exercise on your own computer, note that the `Name` property of the table (shown in the figure as "Table_0", may be different in the generated code on your computer. These are system-assigned names, so don't be concerned if you see these kinds of differences between your system and what is shown here in the text.

Figure 4-39. *Changing the Table view name*

To deploy your customized code for the CarModel view, right click in the source code window and select the Deploy option, as shown in Figure 4-40. An alternative way of doing this is to press Ctrl+F5.

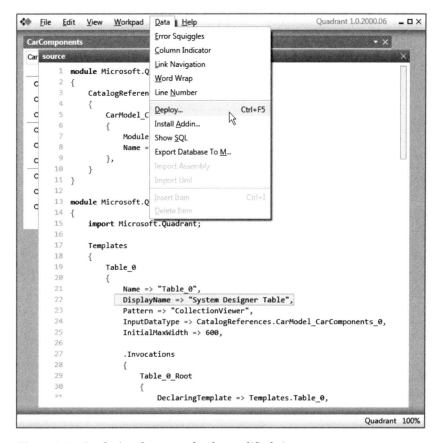

Figure 4-40. Deploying the source for the modified view

This will bring up a Deploy dialog box (see Figure 4-41) to allow you to select which database session to use for deployment. Accept the default Use Existing Database Session and click the Deploy button.

Figure 4-41. Select the existing database session to deploy.

After you've deployed the code changes, if everything goes as planned, you should see a notification dialog saying the deployment was successful (shown in Figure 4-42).

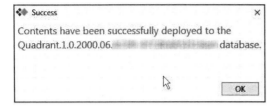

Figure 4-42. Successful deployment of the modified source

You'll likely notice that nothing has changed in the Explorer view (shown in Figure 4-43) after the customized code has been successfully deployed. This is because the customized view was saved under its new name: System Designer Table. To see the new custom view, click on the down arrow at the right of the view's title bar and select the new name.

	Id	Name	Level	Description	Quantity	PartOfCompone		
○	1	My Car	1	1954 Buick Wildcat II	1	○ <null>		List
○	2	Drive Train	2	Makes the car go	1	○ My Car		Master/Detail
○	3	Suspension	2	Makes the ride more comfortable	1	○ My Car		Table (Default) ✓
○	4	Body	2	Metallic blue, no rust	1	○ My Car		Tree Master/Detail
○	5	Steering	2	Makes the car turn	1	○ My Car	▾	Tree
○	6	Engine	3	220hp V8	1	○ Drive Train	▾	System Designer Table
○	7	Pistons	4	Drive the crankshaft	8	○ Engine	▾	
○	8	Valves	4	1 exhaust, 1 intake per cylinder	16	○ Engine	▾	
○	9	Shock Absorbers	3	1 per wheel	4	○ Suspension	▾	

Figure 4-43. Selecting the customized view: System Designer Table

Figure 4-44 shows your customized view, with the name at the right in the title bar. To show another way of renaming the view, this time without having to modify the code, let's change the name from System Designer Table to System Design Table.

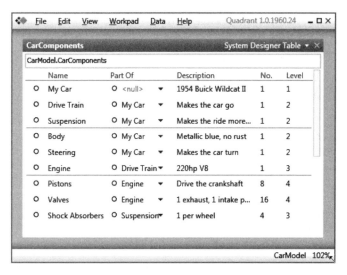

Figure 4-44. *Customized Table view*

Right-click in the title bar of the Table view and select the Save View As option, as shown in Figure 4-45.

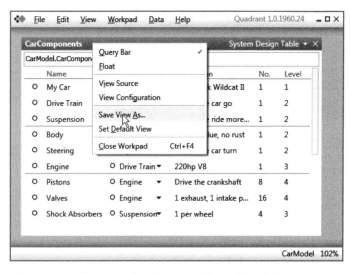

Figure 4-45. *Changing the view name from the title bar context menu*

A dialog box will prompt you for the viewer name. Enter **System Design Table** and click the Save button. Figure 4-46 shows the new title.

As the last requirement of the customization, you'll remove the Query Bar. Right-click on the CarComponents title bar and click the Query Bar option to uncheck this feature. The Query Bar can be restored at any time a particular user my want to execute a query by using the same procedure.

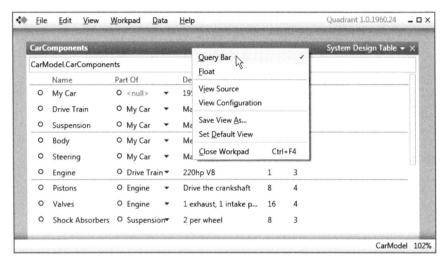

Figure 4-46. Removing the Query Bar

Finally, you'd like to save this customized view as the default view for the CarComponents table so that the user will normally see this view any time she brings up an Explorer view of the table. To do this, right-click on the window's title bar and select Set Default View, as shown in Figure 4-47. The name of the view in the title bar will disappear once it becomes the default view. You can always bring the standard table view back by clicking the Table option on the right side of the title bar.

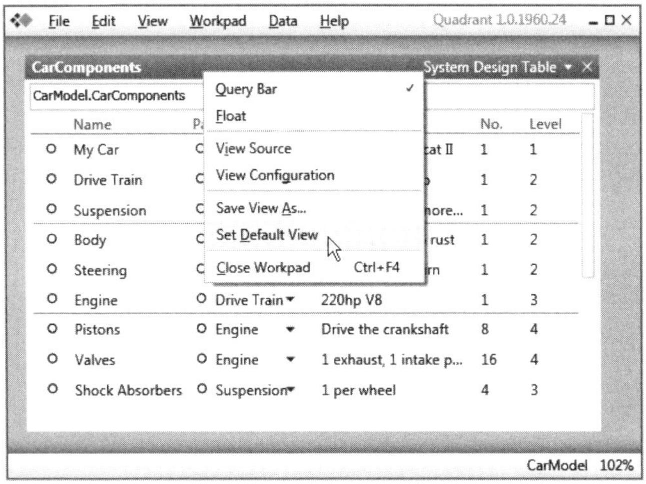

Figure 4-47. Setting the table view to be the default view.

Summary

In this chapter, I have covered some, but certainly not all, of Quadrant's functionality; I've also shown how to build and edit a model using Quadrant's Explorer windows. You used the composite design pattern to build a self-referential design model for a car. This approach could be used to build any model that is amenable to analysis using subsystems and components. Mechanical systems, such as cars or other kinds of machines, can be modeled with this approach, but the composite pattern can be applied to a wide range of other types of entities. I reviewed the facilities for managing and reverting changes to data in the model, reconciling concurrency conflicts, and refreshing data from the database any time you see indications of stale data. I also touched on the use of the Query Bar in the Explorer window and customizing Explorer views to make them more useful to end users, using both source M code for views and menu functions.

In sum, here's a list of what I've covered in this chapter:

- Writing and saving model code in an M file

- Creating types and extents (tables) of types

- Deploying your model to the database

- Viewing and editing the model in SQL Server using SQL Server Management Studio

- Adding new entities and records using Quadrant Explorer views

- Using Quadrant Explorer views to view and edit the model

- Customizing an Explorer view

- Managing changes, concurrency conflicts, and stale data

- Using the Query Bar

CHAPTER 5

M – The Modeling Language

Having covered domain-specific languages and the Intellipad and Quadrant tools in previous chapters, you can turn your attention now to M, the modeling language. M is all about creating, deploying, populating, and using models. It isn't an object-oriented language, like C# or C++ or Java. It is also not a language with procedural constructs (e.g., for/next or do/while or if/else) that you're used to seeing in other languages.

You've already seen some M code in previous chapters, but in this chapter I'll cover the structure and syntax of M in greater detail. I'll start by covering some of the basics you'll need to know in order to write and compile simple M programs. Of course, if you've read and worked through the sample code in previous chapters, you've already done some of this. I'll start off by covering the four basic constructs provided within the M syntax.

Why M?

You probably wouldn't be reading this book if you weren't interested in learning something about the M language. But what, exactly, are the benefits of using M, and why invest the time in learning another language?

M is an integrated part of Microsoft SQL Server Modeling, and is the language "glue" of this framework. If you're going to undertake data modeling using this environment, then developing a knowledge of M is essential. The primary tools of the framework—Quadrant and Intellipad—are "M-aware." M and, more broadly, the SQL Server Modeling framework, provide an environment for creating and deploying domain-specific languages, or DSLs.

M is a more congenial language for developing, maintaining, and deploying data models than T-SQL. By "congenial," I mean that M is more user-friendly and less error prone. You'll have an opportunity to compare the expressiveness and brevity of M for the purpose of building and maintaining model-driven applications in the sections to follow.

Getting Started with M

I'll talk briefly about *modules*, the fundamental namespaces of the M language. Then I'll cover each of the four basic constructs in M: types, extents (which define storage locations—ultimately, these map to SQL Server tables), computed values, and languages (used for building DSLs). Finally, I'll return to modules in the context of import and export directives. The latter have to do with making certain aspects of a module's definitions visible to other modules.

Please don't consider this an exhaustive treatment of the M language—it isn't. It's not my intent to cover every aspect of M here, but rather to provide a flavor of the language's capabilities, and perhaps enough of an introduction for you to feel comfortable moving on to studying Microsoft's "M" Language Specification [http://msdn.microsoft.com/en-us/library/ee730868(VS.85).aspx], the "M" Programming Guide [http://msdn.microsoft.com/en-us/library/dd129568%28VS.85%29.aspx], and other source materials on Microsoft's MSDN website.

Modules

When it comes time to be compiled, all M code must be contained within a module declaration. A module can contain any or all of the type declarations, extent declarations and initializations, computed values (aka functions), or language declarations. I've already touched on types, extents (storage or SQL tables), and languages (i.e., domain-specific languages) in the previous chapters. I haven't yet talked about computed values, but will do so in this chapter.

The simplest possible module declaration would be the empty declaration with no content, shown in Figure 5-1.

```
EmptyModule.m                                              ×

  1   module EmptyModule
  2     {
  3       // Nothing to see here, folks...
  4     }
```

Figure 5-1. An EmptyModule declaration

(Remember, the double-forward slash designates a comment line in the code, and is ignored by the compiler.) This module declaration would be accepted by the M compiler, but it would result in no SQL being generated by the compiler because there is absolutely nothing to compile within the scope of the module.

In M, the module is a top-level namespace containing some M code. Modules cannot be nested or hierarchical (i.e., you can't have modules declared within modules). But several modules can be declared within a single M code file, which is considered a compilation unit.

You can generalize the syntax for a module declaration from the example declaration shown in Figure 5-1, consisting of the following:

- The module keyword. Note that this must be lowercase: Module is not legal.

- The name of the module. This can be up to 400 characters long under the current M language specification, and can contain a dot character (.). If a dot is used in the name, it has no defining syntactic or scoping significance.

- A left brace ({) character.

- Some M code.

- A right brace (}) character below or after the M code.

This is the core of a module definition, but it is not everything. There are times when you may want to use types or computed values (functions) that may be defined in other modules, outside the scope of the module you are working in. You may also want to make types or computed values defined in your current module available elsewhere. This brings me to the concept of import and export directives. But before I talk about this particular subject, I want to cover the four basic constructs of M. Import and export directives will be more meaningful once you've covered that ground.

The Four Basic Constructs of M

There are four basic constructs in M:

- *Types*: These specify the kinds of entities that can occur and the constraints over the sets of values that comprise the type.

- *Extents*: These specify storage locations, usually for instances of types. They typically map to tables in SQL Server.

- *Computed values*: These specify parameterized queries and can be thought of as functions with zero or more parameters.

- *Languages*: These define the tokens and syntax rules for domain-specific languages.

The first three of these constructs are covered in the following sections. The syntax for defining a language in the context of M will be briefly reviewed here, but for a more detailed discussion of domain-specific languages, refer to Chapter 2.

Types

In developing a model, you often want to categorize values that may occur within the context of the model in certain ways. Numbers and text strings are of different value categories because the manner in which you test, combine, or work with them is different in each case. The idea of multiplying two numbers makes sense, but multiplying two text strings doesn't. Concatenating two text strings makes sense, but concatenating two numbers doesn't.

In M, you use the concept of a type to define a category of values, so a type describes a collection of acceptable or *conformant* values. *Collection* and *conformant* are the operative words here: With a few notable exceptions, a type defines a constrained collection. For example, you can use the in operator to test whether a value conforms to a particular type:

```
9 in Integer
```

and

```
"amazing" in Text
```

both evaluate to true.

You know that certain operations or tests can be applied to any or all values of a type, as long as those operations or tests are defined for that type. Any number can be added to any other number. Any text string can be uppercased, concatenated to another text string, or tested whether its length exceeds 20 characters.

Employees, for example, are in a different category than Cars. In the context of the M language, you use types for defining or expressing these categories.

Intrinsic and Derived Types

There are two type categories in M: intrinsic types and derived types. *Intrinsic* types, like Integer, Text, or Logical (true/false), are pre-defined in M and are understood by the M compiler. *Derived* types must be explicitly defined somewhere in M code, and a derived type definition will invoke one or more intrinsic types and/or other derived types.

Let's start with a very simple example of what I mean by a derived type. I'll stick with the subject matter used in the last chapter for the time being: Cars. Figure 5-2 shows what you might have for a very simple definition of a Car type.

```
CarTypeExample1.m                                    ×

  1  module CarTypeExample
  2  {
  3    type Car
  4      {
  5      Mfr : Text; // Manufacturer
  6      Model : Text;
  7      Year : Integer16;
  8      }
  9  }
```

Figure 5-2. *CarType module—an example of a type definition*

The Car type definition in Figure 5-2 starts with the type keyword, followed by the name of the type. The type definition then follows, scoped within braces. In this example, I've named the type Car—no surprise there. And I've given the type three values: Mfr, Model, and Year. Mfr and Model must both conform to the intrinsic type Text, and Year must conform to the intrinsic type Integer16. The colon (:) operator following Mfr, Model, and Year in the type definition is called the *ascription* operator. It designates the ascribed type for the value. So Mfr and Model have the ascribed intrinsic type of Text, while Year has the ascribed intrinsic type of Integer16.

The attributes, or *values*, of a given type are not necessarily constrained to be of an intrinsic type, like Text or Integer. Other derived types may be part of a new type definition. These other derived types may be defined within the module (namespace) of the type that requires it, or they may be defined within the scope of another module if they are made visible through import/export directives. (I'll talk about import/export in the section titled "Modules Revisited: Import and Export Directives.")

So let's take this to the next step by adding a value that has a derived, or non-intrinsic, type: Engine. I'll add a new derived type for Engine within the scope of the module shown in the last code snippet, and add an Engine value to the Car type definition (see Figure 5-3).

```
CarWithEngineExample.m                                                    ×
 1  module CarTypeExample
 2  {
 3    type Car
 4      {
 5      Id : Integer64 => AutoNumber();
 6      Mfr : Text; // Manufacturer
 7      Model : Text;
 8      Year : Unsigned16 where (value >= 1769 && value <= 2020);
 9      Engine : Engine;
10      } where identity Id;
11
12    type Engine
13      {
14      Id : Integer32 => AutoNumber();
15      Cylinders : Unsigned8 where (value >= 1 && value <= 12);
16      Horsepower : Unsigned16 where value < 1000;
17      Fuel : Text where value in {"gas", "diesel", "propane"};
18      Description : Text; // e.g., "V8"
19      } where identity Id;
20  }
```

Figure 5-3. *CarType module with an Engine type added*

If you compare this code with that shown in Figure 5-2, you'll notice I've changed some of the value definitions (Integer to Unsigned) and added some constraints. Rather than defining the Year of the Car type to be an Integer16 (which could be of any reasonable or unreasonable value, and which would allow the year to be negative), I've reset it to be an Unsigned16 integer in the range 1769 (when the first steam-powered car was made) to 2020. There are similar reality-based constraints on the value definitions for the Engine type: no less than 1 and no more than 12 cylinders and no more than 1,000 horsepower.

I've added an identity, or Id value for both the Car and Engine types. There are several reasons for doing this:

- You might have two distinct cars with the same manufacturer, model, year, and engine type, and no definitive way of distinguishing these two instances without having unique identities.

- The M language specification requires that if a derived type (Car in this context) includes another derived type as a value (such as Engine), the included type must have a unique identity.

- If the type is used to define an extent (→ SQL table), the type should provide a unique identity that can map to the primary key of the table.

The AutoNumber() function provides a way of establishing a unique identity for any type instance.

With this example in hand, let's look at types from a more abstract level. Types are simply a way of defining a collection of values. The M language is *structurally* typed rather than *nominally* typed. This is a fancy way of saying that if a collection of values conforms to two types, even though the types have different names, the types are equivalent as far as the M compiler is concerned. If you were to define a type named Boat that had the same structure as defined in Figure 5-3 for Car, the M compiler would be indifferent between the two types.

Types do not necessarily need to be named in M. You could define an anonymous type by simply enumerating a collection. For instance, the unnamed collection in Listing 5-1 could be treated as a perfectly valid type in M, since it is an expression that returns a set of values.

Listing 5-1. An Anonymous Type

```
{
    "Red",
    "Green",
    "Blue"
}
```

One might ask, "Could you have an instance of Car and an instance of Boat (if defined with the same structure as that of the Car type) that are equivalent?" The answer is yes.

If you refined the two types, say by adding a

```
WheelBase : Decimal19
```

attribute to the Car type definition and a

```
PropType : Text
```

to the Boat type definition, then the two types would no longer have the same structure, and the answer would be no.

M's Built-Ins: The Intrinsic Types

Table 5-1 lists all of the intrinsic types included in the M language. If you've used typed programming languages, nearly all of these types (numbers, dates, times, text, logical, and binary) and their operators should be familiar to you. The last two types listed in this table, Collection and Entity, are particularly important in M because of its modeling orientation, and will be given further treatment throughout this chapter.

Table 5-1. M Intrinsic Types

Intrinsic Name	Description
Any	All possible values.
General	All possible values except the Entity and Collection types.
Number	Any numeric value.
Decimal	A fixed point or exact number.
Decimal9	A fixed point or exact number.
Decimal19	A fixed point or exact number.

Decimal28	A fixed point or exact number.
Decimal38	A fixed point or exact number.
Integer	A signed integer.
Integer8	A signed integer with fewer than 9 bits of precision.
Integer16	A signed integer with fewer than 17 bits of precision.
Integer32	A signed integer with fewer than 33 bits of precision.
Integer64	A signed integer with fewer than 65 bits of precision.
Scientific	A floating-point or exact number.
Single	A 32-bit floating-point or exact number.
Double	A 64-bit floating-point or exact number.
Unsigned	An unsigned integer.
Unsigned8	An unsigned integer with fewer than 9 bits of precision.
Unsigned16	An unsigned integer with fewer than 17 bits of precision.
Unsigned32	An unsigned integer with fewer than 33 bits of precision.
Unsigned64	An unsigned integer with fewer than 65 bits of precision.
Date	A calendar date.
DateTime	A calendar date and time of day independent of time zone.
DateTimeOffset	A calendar date and time of day within a specific time zone.
Time	A time of day and time zone.
Text	A sequence of characters.
Logical	A logical flag.
Binary	A sequence of binary octets.
Guid	A globally unique identifier

Byte	A single binary octet.
Collection	An unordered group of potentially duplicate values.
Entity	A collection of labeled values.

The Collection Type

The collection type is an unordered group of potentially duplicate values. A collection can be constructed as an expression with a beginning brace ({), a type reference, an optional multiplicity (described shortly), and an ending brace (}). So the following examples are all valid collections:

- {"NPR", "ABC", "CBS", "NBC"}   // a collection of four broadcast network names

- {"Red", "White," "Blue"}   // a collection of three color names

- {"Baseball", "Basketball", "Soccer"}   // a collection of three ball game names

- {3.141, 2.718}   // the collection of the two transcendental numbers π and e, expressed to a 3-decimal precision

- {Integer#8}   // a collection of any eight integers

- {Unsigned16#1..8}   // a collection of one to eight Unsigned16 integers

- {Date#4..}   // a collection of four or more Date types

- {Single*}   // a collection of zero or more 32-bit floating point numbers

- {Double+}   // a collection of one or more 64-bit floating point numbers

- Cars : {Car*}   // defines the Cars extent as the collection of all values of the Car derived type

- {"Red", 32, { }, "NPR"} // defines a collection with two text values, an integer value, and an empty collection value

The last example in the preceding list shows that the elements of a collection do not necessarily have to be of the same type, and that collections can contain other collections.

The next to last expression uses the ascription operator (:), (as in, "ascribe this identifier to this type") to define the Cars extent. I'll talk about this in the section titled "Extents."

Note that the definition of the collection type said that the collections can have duplicate values. So the collection {1, 2, 3, 1, 1, 3, 4, 98} would conform to an {Integer}#8 definition because it is a collection of eight integers, though with some duplicates. Collections also have no positional or sequential information (unlike lists), so the following expression would be true:

{1, 2, 3, 4} == {4, 1, 3, 2}.

Multiplicity Constraints

Table 5-2 shows the different kinds of multiplicity operators that can be used in defining or constraining a collection. Since types are simply collections of conforming values, multiplicity operators are important in type definitions.

Table 5-2. *Multiplicity Operators*

Multiplicity Operator	Constraint
*	Requires zero or more values (allows an empty collection).
+	Requires one or more values.
?	Requires zero or one value.
#N	Requires the collection to have exactly N values, (have a size of N). N must be a positive integer.
#M..N	Requires the collection to have at least M values, and at most N values. M and N must be positive integers, and M must be less than N.
#M..	Requires the collection to have M or more values. M must be a positive integer.

The first three multiplicity operators listed in this table (*, +, and ?) are sometimes called Kleene operators. (The term comes from generative grammar theory).

Lists are ordered collections, and are denoted with brackets ([ ]) rather than braces. The collection {1, 2, 3, 4} is identical to the collection {4, 3, 2, 1} because order is immaterial for collections. This would not be the case for the lists [1, 2, 3, 4] and [4, 3, 2, 1].

Collection Operators

Some intrinsic types have one or more operators defined for manipulating or testing instances of the type. In the case of collections, the following operators are defined in Table 5-3.

Table 5-3. *Collection Operators*

Operator	Right Operand	Returns	Description
#	Not Applicable	Integer	# is a unary postfix operator that returns the size (or count) of the collection.
<	Collection	Logical	A < B ~ B > A

>	Collection	Logical	A > B ~ A >= B && A != B
<=	Collection	Logical	A <= B ~ B >= A
>=	Collection	Logical	A >= B returns true if collection A has every element of collection B with equal or greater multiplicity.
==	Collection	Logical	A == B ~ A >= B && B >= A
!=	Collection	Logical	A != B ~ !(A == B)
Where	Logical	Collection	Returns a new collection containing only the elements from the left operand that satisfy the predicate on the right when evaluated on the iteration variable value. If the type of the left operand is {T*} the type of the result will be {T*}.
Select	Any	Collection	Returns a new collection containing an equal number of elements as the left operand that is the result of evaluating the expression on the right over the iteration variable value. If the type of the left operand is {T*} and the result of evaluating the expression on the right is R, then the type of the result is {R*}.
&	Collection	Collection	Intersect operator. Converts the right and left operands to sets and returns the set intersection.
|	Collection	Collection	Union operator. Converts the right and left operands to sets and returns the set union.

If you are unused to reading logical expressions, like those in the right column of the first few rows of Table 5-3, here's the key to reading the descriptive statements for the relational operators (<, >, <=, >=, ==, !=) in rows 2 through 6 in plain English:

~ (tilde) is the equivalence operator: A ~ B, means "A is equivalent to B."

&& is the logical AND operator.

! is the logical negation operator: !true == false and !false == true.

The shaded description cell in the right column of Table 5-3 for the >= operator is the key to understanding the semantics of the logical statements in the right column, from which the meaning of the logical descriptions for the other relational operators can be derived.

Relational Operators

Here are some examples of expressions using the relational operators described in Table 5-3 with small integer or text collections as the operands. All expressions in this list evaluate to true:

- {'a', 'b', 'c'}# == 3
- {"three", "text types", "here"}# == 3

- {1, 2, 1} < {1,2,3,1}
- { } < {5} // { } is the empty collection
- {1, 2, 3, 4} > {1, 2, 3}
- {2, 3, 4} <= {2, 3, 4, 5}
- {2, 3, 4} >= {2, 3}
- {2, 3, 4} == {3, 4, 2}
- {4, 5, 6} != {4, 5, 6, 7}
- {1, 2, 3, 4, 1, 2} & {3, 4, 5, 6, 3} == {3, 4}
- {1, 2, 3, 4, 1, 2} | {3, 4, 5, 6, 3} == {1, 2, 3, 4, 5, 6}

Where and Select

The Where and Select operators are generally used in constructing query expressions. Listings 5-2 and 5-3 show some examples. An evaluation of the expression in Listing 5-2 will return *true*.

Listing 5-2. An example of the use of the where and select operators (returns true)

```
(
        from n in {1, 2, 3, 4, 5}
        where n%2 == 0
        select n
) == {2, 4}
```

The % operator is the binary infix modulo operator, so n%2 returns n modulo 2, and n%2 should return 0 for any even number.

Listing 5-3. An example using where and select to return members of the collection named People older than 17

```
from p in People
where p.Age > 17
select p
```

If People is a collection of persons with Age as one of the values, then this query should return the collection of people with age greater than 17.

The Entity Type

Like the collection type, the entity is an intrinsic type. It is a set of zero or more named values, or fields. The Car type I defined earlier (refer to Figure 5-3) is an example of an entity type, often called simply an entity. Any field of an entity can be accessed by the name of the field. An entity can have an identity, which makes it distinct from all other instances of the type, as shown in Figure 5-3. Any or all fields of an entity can be assigned default values when the entity is initialized, and the values of any field can be constrained by an expression, just as I constrained the year of manufacture in the Car type in Figure 5-3.

The field names of an entity must be distinct. (That's why in entities named values must be a set: Sets do not allow duplicate values.)

Entity Value Initializers

Entity values can be assigned default values when the entity is constructed and initialized. M does not provide for altering an entity's member values once it is constructed. Changes in an entity's values will normally occur through data store (SQL Server) operations, or through operations that occur in an application using the data store.

Member Names

An entity member name can be arbitrary Unicode text, meaning it can contain spaces or dots or symbols. As such, when the name violates the requirements of M restrictions on identifiers (say, by containing spaces or dots), the name can be escaped with square brackets. For example:

```
{ [QC Passed] => true, [Assembly Date] =>System.Date.Today] } ;
```

Developers would normally want to avoid using escaped identifiers, but there may be situations where they may be needed.

Entity Values

There are no restrictions on the kinds of values that can be defined for an entity. For example, you could have an entity with an Integer8 value, a list value, and another Integer8 value, as shown in Figure 5-4.

```
RaceData.m                                                                    ×
 1  module RaceData {
 2  // example of entity type where a member is a list or collection
 3      type RaceResult {
 4          RaceNo : Integer8;
 5          CarNumbers : [Integer8#3..15]; // track rules say min of 3, max of 15 cars
 6          WinningCar : Integer8;
 7      }
 8      RaceResults : {(RaceResult where value.CarNumbers <= [Integer8#3..15])*};
 9
10      RaceResults {
11                  {
12                      RaceNo => 1,
13                      CarNumbers [3, 9, 12, 14, 37, 48, 52],
14                      WinningCar => 37
15                  },
16                  {
17                      RaceNo => 2,
18                      CarNumbers [5, 16, 28, 32, 44, 53, 68],
19                      WinningCar => 32,
20                  }
21              }
22  }
```

Figure 5-4. Example of an entity type where one of the members is a list

In the case of the `Car` example discussed earlier, the `Engine` value of the `Car` entity is itself set to a derived type.

Entity Value Operators

Entity values can be accessed using the dot (.) operator. To provide an example of the use of the dot operator to access entity values, let's define `Car` and `Engine` entities with the values shown in Listing 5-4

Listing 5-4. Car and Engine Entities

```
Car => {
                              {Id     => 1,
                              Mfr     => "Acme",
                              Model   => "Runabout",
                              Year    => 1954,
                              Engine  => 100}
               };
Engine => {
                              {Id => 100,
                              Cylinders => 4,
                              Horespower => 98,
                              Fuel => "gas",
                              Description => "42 mpg"}
                  };
```

The following statements will be true for these `Car` and `Engine` entities:

```
Car.Mfr == "Acme"
Car.Engine.Cylinders == 4
```

Modules Revisited: Import and Export Directives

In talking about modules earlier in the chapter, I mentioned the subject of scoping (i.e., visibility) and import/export directives. Normally, a module is entirely self-contained in terms of its scope—code that is defined other than within the module is not visible to types or other constructs within the module, and vice versa. Intrinsic types are, of course, an exception: They are built into M, and can be invoked within any module. But if a derived type or extent or computed value is defined in a different module, it will be unavailable for use outside of the module it is defined in.

Let's go back to the earlier `Car` example shown in Figure 5-3, but this time introduce the convention that you want to define only one type per module. (This can often be a good idea, especially with large projects.) Figure 5-5 shows how the code from this example might change, with the `Engine` type definition moved to its own module (but still within the same M file, or compilation unit).

```
CarTypeExampleWithoutImportExport.m                                    ✕
  1  module CarTypeExample
  2  {
  3    type Car
  4      {
  5      Id : Integer64 => AutoNumber();
  6      Mfr : Text; // Manufacturer
  7      Model : Text;
  8      Year : Unsigned16 where (value >= 1769 && value <= 2020);
  9      Engine : Engine;
 10      } where i Cannot resolve the reference to 'Engine'.
 11  }
 12
 13  module EngineModule {
 14    type Engine
 15      {
 16      Id : Integer32 => AutoNumber();
 17      Cylinders : Unsigned8 where (value >= 1 && value <= 12);
 18      Horsepower : Unsigned16 where value < 1000;
 19      Fuel : Text where value in {"gas", "diesel", "propane"};
 20      Description : Text; // e.g., "V8"
 21      } where identity Id;
 22  }
 23
```

Figure 5-5. The Car example with Engine type moved to its own module without import/export

As you can see, there is an error indication (red squiggles) under the Engine type ascription and an annotation that the Engine reference can't be resolved. This shows that the Engine type definition is not visible and is outside the scope of the CarTypeExample module. You can fix this problem by adding an import directive for EngineModule within the CarTypeExample module, and an export directive for the Engine type in EngineModule. The resulting code is shown in Figure 5-6.

```
CarTypeExampleWithImportExport.m                                       ✕
  1  module CarTypeExample
  2  {
  3    import EngineModule;
  4    type Car
  5      {
  6      Id : Integer64 => AutoNumber();
  7      Mfr : Text; // Manufacturer
  8      Model : Text;
  9      Year : Unsigned16 where (value >= 1769 && value <= 2020);
 10      Engine : Engine;
 11      } where identity Id;
 12  }
 13
 14  module EngineModule {
 15    export Engine;
 16    type Engine
 17      {
 18      Id : Integer32 => AutoNumber();
 19      Cylinders : Unsigned8 where (value >= 1 && value <= 12);
 20      Horsepower : Unsigned16 where value < 1000;
 21      Fuel : Text where value in {"gas", "diesel", "propane"};
 22      Description : Text; // e.g., "V8"
 23      } where identity Id;
 24  }
 25
```

Figure 5-6. The Car example with Engine type moved to its own module with import/export

The Engine type is now resolved within the CarTypeExample module. The import and export directives provide the means for managing modules more logically and keeping them trim. Note that the import directive refers to one or more module names. Several modules can be imported under a single directive, with the module names separated by commas, or they can be imported by separate import directives, one line for each. This is a matter of style. export directives must refer to type definitions, extents, or computed values defined within the module where the export directive is invoked.

Labeled entity instances can be referenced across modules contained in separate M files and compiled in separate compilation episodes, as long as the proper export/import directives are defined. For instance, the Engine type definition shown in Figure 5-6 could have been defined in a separate M file and compiled at a different time (again, with the necessary import/export directives in the respective M files).

Figure 5-10 in the following section shows the extent definitions for Cars and Engines added in the respective modules.

Extents

Extents in M specify storage locations. In the context of SQL Server, extents correspond to SQL tables. Types in M will map to table definitions in T-SQL, but do not result in actually creating the tables in SQL Server. Code that results in a T-SQL table creation requires an extent definition.

Listing 5-5 shows an example of how an extent is defined in M.

Listing 5-5. Defining an Extent

```
Cars  :  {Car*};
```

So an extent is simply defined as a collection of zero or more type instances. If a type is to provide the basis of a SQL table definition, there must be a unique identity for each instance of the type that maps to a primary key in the SQL world. This is why you used the AutoNumber() function to define the Id of each instance of Car and Engine in the Car example (see Figure 5-7). Extents, as a matter of convention, are normally given the plural name of their contained type. Cars would be the usual name of the extent for the Car type, and Persons or People would be the usual name for a Person type, if you defined such a type.

So let's expand the Car example to provide the extents needed for creating the actual Cars and Engines tables of the domain values in SQL. I'll add the extent definitions for Cars and Engines shown in Figure 5-7 (grayed lines).

```
CarTypeExampleWithImportExport&Extents1.m                                        ×
  1   module CarTypeExample
  2   {
  3     import EngineModule;
  4     type Car
  5       {
  6       Id : Integer64 => AutoNumber();
  7       Mfr : Text; // Manufacturer
  8       Model : Text;
  9       Year : Unsigned16 where (value >= 1769 && value <= 2020);
 10       Engine : Engine;
 11       The entity field 'Engine' requires a membership constraint ('in' or '<=').
 12
 13     Cars : {Car*};  // extent definition for Cars
 14   }
 15
 16   module EngineModule {
 17     export Engine;
 18     type Engine
 19       {
 20       Id : Integer32 => AutoNumber();
 21       Cylinders : Unsigned8 where (value >= 1 && value <= 12);
 22       Horsepower : Unsigned16 where value < 1000;
 23       Fuel : Text where value in {"gas", "diesel", "propane"};
 24       Description : Text; // e.g., "V8"
 25       } where identity Id;
 26
 27     Engines : {Engine*}; // extent definition for Engines
 28   }
```

Figure 5-7. The Car example with Cars and Engines extents (→ SQL tables) added.

It isn't correct, however, because the error annotation on the Engine value of the Car type definition indicates that there must be a membership constraint. This means, since there is an Engines extent defined in EngineModule, the Engine value of Car type (line 10) must be constrained to be in the Engines extent. The EngineModule code also needs to be changed to export the Engines extent, along with the Engine type (line 17), since there is now a reference to the Engines extent in the CarTypeExample module. Finally, it's generally a good idea to export types and extents defined in a module if there is a prospect that these should be exposed to other modules as you continue to refine your model. So you still add a declaration to export the Car type and Cars extent, as shown in line 4 of Figure 5-8 (which shows the corrected code).

```
Car&EngineModel.m                                                    ✕
  1  module CarTypeExample
  2  {
  3    import EngineModule;                              I
  4    export Car, Cars;
  5    type Car
  6      {
  7      Id : Integer64 => AutoNumber();
  8      Mfr : Text; // Manufacturer
  9      Model : Text;
 10      Year : Unsigned16 where (value >= 1769 && value <= 2020);
 11      Engine : Engine where value in Engines;
 12      } where identity Id;
 13
 14      Cars : {Car*};  // extent definition for Cars
 15  }
 16
 17  module EngineModule {
 18    export Engine, Engines;
 19    type Engine
 20      {
 21      Id : Integer32 => AutoNumber();
 22      Cylinders : Unsigned8 where (value >= 1 && value <= 12);
 23      Horsepower : Unsigned16 where value < 1000;
 24      Fuel : Text where value in {"gas", "diesel", "propane"};
 25      Description : Text; // e.g., "V8"
 26      } where identity Id;
 27
 28      Engines : {Engine*}; // extent definition for Engines
 29  }
```

Figure 5-8. The Car example with the membership constraint for the Engine value in Car added

You no longer have any error indications for the two modules in this code. This means that this code should successfully create the T-SQL code for generating the schema and table definition on the SQL Server side of the house.

Generating T-SQL Code for the Car Model

To generate the T-SQL code for this model, you will need to switch to Intellipad. Save your code in Quadrant as Car&EngineModel.m, and then exit Quadrant. Next bring up Intellipad and open this file. When the file is loaded, Intellipad will switch to M mode, which you will see in the menu bar. Select the M Mode → T-SQL Preview menu option (as shown in Figure 5-9).

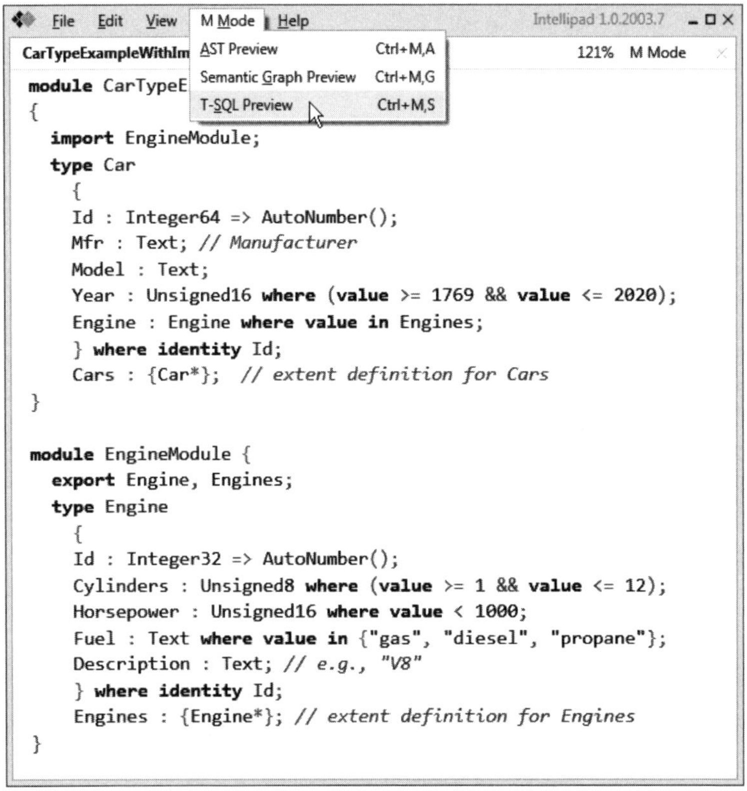

Figure 5-9. Setting up to generate a T-SQL code preview

Figure 5-10 shows the generated T-SQL in the Intellipad right pane.

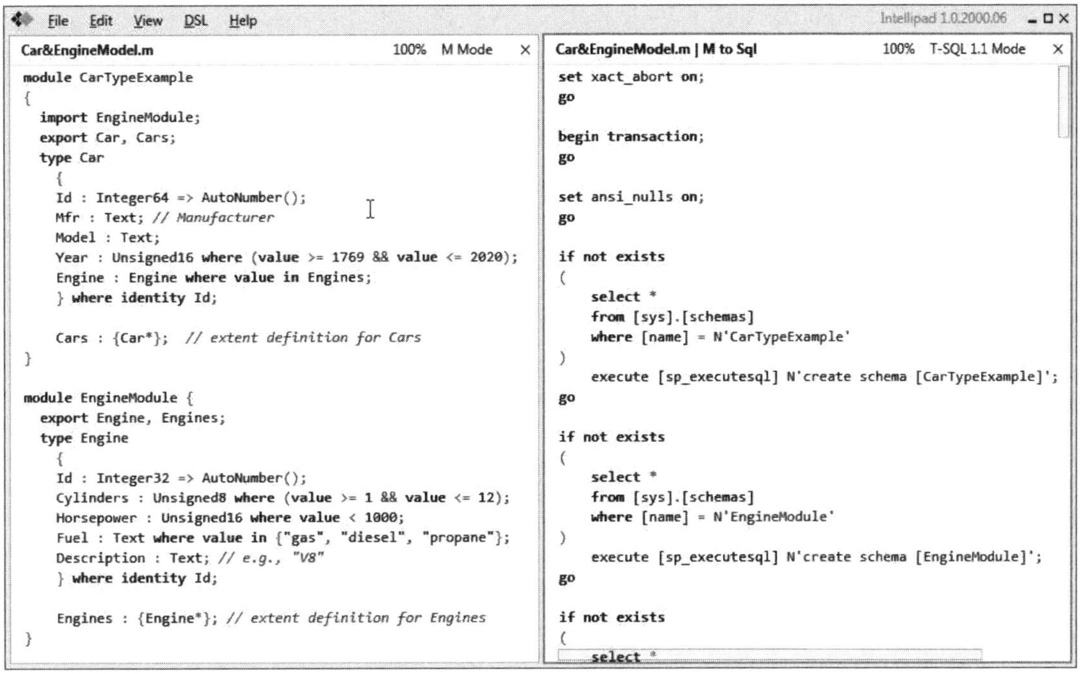

Figure 5-10. *CarTypeExample with generated T-SQL*

Appendix E shows the complete listing for the generated T-SQL. You can see that the generated T-SQL is substantially more complex than the M code used to define this simple two-type model. (There are a total of 254 lines in the generated T-SQL, including blank lines.) Defining a model in T-SQL from the ground up can be complex, error prone, and difficult to debug.

This illustrates an important advantage of the M language and the SQL Server Modeling framework, which is the relative ease of defining a model quickly. The generated T-SQL could be used to deploy this model directly to SQL Server by creating the tables and schema, but this could also be done directly using the deployment facility in Quadrant.

Computed Values

M provides two ways in which values can be created:

- *Stored values*: You've already seen stored values defined in type definitions—for example, Mfr is a stored value of type Text for the manufacturer in a Car type definition. Stored values are also called *fields*, and translate to columns in a SQL table definition.

- *Computed values*: Computed values are derived by evaluating an expression and always occur within a module declaration, just as do type and extent definitions. Computed values can be considered equivalent to functions and can have zero or more arguments.

An example of a computed value definition might be one that returns the sum of two numbers:

```
Add(x : Integer32, y : Integer32) {x + y};
```

Here's an example of a computed value definition for the square of a number:

```
Square(x : Integer32) {x*x};
```

In the instance of the CarTypeExample, you could add a HorsepowerPerCylinder computed value in EngineModule with the following line:

```
HorsepowerPerCylinder(Eng : Engine) {Eng.Horsepower / Eng.Cylinders}
```

Figure 5-11 shows the code in Intellipad with this computed value definition added, but the return value and arguments are ascribed to a Decimal19 so that a reasonable precision can be returned from dividing the two integers.

```
1   module CarTypeExample
2   {
3     import EngineModule;
4     export Car, Cars;
5     type Car
6       {
7       Id : Integer64 => AutoNumber();
8       Mfr : Text; // Manufacturer
9       Model : Text;
10      Year : Unsigned16 where (value >= 1769 && value <= 2020);
11      Engine : Engine where value in Engines;
12      } where identity Id;
13
14      Cars : {Car*};  // extent definition for Cars
15   }
16
17   module EngineModule {
18     export Engine, Engines;
19     type Engine
20       {
21       Id : Integer32 => AutoNumber();
22       Cylinders : Unsigned8 where (value >= 1 && value <= 12);
23       Horsepower : Unsigned16 where value < 1000;
24       Fuel : Text where value in {"gas", "diesel", "propane"};
25       Description : Text; // e.g., "V8"
26       } where identity Id;
27
28      Engines : {Engine*}; // extent definition for Engines
29      // Example of a computed value:
30      HorsepowerPerCylinder (Eng : Engine) : Decimal19
31        {(Eng.Horsepower : Decimal19) / (Eng.Cylinders : Decimal19)}
32   }
```

Figure 5-11. *The Car example with a computed value definition.*

M generates a T-SQL function definition for this computed value definition, as shown in the Intellipad T-SQL preview pane in Figure 5-12.

```
File    Edit    View    DSL    Help                           Intellipad 1.0.2000.06    _ □ ×

CarWithEngine&HorsepowerPerCylinder.m | M to...               100%    T-SQL 1.1 Mode
70                    then 1
71                    else 0
72              end
73         end;
74   go
75
76   create function [EngineModule].[HorsepowerPerCylinder]
77   (
78         @Eng as xml
79   )
80   returns decimal(19,6)
81   as
82         begin
83              return convert(decimal(19,6),
84              (
85                    select (@Eng).value(N'(/entity/Horsepower)[1]', N'int') as [Item]
86              )) / convert(decimal(19,6),
87              (
88                    select (@Eng).value(N'(/entity/Cylinders)[1]', N'tinyint') as [Item]
89              ))
90         end;
91   go
92   |
93   create function [EngineModule].[Check_Engines_Func]
94   (
95         @Cylinders as tinyint
96   )
     returns bit
```

Figure 5-12. *T-SQL code generated for the HorsepowerPerCylinder computed value in the M code.*

You might have noticed that this definition for the computed value could potentially have resulted in a divide-by-zero error in certain situations had you not constrained the number of cylinders to be an integer between 1 and 12 (line 15 back in Figure 5-3).

The generated T-SQL code for this example, including the computed value, is shown in Appendix E.

Overloading

Overloading of computed value definitions is supported in M. This means that multiple computed values with the same name can be defined, as long as each definition has a different number of arguments. Selection of which definition is used by the compiler is determined by the number of arguments in the invocation. For example, the formula for the volume of a sphere, given the radius r is:

$$V(r) = 4/3\ \pi r^3 \text{ (where } \pi \approx 3.14159)$$

and would translate into the following expression for a computed value in M:

```
Volume(R : Decimal19) {((4/3) : Decimal19) * 3.14159 * (R*R*R)}.
```

You could have another computed value with the same name (Volume) for a rectangular cuboid with sides of length A, B and C:

```
Volume(A : Decimal19, B : Decimal19, C : Decimal19) {A*B*C}.
```

Both computed values have the same identifiers (or names), but overloading allows you to define both within a given module, since they have a different number of arguments. In this case, you could avoid some possible confusion by renaming the computed values to SphereVolume and CuboidVolume, but there may be stylistic reasons in certain domains to take advantage of overloading and retain the same computed value identifier across several different implementations, each with differing argument counts.

Two computed value definitions with the same name and the same number of arguments will result in an error.

Languages

Languages are the fourth basic construct included in the M language. Language constructs were provided in M with the primary intent of enabling the development of domain-specific languages, or DSLs, which can be a useful tool in model-driven development. This subject was covered in Chapter 3.

Summary

In this chapter I've provided a quick overview of the M language. M is a central component of the SQL Server Modeling framework, and is intended primarily as a language for defining and managing models and domain-specific languages. It can be used for transforming and deploying models defined in the language into SQL Server schemas in SQL Server via T-SQL code generation.

Four central elements are important in developing an understanding of M:

- Types

- Extents, which map to SQL Server tables

- Computed values

- Languages

The first three of these are covered in this chapter, while Chapter 3 discusses languages from the perspective of Domain-Specific Languages (DSLs).

I also covered modules and how type, extent, and computed value declarations in one module can be made visible to other modules via Import/Export declarations.

For further reading on the M language, please refer to Microsoft's "M" Language Reference (http://msdn.microsoft.com/en-us/library/ee730868(VS.85).aspx), and the "M" Programming Guide (http://msdn.microsoft.com/en-us/library/dd129568%28VS.85%29.aspx).

■ ■ ■

CHAPTER 6

SQL Server Modeling Services – The Folder Pattern

SQL Server Modeling Services is the name of what, at one time, was termed the Repository. This was back in the days of Code Name Oslo. In November 2009, Microsoft held its annual Professional Developers Conference, and announced a number of name changes. Oslo became SQL Server Modeling, and the Repository became SQL Server Modeling Services. (I will sometimes use SSMod as a short form for the longer name.) SSMod Services, née Repository, was developed with two goals in mind: 1) to provide a database geared to storing application models, and 2) to provide for common model database schemas.

Enterprise application models can come with a large amount of associated metadata: database schemas representing the models, design requirements, config files, application binaries, team documentation, and versioning information are some examples. Using an optimized central repository for storing and managing this metadata can make the application life cycle significantly more productive and efficient.

Schemas or domain models are often found in common across a wide range of applications. SQL Server Modeling Services provides a set of these common schemas or domain models for use wherever they might be appropriate in developing a model-based application. These can be provided either by Microsoft or by third parties.

The SSMod Services are built on the SQL Server platform, but they are enhanced and optimized for supporting model-based development. These enhancements mean that a Modeling Services database will

- Contain each application model in its own SQL Server schema

- Support fine-grained (i.e., row-level) security

- Support localized strings and resources

- Support hierarchical (i.e., folder-structured) data organization across all types or tables, as needed

- Support change tracking and auditing

- Still provide a natural database structure that supports standard access technologies and ad hoc queries

Put another way, the Modeling Services component of SQL Server Modeling encompasses features that embody the enterprise capabilities of the new .NET framework.

So to sum up, when an IT manager contemplates the use of a new technology for mission-critical software, he or she will usually be thinking about at least some combination of the following issues:

- Security

- Scalability

- Availability

- Auditing

- Change tracking

- Version management

- Localization

Woven together, the capabilities represented in this list provide the components of a system that might qualify the modeling framework as enterprise-ready. All of these capabilities are provided within the framework of SSMod Services. Covered in any depth, each would require a book in itself. This chapter and the next one will provide an overview of two important facets of SQL Server Modeling Services: the Folder Pattern and security.

The Modeling Services Folder Pattern

Modeling Services uses a folder pattern as the foundation of several of its services, including claims-based Security, Versioning and Change Management, as well as Auditing. Any table can be given a folder field, so Modeling Services support organizing data into logical folders. In other words, any row from any table can belong to a given folder, and, like file system folders in DOS, Windows, or UNIX, repository folders can be organized in a hierarchical structure.

The folder structure in Modeling Services is very simple and is illustrated in Table 6-1. Each folder has three values:

- An integer Id, which corresponds to its primary key in the folders table

- A text name

- An integer folder field, which is null if it is a top-level folder, or the Id of a higher level folder if it is a child folder of the higher level folder.

Table 6-1 is an example of a folder structure for a very simple quality control (QC) system that you will apply to the CarComponents model discussed in Chapter 4.

Table 6-1. QC Folders for CarComponents

Id	Name	Parent Folder
1 Repository		NULL
500 QC	Level	NULL
510 QC	Critical	500
520 QC	High	500
530 QC	Standard	500

Example: A Quality Control System for CarModel

Following along the lines of Table 6-1, you will name three QC levels of Critical, High, and Standard. A QC level of *Critical* might be applied to components that have an important impact on safety-related aspects of the car, such as brakes, air bags, seat belts, suspension, and so forth. A QC level of *High* might be required for components that affect the mechanical performance of the car, such as the drive train components. A QC level of *Standard* would be required of the parts not classified in the first two categories, and could include items such as carpeting, dome lights, and so on. QC ratings and criteria apply to all components of the system, so this is a natural area where a horizontal partitioning of the data (across a number of tables or types) works very well. Table 6-2 shows the earlier car components table (cf. Chapter 4), with a QCFolder column added, and a QC Folder Id corresponding to one of those enumerated in Table 6-1 assigned for each component.

Table 6-2. CarComponents Model with QC Folders Added

Id	Name	Level	Description	Quantity	Part Of	QC Folder
1 C	ar	1	Top Level	1	NULL	520
2	Drive Train	2	Makes the car go	1	Car	520
3	Suspension	2	Makes the ride smoother	1	Car	520
4 Bo	dy	2	Metallic Blue	1	Car	520
5	Interior	3	Seats, carpeting, etc.	1	Body	530
5 St	eering	2	Makes it turn	1	Car	510
6	Engine	3	220hp V8	1	Drive Train	520

7	Pistons	4	Drive the crankshaft	8	Engine	520
8	Valves	4	8 intake, 8 exhaust	16	Engine	520
9	Shock Absorbers	3	One for each wheel	4	Suspension	520
10	Wheel Assembly	3	One for each wheel	4	Drive Train	510
11	Disk Brake	4	One for each wheel	4	Wheel Assembly	510
12	Floor Covering	4	Carpeting and Mats	1	Interior	530

A note to the reader: This very simple QC system is just an example intended to illustrate a possible use of the folder pattern provided by the SQL Server Modeling Services. It isn't intended to emulate the design for a real-world manufacturing QC system, which would be considerably more complex. I could just as easily have said that all parts are painted one of three colors (red, green, or blue) for the purpose of this example. Also, for the purpose of illustrating the folder model, I've added a few more components than what you saw in the `CarModel` example used in Chapter 4. Finally, the term "CarModel" refers to the name of the overall model in that example, which is also the name of the M module. (To be entirely accurate, the module name was "Car.Model", but I've dropped the period for the purposes of this discussion.) CarComponent is the type that is defined in that module, and CarComponents is the name of the extent for the CarComponent type.

Here is where I can talk about how Repository folders are created, organized, and managed using the SSMod tool set (Intellipad, Quadrant, and the command-line tools) and Visual Studio. Let's open Intellipad and reload (or re-enter) the code for Chapter 4's `CarModel` example. It should look something like that shown in Intellipad Figure 6-1.

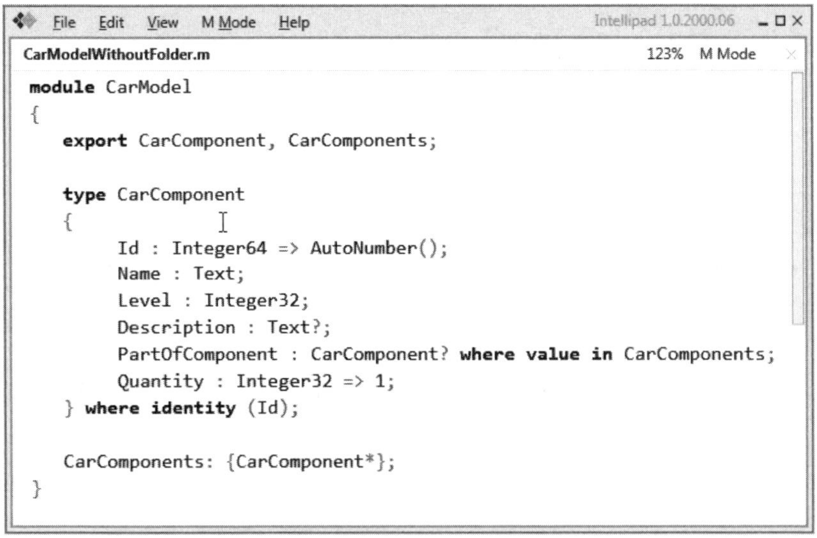

```
File   Edit   View   M Mode   Help                    Intellipad 1.0.2000.06   _ □ X

CarModelWithoutFolder.m                                      123%   M Mode      ×

module CarModel
{
    export CarComponent, CarComponents;

    type CarComponent
    {
        Id : Integer64 => AutoNumber();
        Name : Text;
        Level : Integer32;
        Description : Text?;
        PartOfComponent : CarComponent? where value in CarComponents;
        Quantity : Integer32 => 1;
    } where identity (Id);

    CarComponents: {CarComponent*};
}
```

Figure 6-1. Original CarModel type definition from Chapter 4

How do you modify this code to add a folder value? Folders are provided by the `Repository.Item` model, so you'll add an import directive for `Repository.Item`. Next you'll add a `Folder` value to the `CarComponent` type definition, ascribed to the `FoldersTable` type: This is shown in Figure 6-2.

```
File   Edit   View   M Mode   Help                Intellipad 1.0.2000.06  _ □ ×

CarModelWithFolder.m                                   123%   M Mode      ×

module CarModel
{
    import  Repository.Item;
    export  Cannot resolve the reference to 'Repository.Item'.

    type CarComponent
    {
        Id : Integer64 => AutoNumber();
        Name : Text;
        Level : Integer32;
        Description : Text?;
        PartOfComponent : CarComponent? where value in CarComponents;
        Quantity : Integer32 => 1;
        Folder : FoldersTable;
    } where identity (Id);

    CarComponents: {CarComponent*};
}
```

Figure 6-2. *Adding the Folder value, showing two reference errors*

But there's a hitch: The M compiler is unable to resolve the `Repository.Item` model and `FoldersTable` type references. You need to specifically add a reference to the `Repository.Item` model, which, as it turns out, is contained in the Repository.dll file. Adding a reference to the Repository.dll file must be done in the context of a Visual Studio project, and Intellipad provides a way of doing this:

1. Expand the Intellipad window horizontally to make room for a split window by dragging the right edge of the window to the right (see Figure 6-3).

2. Click on the View tab of the Intellipad window.

3. Select the Split Vertically option. This will split the Intellipad window vertically into two M mode panes, each with the same M code as appeared before the split.

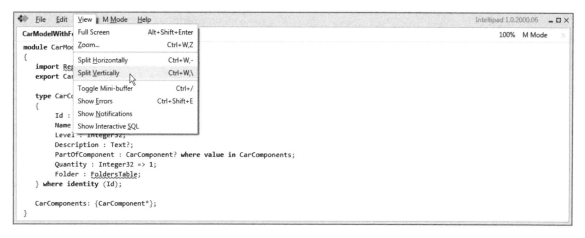

Figure 6-3. *Splitting the Intellipad window vertically to allow room for opening a new project*

Now you can add the new project:

1. Click the File tab of the Intellipad window.

2. Select the New Project option (as shown in Figure 6-4).

3. A Save Project As dialog box will pop up to allow you to name the new project file to be saved. Enter a project filename of **CarModelWithFolder** (see Figure 6-5). This will display a new project template in the right pane (see Figure 6-6).

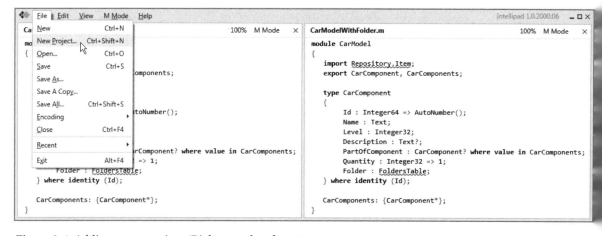

Figure 6-4. *Adding a new project. (Right pane has focus.)*

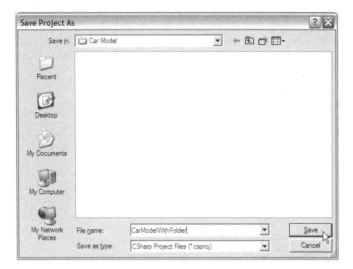

Figure 6-5. Saving the new project file as CarModelWithFolder.csproj

```
File   Edit   View   Project   Help                                                    Intellipad 1.0.2000.06   _ □ ×

CarModelWithFolder.m                    100%   M Mode   ×   file:///C:/Documents and Setting...      100%   Project Mode   ×

module CarModel                                             CarModelWithFolder.csproj
{                                                             Reference
    import Repository.Item;                                     [System]
    export CarComponent, CarComponents;                        [System.Core]
                                                               [System.Xml.Linq]
    type CarComponent                                          [System.Data.DataSetExtensions]
    {                                                          [Microsoft.CSharp]
        Id : Integer64 => AutoNumber();                        [System.Data]
        Name : Text;                                           [System.Xml]
        Level : Integer32;                                     [System.Configuration]
        Description : Text?;                                   [System.Data.Entity]
        PartOfComponent : CarComponent? where value in CarComponents;  [System.ComponentModel.DataAnnotations]
        Quantity : Integer32 => 1;                             [C:\Program Files\Microsoft Oslo\1.0\Bin\Microsoft.M.dll]
        Folder : FoldersTable;                                 [System.Runtime.Serialization]
    } where identity (Id);                                   MCompile
                                                               [Model.m]
    CarComponents: {CarComponent*};

}
```

Figure 6-6. New project (right pane)

The new project file is based on a generic template, and includes a single generic M file (Model.m under the MCompile section) and a number of models under the Reference section. These are all models provided in the SSMod Services Base Domain Library (BDL). I'll say more about the BDL in the next chapter.

Note that the Reference section doesn't include a reference to Repository, and the CarModelWithFolder.m file is not included in the MCompile section. So the project is initialized as a generic project from a template, and has nothing to do with the model you are working with. Model.m is a placeholder code file, which could be used to flesh out the code you actually want for the domain model definition file. Figure 6-7 shows the generic Model.m code after being created as a result of setting up the new project.

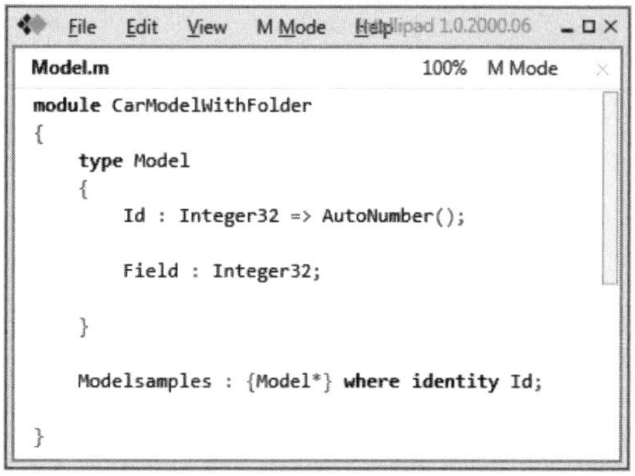

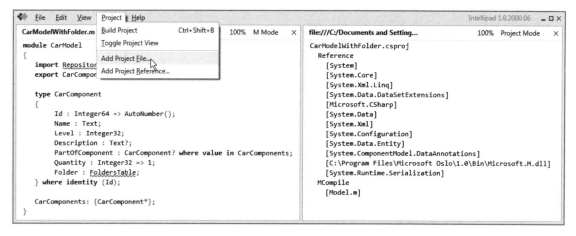

Figure 6-7. Generic Model.m file created with the new project file

Note that the module is named the same as the M code file that was loaded in Intellipad at the time you created the project, but it doesn't reflect the code in that file. If you had started by creating the project file first, then using the Model.m file as the starting point for building the model code, this would have worked just as well. Intellipad, however, currently provides no facility for renaming the M file within the project file.

If you've been following along with this example by executing the steps in Intellipad, you may have noticed that the configuration text in the project file is read-only and can't be modified in this view. You can, however, add the CarModelWithFolder.m file to the project file by clicking the Project menu and selecting the Add Project File option, as shown in Figure 6-8.

Figure 6-8. Setting up to add the CarModelWithFolder.m file to the MCompile section of the project file

This will bring up an Open file dialog box, as shown in Figure 6-9. Select CarModelWithFolder.m and click the Open button.

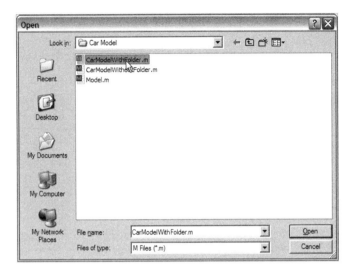

Figure 6-9. Selecting the CarModelWithFolder.m file to add to the MCompile section of the project file

This will add the M file under the MCompile section of the project (see Figure 6-10).

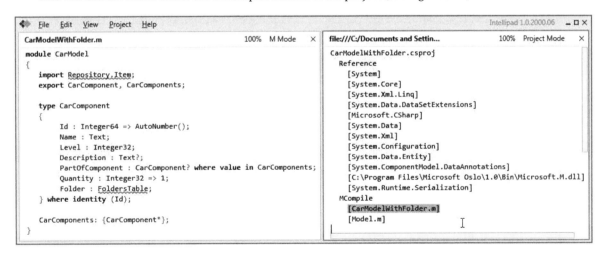

Figure 6-10. CarModelWithFolder.m file added to the MCompile section of the project file

Although you now have the desired CarModelWithFolder.m included in the project, you also still have the unwanted baggage of the Model.m file in this section. Here are the steps you can take to remove it:

1. Click on the Project menu and select Toggle Project View.

2. This displays the project file in XML format. Unlike the read-only Project view, the XML view can be edited.

3. Figure 6-11 is the result. I've highlighted the line for Model.m under the `<ItemGroup>` tag.

4. Highlight and delete this line.

5. Toggle again to the normal Project Mode view.

6. Save the project file with Ctrl+S, or by using the File → Save menu option.

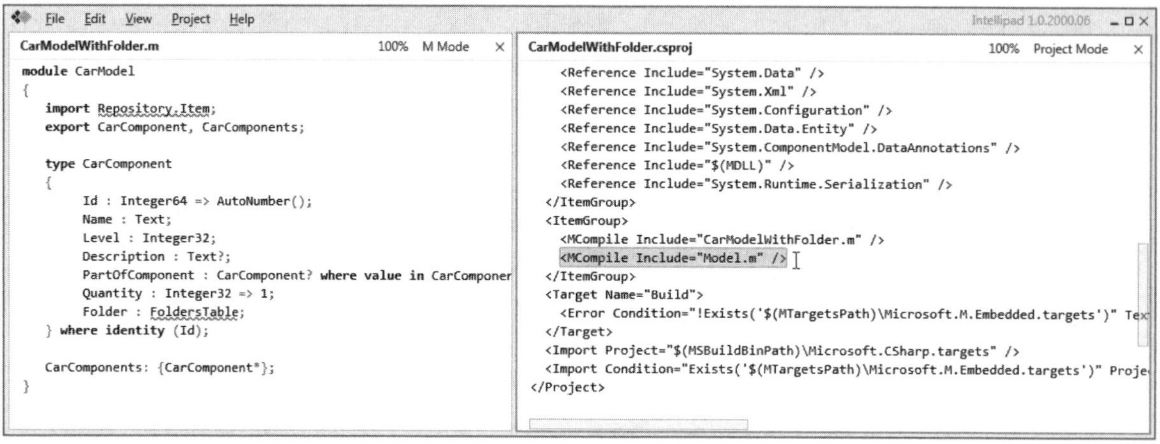

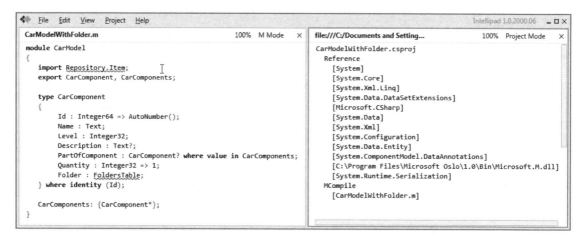

Figure 6-11. Project mode in XML with Model.m line highlighted

Figure 6-12 shows the result.

Figure 6-12. CarModelWithFolder project with the updated MCompile section (bottom of right pane)

You can see that the resolution errors for `Repository.Item` and `Folders.Table` are still occurring, so what's been done so far hasn't fixed this situation. You want to add a reference for the `Repository.Item` model under the Reference section of the project definition. `Repository.Item` (and other SSMod Services models) is defined in the Repository.dll file. This file resides in the bin folder where the SQL Server Modeling framework is installed on your computer. The default path for this file, assuming a standard installation for the SSMod software, is normally C:\Program Files\Microsoft Oslo\1.0\bin\Repository.dll. (If your instance of SQL Server Modeling was installed to a different path, you will need to make the appropriate adjustment in what follows to point to the folder where Repository.dll resides.)

To add this reference, click again on the Project menu, and select the Add Project Reference option (see Figure 6-13).

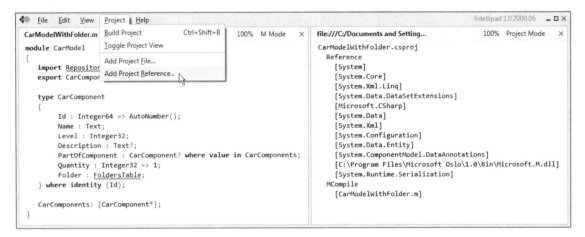

Figure 6-13. *Adding the project reference for Repository.dll*

Navigate to the location of the Repository.dll file, select that file, and click the Open button (shown in Figure 6-14).

Figure 6-14. *Adding the reference to C:\Program Files\Microsoft Oslo\1.0\bin\Repository.dll in the Open dialog box*

The result is shown in Figure 6-15: Repository.dll has been added in the Reference section of the project listing, and the resolution errors have disappeared in the M Mode view of the model M file (left pane).

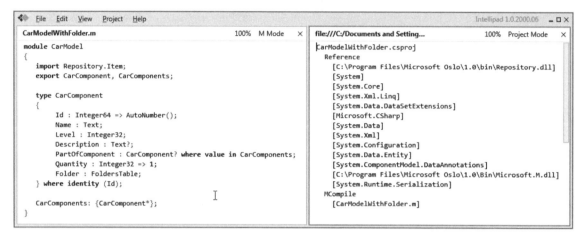

Figure 6-15. Adding Repository.dll as a reference in the project file fixes the resolution errors.

Now that `Repository.Item` and `FoldersTable` can be resolved in the M code, make sure the cursor is in the right pane and use Ctrl+S to save the project file again. (This should save it as the CarModelWithFolder.csproj in the same folder where the CarModelWithFolder.m M code file is located.)

The next step is to deploy the model to SQL Server. This time you'll use Visual Studio 2010, rather than Quadrant, to deploy. Start by opening SQL Server, and select Open Project (see Figure 6-16).

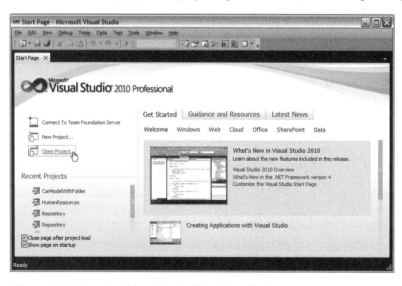

Figure 6-16. Opening the project in Visual Studio 2010

Browse to the folder where CarModelWithFolder.csproj was just saved, and select this file (shown in Figure 6-17). Select the file in the Open Project dialog box.

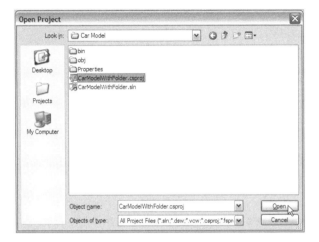

Figure 6-17. Opening the project file in Visual Studio 2010

The title bar of the Visual Studio window should indicate the name of the project. In case the Solution Explorer is not already open in Visual Studio, select the View → Solution Explorer menu option to open it (see Figure 6-18).

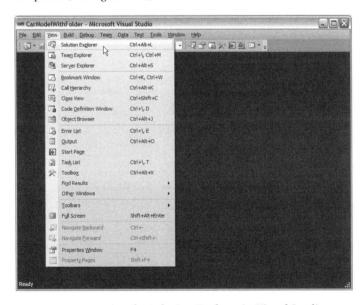

Figure 6-18. Opening the Solution Explorer in Visual Studio

Figure 6-19 shows the Visual Studio window with the Solutions Explorer pane.

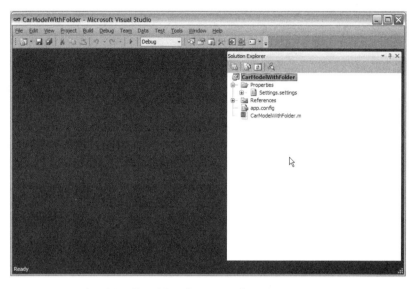

Figure 6-19. Visual Studio with Solution Explorer open

After the Solution Explorer is opened, expand the References section to make sure everything is in order (you want to see that the reference to Repository.dll is still there), and double-click CarModelWithFolder.m to display the M code (as shown in Figure 6-20). Verify that no error indications appear in the M code pane.

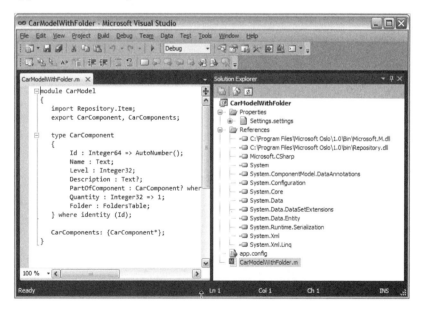

Figure 6-20. CarModelWithFolder.m code (left pane)

Now you should be ready to use the M Deployment facility in Visual studio to deploy the model to SQL Server. Right-click on the project name in the Solution Explorer pane (top line), and select Properties from the context menu that appears (see Figure 6-21).

Figure 6-21. Opening the project properties pane in Solution Explorer

Select the M Deployment section in the project Properties pane on the left (see Figure 6-22).

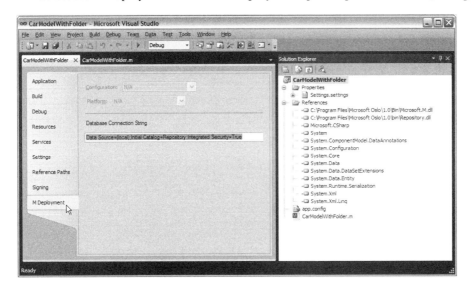

Figure 6-22. Selecting the M Deployment section in project properties

Verify that everything is in order in the Database Connection String. It should look exactly the same as displayed in Figure 6-22, unless you are connecting to a remote database or running with other than Windows security.

Now right-click again on the Project name in Solution Explorer and select Deploy, as shown in Figure 6.23.

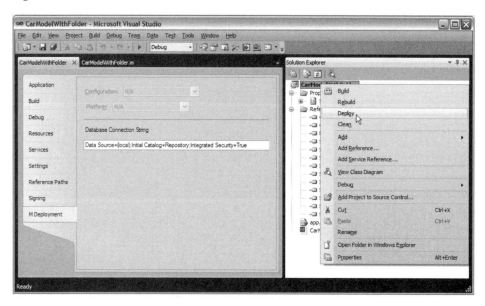

Figure 6-23. Selecting the Deploy option for the CarModelWithFolderProject

Once the deployment has executed, you should see a Deploy Succeeded indication in the lower left of the Visual Studio window (shown in Figure 6-24). If you get a Deploy Failed indication, check the Database Connection String field in the M Deployment pane.

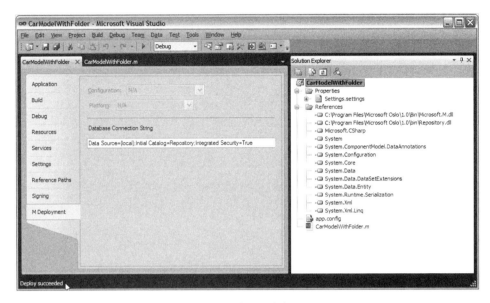

Figure 6-24. Deploy Succeeded indication (lower-left corner)

If everything is correct, you're finished with Visual Studio, and you can go ahead and close it.

To verify that the model has been deployed to SQL Server, open Quadrant and click on View →
Explorer → Repository on the menu (see Figure 6-25).

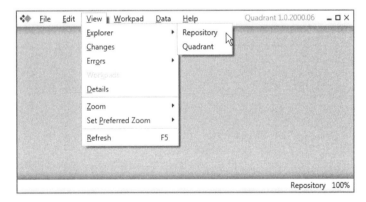

Figure 6-25. Opening an Explorer on the Repository in Quadrant

In the Repository Explorer, expand the CarModel database by clicking the triangle icon to the left of
the label, then left-click and drag the CarComponents table onto the Quadrant canvas, as shown in
Figure 6-26.

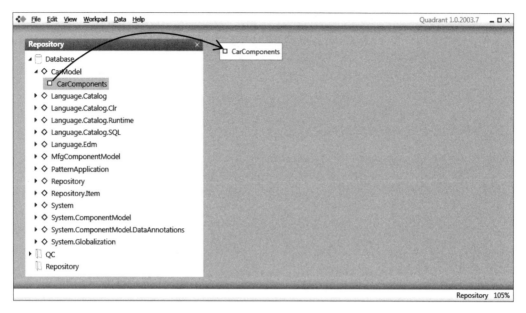

Figure 6-26. *Dragging the CarModel.CarComponents table onto the Quadrant canvas*

This should open a view of the empty CarComponents table, as shown in Figure 6-27. The important thing to check here is that there is a Folder column included in the table column headings.

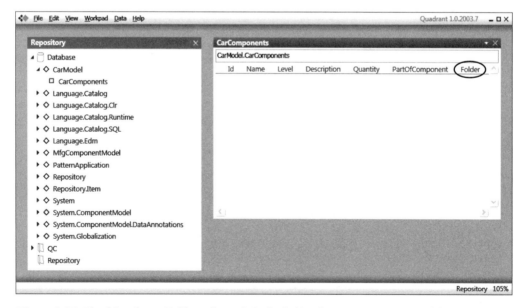

Figure 6-27. *Checking that a Folder column is included in the CarComponents table*

Next, you need to set up the QC folders in the Repository, since these have not been created yet. To do this, start by opening SQL Server Management Studio. Connect to the database where the Repository is defined. This should be the default (local) connection, unless you have been working with a different database connection.

Expand the Databases section (click on the + sign) in the Object Explorer pane, then the Repository, then the Views section (as shown in Figure 6-28). Always use the Views section of the Repository to create and manage folders, not the Tables section. This is important because using the Tables section to create or manage folders can cause inconsistencies or integrity problems within the Repository's folders setup. Correcting such problems can be difficult.

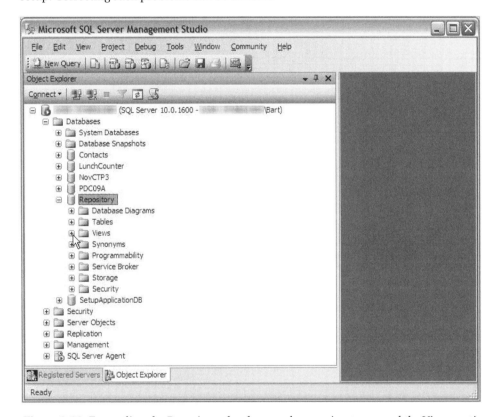

Figure 6-28. Expanding the Repository database and preparing to expand the Views section

After expanding Views, scroll down through the Views listing and right-click on the Repository.Item.Folders view (see Figure 6-29). Select the Edit Top 200 Rows option.

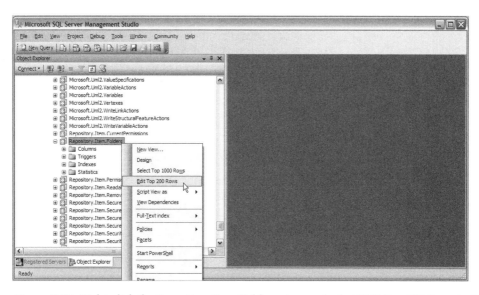

Figure 6-29. *Right-click the Repository.Item.Folders view and select Edit Top 200 Rows in the context menu.*

This should bring up a table view of Repository.Item.Folders in the right pane of SQL Server Management Studio, as shown in Figure 6-30. The view will show all folders defined under the Repository and is updatable. New folders are added simply by entering the Id, folder name, and parent folder Id in the bottom row of the view (the one with all NULL entries). If the folder is to be a top-level folder, leave the Folder value as NULL. The red exclamation point icon ❶ indicates that the row has been changed, but not yet committed.

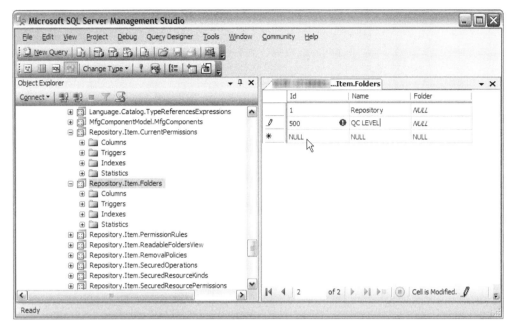

Figure 6-30. *Adding the parent QC Level folder in the Repository.Item.Folder table view*

Clicking in the left cell of the bottom row (the one with all NULL entries) commits the changes just made to the QC Level folder row above. In this bottom row, enter 510 for the next Id, QC Critical for the Name value, and 500 for the parent Folder Id value. Figure 6-31 shows these changes before the row has been committed. After this row is committed, enter and commit the next two folders, with the following values:

- Id: 520; Name: QC High; Folder: 500

- Id: 530; Name: QC Standard; Folder: 500

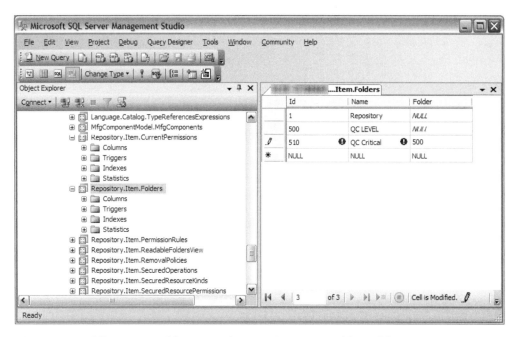

Figure 6-31. *Adding a new Folder row in the Repository.Item.Folders table view*

Figure 6-32 shows the four QC folders in the Repository.Item.Folders table after adding and committing.

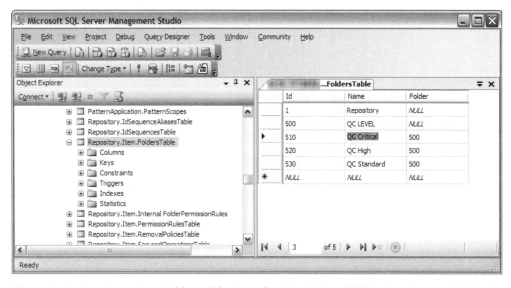

Figure 6-32. *Repository.Item.Folders table view after the QC Level folders have been added and committed*

Returning to the CarComponents Explorer in Quadrant (see Figure 6-33), you can begin filling out your model by entering new component instances (just as you did in Chapter 4, using Data → Insert Item or Ctrl+I), but this time specifying the QC Level of each component by selecting the QC Folder name.

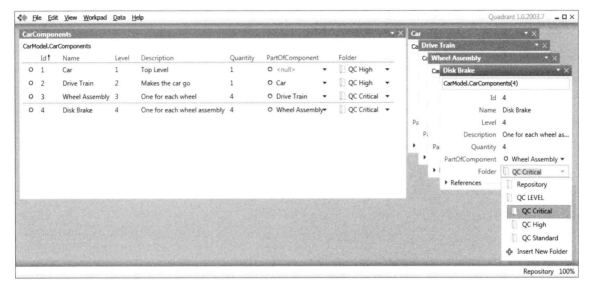

Figure 6-33. Adding new CarComponents values and specifying the QC Level for each

In Figure 6-33, I've defined four CarComponent values with their associated QC Level values. You can see that there are two components with a QC Level of High (the Top Level Car system, and the Drive Train), and two with a QC Level of Critical (Wheel Assembly and Disk Brake). So, theoretically, you should be able to take a look in the QC Level folders and see if the contained component values correspond to this model as it's been configured so far.

If you go back to the Repository Explorer, you can see the top QC Level folder. Expanding the parent QC Level folder (by clicking on the triangle icon on the left), you see the three QC Level child folders: Critical, High, and Standard (shown in Figure 6-34).

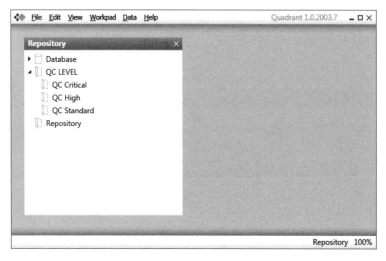

Figure 6-34. Repository Explorer with the QC Level folder expanded

If you drag the QC Level folder onto the Quadrant canvas, this will open a separate Explorer just on the QC folders. Figure 6-35 shows this explorer, and you see exactly what you might have anticipated: two CarComponents with a QC Critical level, and two with a QC High level. The QC Standard folder is showing null, since you haven't yet assigned any CarComponents to that QC level.

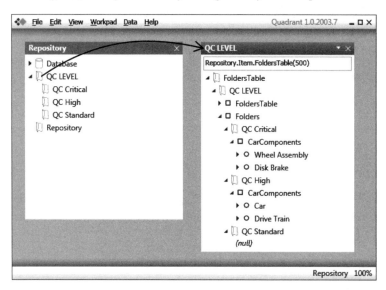

Figure 6-35. Quadrant Explorer showing the QC Level folders and their contained values

If you had defined other types (and their extents) in the application that you wanted to include in the QC system, then those extents (tables) could also be reflected within the QC Level folders. Say that your manufacturer not only made cars, but also toasters and lawnmowers. Then you could also define a `ToasterComponent` type and a `LawnMowerComponent` type, with corresponding ToasterComponents and LawnMowerComponents tables. If the manufacturer had a single QC department that covered all manufacturing lines, then you would have the seed for developing a QC model and application that this department could use for managing its operations across different lines. If the manufacturer decided that each line should have its own QC department (say, for instance, they were made in different plants), then the folder pattern of SSMod could be applied to allow each QC department to view and manage the QC data of its respective line, but not be distracted with data for the other lines. Corporate headquarters would, of course, have access to all QC data if that was how the IT department was asked to structure the system.

In the next chapter, which covers the security services provided by SQL Server Modeling Services, you'll use this basic scenario as the basis of an exercise to illustrate how security can be used to expose or hide data.

CHAPTER 7

■ ■ ■

SQL Server Modeling Services – Security

Security is an essential component of enterprise applications. Since SQL Server Modeling (SSMod) is part of the broader .NET framework, developers have access to a wide range of services and technologies, some of which provide their own security options. Applications and users can query a SQL Server database through Entity Data Modeling (EDM), LINQ, ADO.NET, ODBC, and other systems, including non-Microsoft platforms.

The Modeling Services framework supports granular (row-level) and claims-based security, built on the folder pattern discussed in the previous chapter. It should be clear, however, that a wide range of other security facilities is available, depending on which platforms you involve in creating an application.

Modeling Services uses updatable views in conjunction with the folder pattern to protect the base tables and provide row-level security. A SQL Server view is essentially a named read-only query of one or more tables that you or an application can use with subsequent queries as if it were a table. These queries can result in updating, inserting or deleting actions in the base table (and consequently the view) if the user has been granted the appropriate authority.

A view becomes updatable by using what are called INSTEAD OF triggers. Triggers are a special kind of stored procedure that execute on the database server when a user or application attempts to modify data through a DML (data-manipulation language) event. (There are also data-definition language (DDL) and LOGON events that can be addressed by triggers, but I won't go into these here.)

There are only three categories of DML events, created by INSERT, DELETE, or UPDATE statements. An INSTEAD OF trigger substitutes execution of the trigger code for execution of the statement triggering the DML event. The trigger can implement the security criteria established by the developer or the database administrator. An event can initiate a single trigger, or a specified sequence of triggers, to perform tasks to check user privileges and preserve the data and relational integrity.

How triggers are coded and implemented is a topic beyond the level of this book. In any event, SQL Server Modeling Services already provides the infrastructure, based on the folder pattern and pre-installed INSTEAD OF triggers, to support row-level security.

In this chapter, you will extend the CarComponent model introduced in Chapter 4 to a more general manufacturing component model. I will use this more general model to introduce the idea of using the folder pattern to provide security in a way that manufacturing line managers will be able to see or modify data relating only to components made on the manufacturing lines for which they are responsible.

Using Security to Limit Data Visibility

Consider the following scenario. Your car manufacturer has decided to diversify and has recently purchased a company that manufactures small appliances, like toasters and coffee makers. The two lines of businesses will be kept separate in terms of engineering and management. However, corporate is quite happy with the operations of the QC department, and wants to extend their QC procedures and standards into their newly acquired small appliance manufacturing operations.

For the sake of simplicity, I'll call the original manufacturing line, the one that makes cars, the CarLine. The newly acquired plant, the one that makes toasters, I'll call the ToasterLine. Corporate headquarters has promoted the original QC manager to manage QC standards and procedures across both plants, so I will call her TopQC. She promoted her former deputy to manage QC for the car plant, so he will be known as CarQC. As you might expect, the QC manager at the toaster plant will be ToasterQC.

In terms of IT operations then, you have three users, each needing access to the QC data she or he is responsible for managing:

- **TopQC**: Access to all QC data across both manufacturing lines.

- **CarQC**: Access only QC data for the car line.

- **ToasterQC**: Access only to QC data for the toaster line.

These will be user names created as part of this exercise, with TopQC given read/write privileges to all QC data across the board, and the remaining two QC users given read/write privileges only to the data pertaining to their respective manufacturing domains.

Setting Up – Installing the PatternApplication Sample

Before getting started with this exercise, you will need to install the PatternApplication sample in the Repository. This code is required to enable the use of three patterns that this exercise depends on. One of these patterns, named **AddViewsInsteadOfTriggers**, supports the use of the **INSTEAD OF** triggers I just discussed. Another pattern, named **AlterSchemaPermissions**, supports the security features you will need in this example. Finally, you will use a pattern, named **AddFolderForeignKey**, that supports adding a folder and key more efficiently than explicitly coding it.

The instructions for downloading and installing this sample are available on the MSDN web page: "How to Install the PatternApplication Sample." The URL for this page (as of the Nov. 2009 CTP release) is

`http://msdn.microsoft.com/en-us/library/ee713117(VS.85).aspx`

The download file is a Zip file, so you will need to extract the files to a folder such as

`C:\Temp\PatternApplication.`

Be sure to allow Winzip (or whatever extraction tool you use) to create the embedded directory tree. Make a note of where this sample is installed because you will need this path later on in the exercise.

In case you are reading this after a more recent CTP or beta release has become available, you should be able to find the page with an Internet search on "PatternApplication Sample." Follow the directions on this web page, but also have a look at the readme.htm file that's included in the downloaded Zip file, since the readme page contains additional code and information.

Building on the CarModel

The model for this example is similar to the **CarModel** code you developed in Chapter 4, so let's look at the M code for that model (see Figure 7-1).

```
module CarModel
{
    export CarComponent, CarComponents;

    type CarComponent
    {
        Id : Integer64 => AutoNumber(); // used for the Id, or key for each component
        Name : Text;
        Level : Integer32;      // the system level of the component
        Description : Text?;    // "?" is a "Kleene operator" meaning 0 or 1 occurrences
        PartOfComponent : CarComponent? where value in CarComponents;
        Quantity : Integer32 => 1; // how many needed in top-level system; default to 1
    } where identity Id;

    CarComponents: {CarComponent*};
}
```

Figure 7-1. M code for the original car component model from Chapter 4

To extend this to a more general model for manufacturing components, remove the string **Car** from the code. This is only a lexical change, so the logic doesn't change at all. However, you now need to track which manufacturing line makes a particular component, so I'll add a **MfgLine** text value to the **Component** type. Figure 7-2 shows the revised code. I've also changed the model name to **MfgComponentModel**.

Open Intellipad on your computer. If you saved the CarComponentModel.m file when working through the example in Chapter 4, open this file in Intellipad and modify the code to be the same as that shown in Figure 7-2. If you don't have the code from Chapter 4 saved, it should take only a minute to key in this code. Alternatively, you can download it from the Apress website.

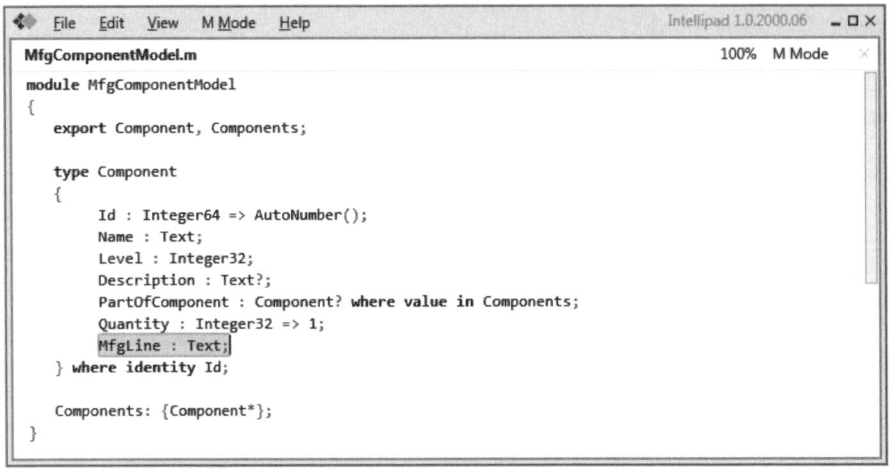

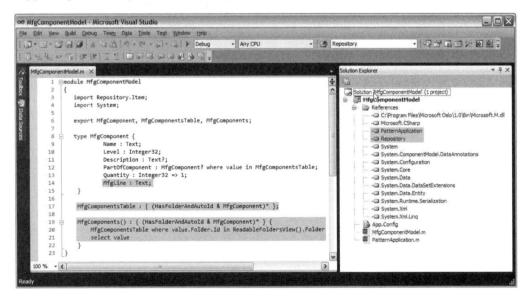

Figure 7-2. Changing the code for MfgComponentModel, and adding MfgLine value to the type

Create a new working directory to save the code and project files to, like C:\MfgComponentModel, and save the M file as MfgComponentModel.m in that directory.

Now, let's jump ahead to a preview of where you're going with this model. I'll switch tools here, from Intellipad to Visual Studio, because you'll be working in Visual Studio from here on. Figure 7-3 shows the M code for the model in the left pane of Visual Studio, once you've added in the code supporting the folder pattern and security.

Figure 7-3. A preview of the final MfgComponentModel code and project solution in Visual Studio

The grayed areas in the left pane of Figure 7-3 are the important changes from the original `CarModel` code that enable the security features in this model (lines 17 and 19–21). I'll talk about these more as you go through this exercise, but here's a quick overview:

- *Line 14*: This is the new text value that references the manufacturing line you added to the `MfgComponent` type. It identifies which manufacturing line produces the component.

- *Line 17*: `MfgComponentsTable:` This was formerly the `MfgComponents` extent and mapped to the `MfgComponents` table in the database. It has been renamed to `MfgComponentsTable` so that an updatable view called `MfgComponents` can be created that provides the actual user view into the table. The `MfgComponentsTable` extent is created as a "mix-in" of two types: `HasFolderAndAutoId` and `MfgComponent`. `HasFolderAndAutoId` actually provides the `Folder` and `Id` values of the extent, without having to add these explicitly in the `MfgComponent` type, as you did before. Note these are no longer included in the `MfgComponent` type declaration, as they were in the `CarModel` code.

- *Lines 19–21*: `MfgComponents():` This is an important part of the model code providing the security capability. It is essentially a query that creates a view of the records in the `MfgComponentsTable` extent constrained to be in the `ReadableFoldersView().Folder` collection. This collection contains only the folder Id's to which the logged-on user has access.

The grayed items (PatternApplication and Repository*)* under the References section of the Solution Explorer (right pane) of Figure 7-3 are references you must add in order for certain parts of the code to work.

Note also, there's a new PatternApplication.m code file at the bottom of the Solution Explorer pane. This file is required to make the code work, specifically, line 17 and lines 19–21 discussed in the second and third items of the preceding list.

Building the MfgComponentModel Project in Visual Studio

Open Visual Studio 2010 and select the File →→ New →→ Project From Existing Code menu item (see Figure 7-4).

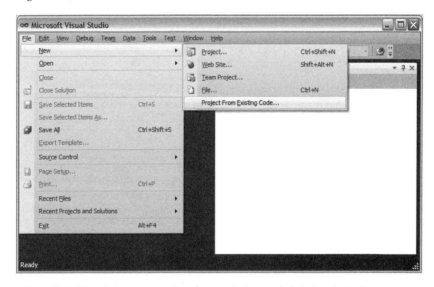

Figure 7-4. *Opening a new project from existing code in Visual Studio*

This will bring up the Create Project from Existing Code Files Wizard (shown in Figure 7-5).

Figure 7-5. *Create Project from Existing Code Files Wizard*

Select Visual C# for the project type, and click the Next button. This should bring up the Specify Project Details panel of the wizard (see Figure 7-6).

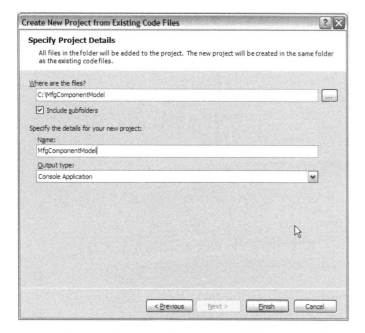

Figure 7-6. Specifying the project details as the last step in the wizard

Enter the path for the Where Are the Files? prompt. This should be C:\MfgComponentModel or whatever path you used to store the MfgComponentModel.m file from Intellipad earlier in the exercise. Under Specify the Details for Your New Project, enter **MfgComponentModel** for the project name, and select Console Application as the output type. You should wind up with a Visual Studio window similar to what appears in Figure 7-7.

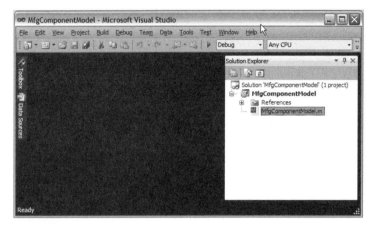

Figure 7-7. *After opening the new project from the existing MfgComponentModel.m file*

In the Solution Explorer pane, expand the References section by clicking the plus sign (+) sign to the left, and then double-click MfgComponentModel.m to bring up a view of the file (see Figure 7-8).

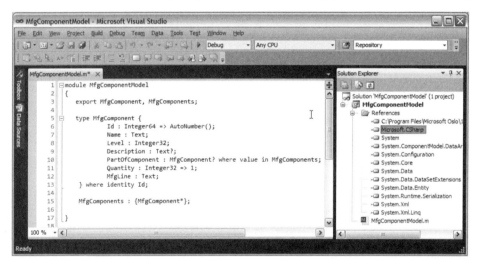

Figure 7-8. *Visual Studio view of the new MfgComponentModel project, showing References and MfgComponentModel.m*

Refining the Model to Include Security

How do you get from the model code shown in Figure 7-8 to the desired end shown in Figure 7-3? Let's work from the top down and add the two import declarations for **Repository.Item** and **System** (see Figure 7-9).

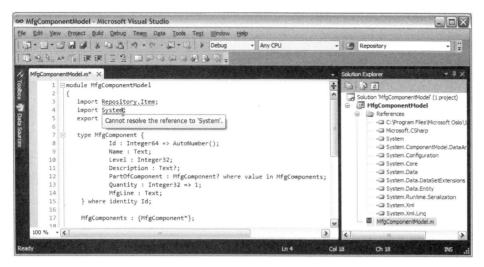

Figure 7-9. *Adding the import declarations for Repository.Item and System results in a "Cannot resolve…" error for both*

As you found in Chapter 6, resolving `Repository.Item` requires adding a reference to the Repository schema, contained in Repository.dll. Let's go ahead and add that reference by right-clicking on References in the right pane, and selecting Add Reference (see Figure 7-10).

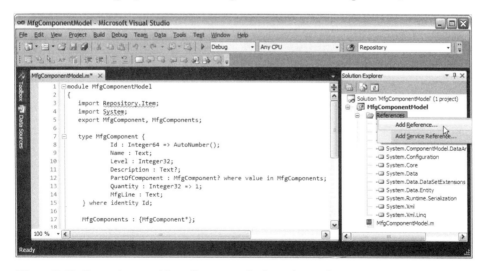

Figure 7-10. *Preparing to add a reference to the Repository schema*

This will bring up an Add Reference dialog box, as shown in Figure 7-11. Click the Browse tab, and browse to the folder containing the Repository.dll file. This will typically be in the Bin folder where Microsoft SQL Server was installed, which for the November CTP is normally

```
C:\Program Files\Microsoft Oslo\1.0\bin\
```

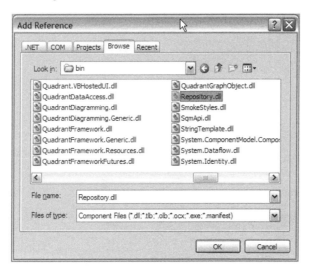

Figure 7-11. Browsing to Repository.dll to add the Repository reference

If you installed SQL Server Modeling to a different location, you will need to make the appropriate adjustment in locating the Repository.dll file.

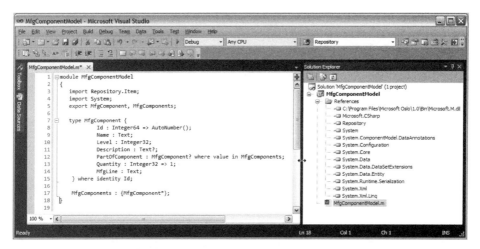

Figure 7-12. Resolution errors for the import declarations are resolved after adding the Repository reference

Figure 7-12 shows the two resolution errors are no longer there.

Next, you want to remove the references to Id and identity (lines 8 and 15), since the **HasFolderAndAutoId** type you will be adding provides the identity constraint required for creating a table in the database. Making these changes in the code results in the error shown in Figure 7-13—an error that is fully expected. (You won't be doing anything with the Solution Explorer for the time being, so you can close it.)

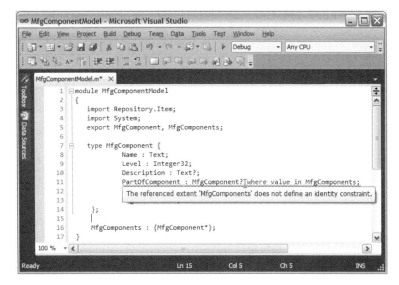

Figure 7-13. Error after removing the Id value in the MfgComponent type, and the identity constraint

This error will be resolved in a moment, after you add the **HasFolderAndAutoId** type, which provides **Folder** and **Id** values without having to code these explicitly. This is an example of one of the services provided by the Base Domain Library (BDL), which is part of SQL Server Modeling Services.

A BRIEF SIDEBAR ON THE VISUAL STUDIO INTERFACE

Before continuing with the exercise, let's take a brief pause to note a few things about the Visual Studio interface. If you're already familiar with Visual Studio, you might want to jump ahead to the next section. If not, please read on.

First, you might have noticed the yellow vertical marker bands to the right of the line numbers. These flag lines that have been modified since the file was loaded or last saved. The asterisk (*) appended to the filename on the top tab of the code pane also indicates the file has been modified but not saved. If the file is saved (use Ctrl-S to save the active pane, and Ctrl-Shift-S to save all files in the project), the color of the vertical marker bands will change from yellow to green. This way, you don't lose the information about changes that have occurred during the current session, even if you save as you go along.

Next, Visual Studio 2010 is "M-aware," which means it has the Intellisense facility for colorizing keywords in the code and for providing suggestions or choices of values or entities that fit in the context of the code. As you've already seen, it flags reference or syntactic problems in the code with red-squiggle underlining, and it will present an error annotation if you cursor over one of these error flags in the code. As you've seen in earlier chapters, Intellisense and this error-flagging facility also show up in Intellipad and Quadrant.

Finally, Visual Studio provides an outlining facility that can be helpful when working with large code files. The vertical lines to the right of the change bands with the minus (–) signs (lines 1 and 7 in Figure 7-13) allow you to collapse or expand the designated sections of code as you need to.

Figure 7-14 shows the left pane before saving the file, so the vertical bands are yellow, indicating unsaved changes. The section of code defining the **MfgComponent** type (line 7) has been collapsed by clicking the minus sign. Now an ellipsis (. . .) appears immediately to the right of the collapsed code section. If you need to have a quick look at the code contained in a collapsed section, you can cursor over the ellipsis, and a pop-up text box will show the code until you move the cursor elsewhere. Note, however, that error indications are not provided in this pop-up text, so if you're looking for code that needs fixing, you will have to expand any collapsed sections. Clicking the plus sign at line 7 would again expand that section of the code.

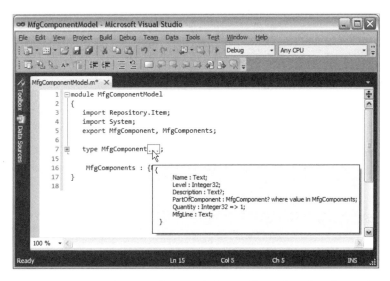

Figure 7-14. Cursoring over the ellipsis for a collapsed section shows the contained code.

Visual Studio is a rich development environment, and can be customized with add-ons and tools. Investing the time to become familiar with its interfaces and features will pay off in greatly improved productivity.

It doesn't hurt to be aware of the info displayed at the bottom of the main window, which can include the status of the last action, the current cursor location, and whether you are in Insert or Overwrite mode. The kind of information can vary, according to what type of pane is active.

HasFolderAndAutoId

I've already mentioned the built-in type **HasFolderAndAutoId**, provided in the Base Domain Library. Consider line 16 in Figure 7-15. The extent declaration in the earlier version of the code was

```
MfgComponents : {MfgComponent*}
```

This was dependent on the identity constraint in the earlier **MfgComponent** type declaration, so it broke when you removed that identity constraint. Since you are getting ready to add an updatable view called **MfgComponents**, you must rename the actual extent to **MfgComponentsTable**. This is (usually) the convention whenever the folder pattern is retrofitted into a model. So the new line of code becomes

```
MfgComponentsTable : { (HasFolderAndAutoId & MfgComponent)* }
```

The new name of the extent becomes **MfgComponentsTable**, and the collection becomes **(HasFolderAndAutoId & MfgComponent)***. **HasFolderAndAutoId** is essentially a type that has a **Folder** value and an auto-incremented identity, and nothing else in terms of attributes. As I mentioned in the first section of the chapter, **(HasFolderAndAutoId & MfgComponent)** is called a *mix-in* type: It combines the values of both types. It's like saying "I'm a **MfgComponent** type, and, by the way, I have a Folder and an AutoNumber Id."

Figure 7-15 shows the model code with the new extent definition added.

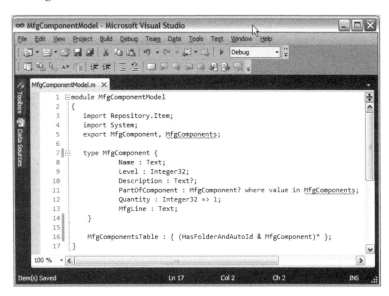

Figure 7-15. *Renaming the MfgComponents extent to MfgComponentsTable, and adding in HasFolderAndAutoId*

Note that by reconfiguring the extent declaration in this way, you have removed the previous identity constraint error (shown in Figure 7-13), but you now have a resolution error on the **MfgComponents** identifier. Of course, this happened because you just renamed it to **MfgComponentsTable**. So let's rename the old extent name **MfgComponents** on lines 5 and 11 to **MfgComponentsTable**. But you are about to define a declaration for an updatable view called **MfgComponents**, so is this really what you want to do? Yes, in the case of the **MfgComponent** type declaration, you want the **PartOfComponent** value constrained to be in **MfgComponentsTable** extent, not in the **MfgComponents** updatable view. Making these changes fixes the two resolution errors, and the compiler is happy.

Next, you need to add the code creating the **MfgComponents** updatable view (see Figure 7-16). This is a key part of the code because it's the part that provides the security functionality.

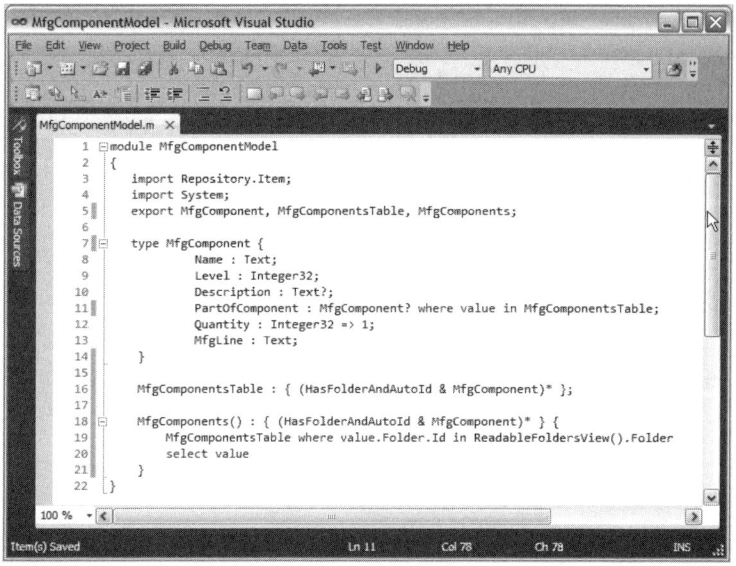

Figure 7-16. Code for the MfgComponents updatable view declaration (lines 18-20)

So what was formerly the **MfgComponents** extent has now become **MfgComponentsTable**, and you have added the **MfgComponents** updatable view, which exposes only the data the user should see. **ReadableFoldersView()** is a built-in function provided in the **Repository.Item** module that returns the list of folder identifiers the user has permission to read. Lines 19-20 of this new code are responsible for providing the security constraint to what the user can view or update.

Adding the PatternApplication Module

You're not finished yet, because you don't have code to hook into the part of the BDL that provides the infrastructure of **INSTEAD OF** triggers and other machinery necessary to implement the desired security capability. Use the Ctrl-Alt-L shortcut key combo to bring up the Solution Explorer (shown in the right pane of Figure 7-17).

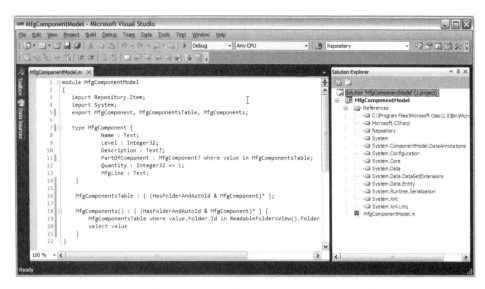

Figure 7-17. Use the Ctrl-Alt-L shortcut to bring up the Solution Explorer (right pane)

You need to add a new M code file for a module called **PatternApplication**. To do this, right-click on the MfgComponentModel project name at the top of the Solution Explorer, and select Add → New Item. As the pop-up menu indicates, you can also use the Ctrl-Shift-A shortcut to do this (see Figure 7-18).

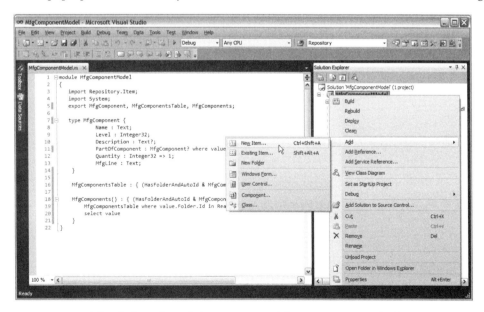

Figure 7-18. Right-click on the MfgComponentModel project name and select Add → New Item

This will bring up an Add New Item dialog, as shown in Figure 7-19. Select the "M" Model option.

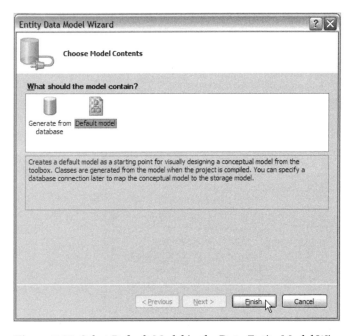

Figure 7-19. Selecting "M" Model as the type of new item to add

This will bring up the Entity Data Model Wizard (shown in Figure 7-20). Select Default Model and click the Finish button.

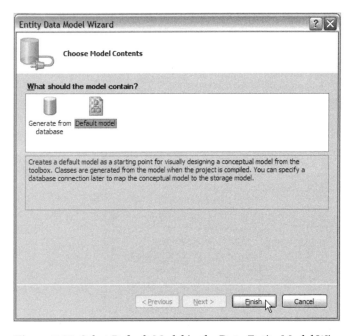

Figure 7-20. Select Default Model in the Data Entity Model Wizard, then Finish

This will add a new M code file template under the previous MfgComponentMode.m file, as shown in Figure 7-21. To rename this file to the desired name of PatternApplication.m, right-click on the name, select the Rename option, then type in the name **PatternApplication.m**. As soon as you press the Enter key to accept the new file name, the tab on the left code editor pane should change accordingly.

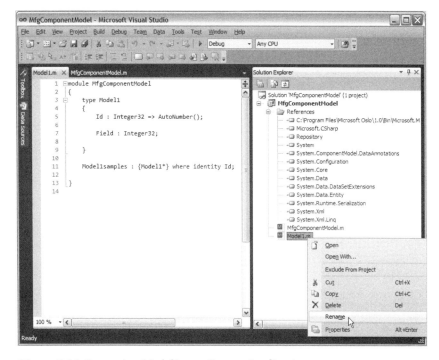

Figure 7-21. Renaming Model1.m to PatternApplication.m

Now you need to replace the generic template code with the M code for the `PatternApplication` module, shown in Figure 7-22. If the resolution error indications shown in the figure do not appear after you've finished entering this code, save all files in the project with Ctrl-Shift-S, close the project, then reload it, and the error indications should appear.

The `Patterns` identifier is not being resolved because, as you might again expect, you need to add a reference to a new schema, or model. In this case, it is called `PatternApplication` (discussed earlier in the chapter), and it is contained in the PatternApplication.dll file. This should be installed on your computer if you followed the instructions in the previous section called "Setting Up – Installing the PatternApplication Sample." If not, you will need to go back and do that now. If it is, you can add the reference to this schema using the same procedure you went through before.

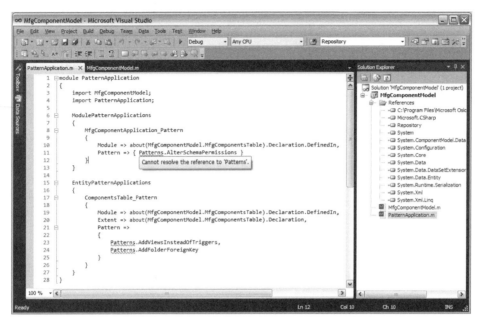

Figure 7-22. *M code for the PatternApplication module (left pane)*

In the Solution Explorer, right-click on References under **MfgComponentModel**, and select Add Reference. This will bring up the Add Reference dialog box. Click the Browse tab and navigate to the location of the PatternApplication.dll file (as shown in Figure 7-23). If you installed the sample to the following path

```
My Documents\Oslo\PatternApplication\
```

Then the path of the DLL file should be

```
My Documents\Oslo\PatternApplication\bin\Debug\PatternApplication.dll.
```

Figure 7-23. *Browsing to the PatternApplication.dll location*

If this resolves the error, then save all files (Ctrl-Shift-S), and you should be ready to build and deploy to the database.

Building the Project

Right-click the project name and select the Build option (see Figure 7-24).

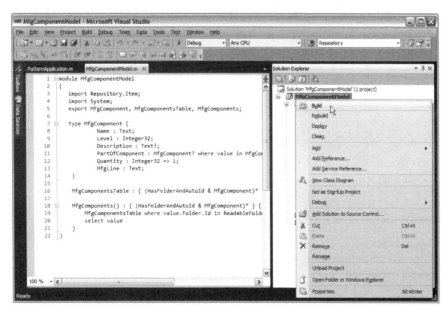

Figure 7-24. *Executing the build*

If the build is successful, you should see results similar to that shown in the Output window in Figure 7-25.

Figure 7-25. *Successful build results shown in the Output window*

Deploying to the Database

Once the build is accomplished, you should be ready to deploy the model to SQL Server. First, however, you need to make sure you have a valid connection string to the database.

Right-click again on the project name and select Properties, which should be at the bottom of the context menu (Figure 7-26).

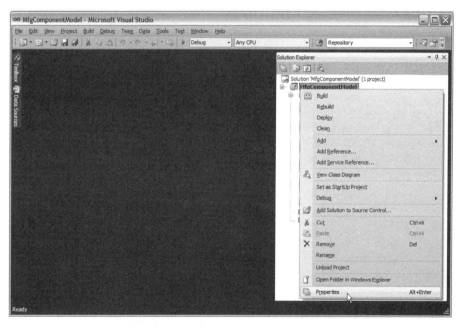

Figure 7-26. *Selecting the project Properties window in the drop-down context menu*

Select the M Deployment at the bottom-left of the Properties pane (see Figure 7-27).

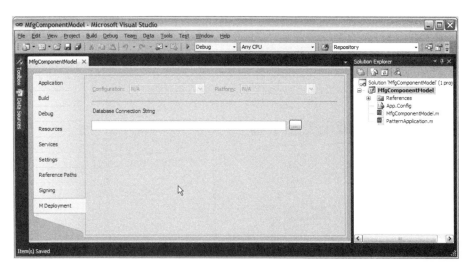

Figure 7-27. Preparing to configure the database connection string in the Properties pane

Click the ellipsis button  to the right of the connection string prompt. This will bring up the Connection Properties dialog (see Figure 7-28).

Figure 7-28. Connection Properties dialog box

Enter (**local**) for the server name, enter **Repository** for the database name, and click the OK button. You should see the connection string displayed in the M Deployment area of the Properties pane (shown in Figure 7-29). Look at this connection string to make sure everything makes sense. If you need to change something, it can be directly edited in the prompt.

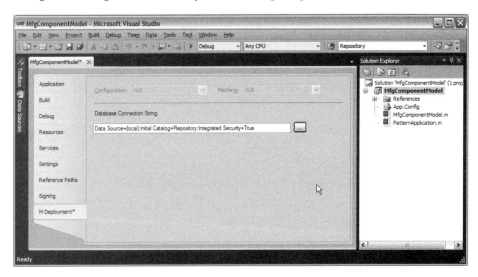

Figure 7-29. *M Deployment area showing the connection string for the newly created* *MfgComponentModel database*

If you want to make sure everything is in order after setting up the connection string, click again on the ellipsis button to the right of the connection string prompt to bring up the Connection Properties dialog, and then click the Test Connection button in the lower-left corner. You should get a notification that the "Test connection succeeded" (see Figure 7-30). Click OK in the notification window, then the Cancel button in the Connection Properties dialog to return to the M Deployment area in the Properties pane.

Figure 7-30. *Testing the database connection string*

At this point, you should be ready to deploy the model to the Repository database. Make sure you've saved all files by using the Ctrl-Shift-S Save All action. (No asterisk should appear on any tab.) Right-click again on the MfgComponentModel project in the Solution Explorer, then select Deploy (as shown in Figure 7-31).

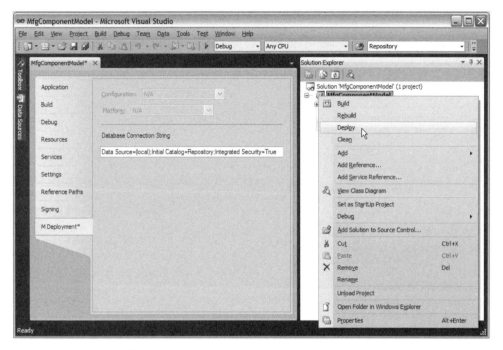

Figure 7-31. *Selecting the Deploy option in the project context menu*

The deployment process writes a log to the Visual Studio Output window. If the deployment is successful, you'll see an indication in the last line of this window, as shown in Figure 7-32.

Figure 7-32. *Visual Studio Output window, showing the deployment succeeded*

If, for some reason, the deployment is unsuccessful, you may get a partial deployment of the database, with the SQL Server system tables, but without the MfgComponentModel schema. You may be able to delete the database by right-clicking on the MfgComponentModel database name in the SSMS Object Explorer, and start over. If that doesn't work, follow the recovery procedure described in the sidebar.

REFRESHING THE COMPONENTMODEL DATABASE

A corrupted or nonworking ComponentModel database can be restored using the `mx.exe` command-line tool. This involves entering three `mx.exe` commands:

1. `mx.exe create /database:ComponentModel /force`. This forces a re-creation of the ComponentModel database. Existing data will be overwritten.

2. `mx.exe install Repository.mx /database:ComponentModel /server:(local) /property:rct=+ /property:ra=+.` (The command should be entered in the command-prompt window as all one line.) This installs the Repository schema in the database, enables change tracking (rct=+), and enables auditing (ra=+).

3. `mx.exe install C:\Oslo\PatternApplication\bin\Debug\PatternApplication.mx /database:ComponentModel.` (Again, all one line.) This installs the PatternApplication code for supporting the pattern hooks. The path used in this command assumes you downloaded and installed the pattern application image to `C:\Oslo\PatternApplication`. If this was installed to a different location, make the appropriate adjustment in the path.

If you find yourself using this restore procedure more than once, it may be easier to create a `refreshdb.bat` batch file containing these three commands, using a text editor. This batch file should be located in the same folder as the mx.exe executable, which would normally be `C:\Program Files\Microsoft Oslo\1.0\bin`

It can be executed from the SQL Server Modeling CTP command prompt.

Creating the QC Folders

Recall that you have two manufacturing lines at two different plants: Cars at one plant, and toasters at another plant. You want to design your QC system so that the CarQC manager can manage his data, the ToasterQC manager can manage her data, and the top-level QC manager has access to all QC data.

You will set up the QC folders to reflect this, so the folder hierarchy should look like the following (numbers in parentheses are the assigned folder Id):

QC (100)

- QC-Cars (110)

    - QC-Cars-Critical (111)

    - QC-Cars-High (112)

    - QC-Cars-Std (113)

- QC-Toasters (120)

    - QC-Toasters-Critical (121)

- QC-Toasters-High (122)

- QC-Toasters-Std (123)

To create this folder structure, bring up SQL Server Management Studio, select the Repository database in the Databases section, and expand the Views section of the Repository (see Figure 7-33). Hit the R key to home in on the view names starting with Repository, and select Repository.Item.Folders. Right-click on the view name, and select Edit Top 200 Rows. Since any user has rights to view the top-level Repository folder, this view (and its table) should have only one row for the Repository folder and nothing else, unless folders have been previously created because of other activities. This is shown in Figure 7-33.

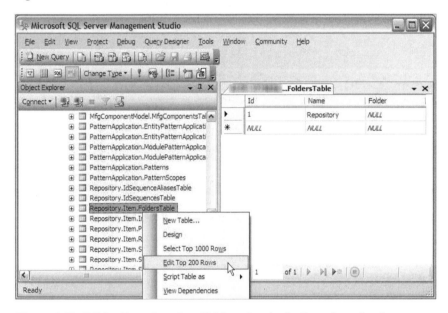

Figure 7-33. *Editing Repository.ItemFolders view in the Repository database*

Click in the Id column of the second row and enter **100** for the Folder Id, and **QC** for the Name. Leave the Folder value as NULL, since you want the QC folder to be a top-level folder, with no parent folder (see Figure 7-34). The exclamation points in the red circles indicate that the cells have changed, but the data is not committed. As soon as you click on the next row, the data in this row will be committed.

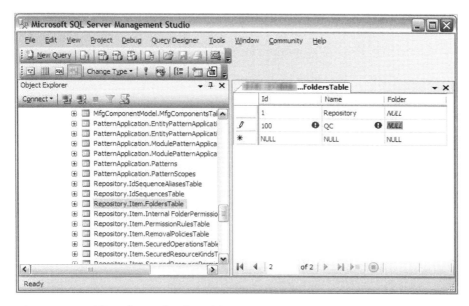

Figure 7-34. Adding the top-level QC folder to Repository.ItemFolders view

Continue to add new folder rows according to the plan laid out at the start of this section. When you're finished, the Repository.Item.Folders data should look like the right pane shown in Figure 7-35.

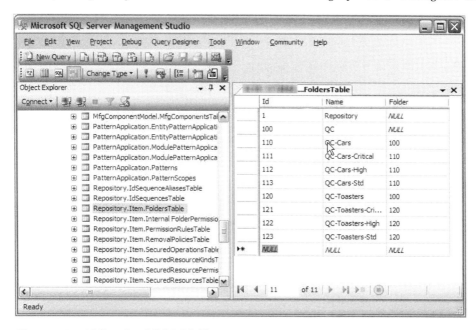

Figure 7-35. Adding the child QC folders to Repository.Item.Folders

Building the Sample Data

Now you're ready to build some sample manufacturing component data to test your security sample design. You can use Quadrant to do this, so open Quadrant. If any sessions or workpads were left open in the interface when you exited the last time Quadrant was being used, close these so that you have a fresh canvas with nothing on it. Also, use the File → Delete Session menu option to delete any existing sessions (named other than Quadrant) left over from the last time you closed Quadrant. Quadrant is the name of the default session, which can't be deleted.

On the top menu, select File → New → Session (or use the Ctrl-Shift-N shortcut) to open a new database session (see Figure 7-36). The default in the Server prompt of the resulting New Database Session dialog should be a period (.), which is the equivalent of the (local) instance of SQL Server. Accept the default for the server instance, or change it to whatever server instance you have been using for this exercise. (Remember: You need to be working with SQL Server 2008 or newer in order to have the features that work with M and SQL Server Modeling.) In the Database prompt, select Repository from the drop-down menu, or simply enter **Repository**. For the session name, enter **Loading MfgComponent Data**. Click the Create button to open the session.

Figure 7-36. *Creating a new Quadrant session on Repository to load MfgComponentsTable*

This should bring up a database Explorer pane on the canvas, showing three items: Database, QC, and Repository. Note the icons associated with each item: The QC and Repository items each show a folder symbol, while the Database item shows (of course!) a database symbol (see Figure 7-37).

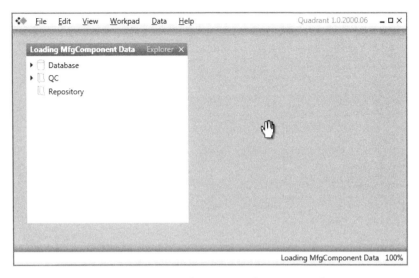

Figure 7-37. Initial Quadrant Explorer pane after opening the new Repository database session

Just to assure yourself everything is good as far as the folder setup us concerned, expand the QC item by clicking the triangle to its left, and then expand the two items at the next level: QC-Cars and QC-Toasters. You should see something very close to what's shown in Figure 7-38.

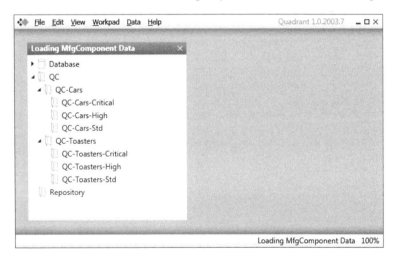

Figure 7-38. MfgComponentModel database Explorer with QC folders expanded

The folder structure looks good—at least if it looks like Figure 7-38—so let's expand the Database item by clicking in the triangle symbol (see Figure 7-39). Click and drag the square symbol for MfgComponentsTable onto the Quadrant canvas (as shown by the arrow in the figure). This will open an Explorer pane for MfgComponentsTable, which will be empty, since you haven't created the sample data.

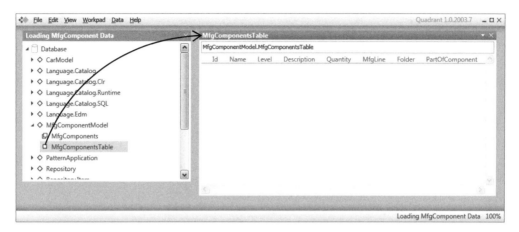

Figure 7-39. Dragging the MfgComponentsTable onto the Quadrant canvas to open a new Explorer pane

Click on an empty part of the grayed background canvas (you should see a hand cursor  appear), and drag the canvas with the two explorer panes to the left until only the **MfgComponentsTable** Explorer pane is visible in the main window (as shown in Figure 7-40).

Figure 7-40. After dragging the canvas to the left to isolate the MfgComponentsTable Explorer pane

To load the sample data, use the same procedure you used in Chapter 4 for creating the sample records for the car example. Click in the Explorer pane, then use the Ctrl-I shortcut to bring up a form for adding a new record (see Figure 7-41). (This is equivalent to using the Data → Insert Item menu option.)

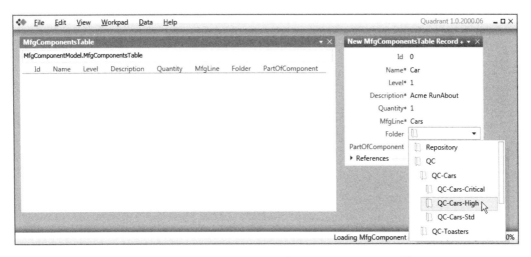

Figure 7-41. Adding the top-level instance of Car to the MfgComponentsTable

Note that in the prompt for the Folder value, you have a drop-down list that allows you to choose the appropriate QC folder. Even the top-level instance (in this case, named Car) must pass QC certification, so let's assign it a QC level of High. Leave the PartOfComponent prompt as Null, since the Car value is a top-level item and has no parent component. Once you've entered all the values for the new record, press Ctrl-S to save it. It should immediately appear in the table.

Table 7-1 shows the sample data to enter into the `MfgComponentsTable` in Quadrant. There are four Car component rows and three Toaster component rows. The CarQC manager should only see the four Car rows, and the ToasterQC manager should see only the three Toaster rows when they query the table.

Table 7-1. Sample Data for the MfgComponentsTable

Name	Level	Description	Qty	MfgLine	Folder	PartOfComponent
Car	1	Acme Runabout	1	Cars	QC-Cars-High	\<null\>
Drive Train	2	Makes the car go	1	Cars	QC-Cars-High	Car
Rear Wheel Assembly	3	Includes brake Assembly	2	Cars	QC-Cars-Critical	Drive Train
Brake Assembly	4	Disk Brakes	4	Cars	QC-Cars-Critical	Rear Wheel Assembly
Toaster	1	Acme Bunmaster	1	Toasters	QC-Toaster-High	\<null\>
Heater Assembly	2	1 per slot	4	Toasters	QC-Toaster-Critical	Toaster
Heater Element	3	2 per heater Assembly	8	Toasters	QC-Toaster-Critical	Heater Assembly

After entering this data for the seven sample records, the `MfgComponentsTable` Explorer in Quadrant should look similar to that shown in Figure 7-42.

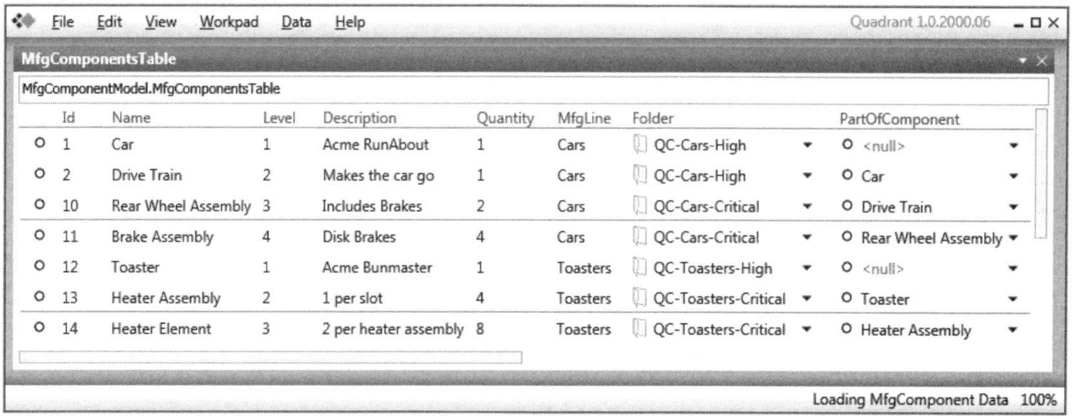

Figure 7-42. Sample ComponentsTable data loaded for Car and Toaster

Now that you've set up the sample data, take a peek in your QC folders and see if those make sense. To do this, click and drag the Quadrant canvas back to where the MfgComponentModel Explorer pane is visible. Drag the top-level QC folder onto an empty part of the canvas (see Figure 7-43). Expand the FoldersTable in this pane, and drill down (expand) on the Folders items, then the `MfgComponents` items, until the individual Car component names are visible. Check which item is in which QC folder to make sure everything makes sense, according to the model and folder hierarchy. Since you assigned the wheel assemblies and the brakes a QC level of Critical, you would expect these items to be included in the QC-Cars-Critical folder. The two remaining car components, the car itself and the drive train, have QC levels of High, so these two components should be in the QC-Cars-High folder. Looking at Figure 7-43, this is indeed what you see, so things appear to be going according to plan. Looking at the QC-Toasters set of folders also confirms you're on track.

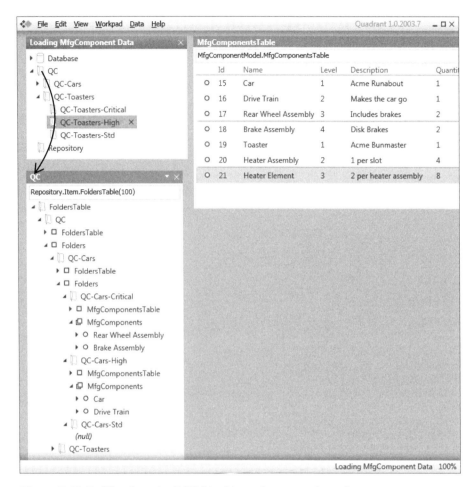

Figure 7-43. Drilling into the QC folder hierarchy to see where the components are

Setting Up the QC Manager Test Users

The fastest way of setting up your test users is to utilize the SQL Server Modeling command prompt. Go to the Windows Start button → All Programs, and select the Microsoft SQL Server Modeling group. One of the options in this group should be the Microsoft SQL Server Modeling Command Prompt. If you want, you can right-click on this item to create a shortcut, and then drag the shortcut to your desktop for quicker access. Click on the Command Prompt item, or execute the new shortcut from your desktop.

Use the **net** command to create each of the three users by entering the command

```
net user <user name> <password> /add
```

for each user: CarQC, ToasterQC, and TopQC. Since these are short-lived test users, use a password that is easy to remember for the purpose of this exercise. Setting the password to be the same as the user name should work, as long as you remember to go back after you're finished and delete these three user accounts in Windows. You should see the message "The command completed successfully" each time you execute the command to create one of the user accounts. Figure 7-44 shows a screen shot of the Command Prompt window after this operation is completed.

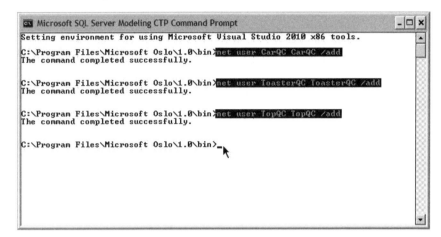

Figure 7-44. Creating the QC manager users in the SQL Server Modeling Command Prompt window

Since these are created as Windows user accounts, you will see these users on your logon window the next time you log on to Windows. You can remove these users by going to User Accounts in the Windows Control Panel and deleting them.

You should also add these as SQL Server users, since you want to test their security access in the SQL Server Modeling environment. To do this, bring up SQL Server Management Studio, and click on the New Query button in the upper-left corner (under the File menu option). You can close the Object Explorer pane (if it's open) to give you more real estate to work with.

Enter the SQL code shown in Figure 7-45. For **<your domain here>**, substitute the host domain name of your computer. Normally this will be the Windows domain name of your computer, which might be something like ACME-638AC9C5AC. In SQL Server Management Studio, the domain name will appear at the bottom of a query window followed by a forward slash and your Windows user account name. (It's in the same location I've obscured for security reasons at the center bottom of Figure 7-45.)

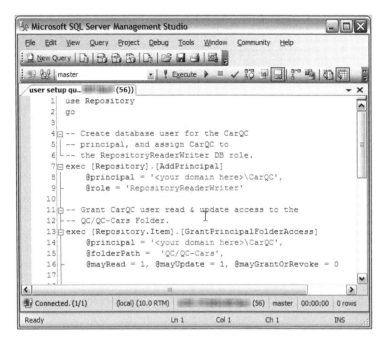

Figure 7-45. SQL code to set up the CarQC user and grant access

You can select code in an SSMS query pane and then execute it with the F5 key. This is equivalent to pressing the Execute button at the top-center of the window, next to the exclamation point (!). Highlight lines 1–2 at the top and press F5. This sets any following actions to run against the Repository database. Then highlight lines 7–9 and press F5. This runs the **[Repository].[AddPrincipal]** stored procedure with the parameters shown on lines 8 and 9. Be sure to put in the proper domain name before executing the action, however. Finally, highlight lines 13–16 and press F5 to execute. This will run the **[Repository.Item].[GrantPrincipalFolderAccess]** stored procedure to give read and update privileges for data in the QC/QC-Cars folder path to the **<domain>\CarQC** user.

Repeat this procedure for the QC-Toasters and QC-Top users, making the necessary changes in lines 8, 14, and 15 of the T-SQL code shown in Figure 7-45. After you've done this for each of the three users, the folder access paths should be the same as those shown in Table 7-2.

Table 7-2. Test User Folder Access Paths

User Name	Folder Path
TopQC	QC
CarQC	QC/QC-Cars
ToasterQC	QC/QC-Toasters

Configuring Test-User Permissions in SQL Server Management Studio

So far, you've created the test users and granted read permissions to their principal folder paths. In order for the users to see the QC data associated with their respective roles, they also need to have read/write access to two views:

- The MfgComponentModel.**MfgComponents** updatable view. (Remember you defined this view via the M code shown in Figure 7-16 in the previous "HasFolderAndAutoId" section.)

- The Repository.Item.ReadableFolders view.

Here's the procedure for establishing the appropriate permissions:

1. In SSMS, open the Object Explorer pane, and select and expand the Repository database.

2. Under Repository, select and expand the Views section.

3. Under Views, select and expand the **MfgComponentModel.MfgComponents** view (see Figure 7-46).

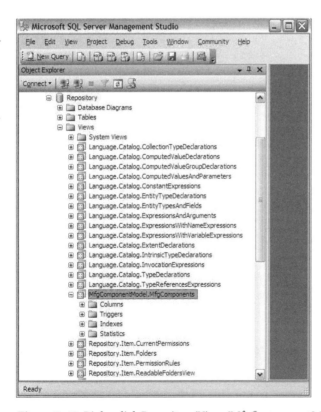

Figure 7-46. Right-click Repository/Views/MfgComponentModel.MfgComponents

4. Right-click this item and select Properties. This should bring up the View Properties dialogue box for the MfgComponents updatable view (see Figure 7-47).

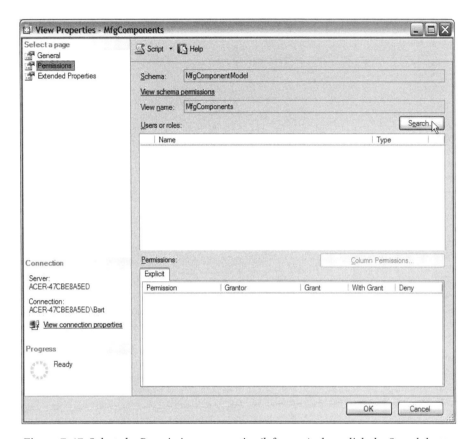

Figure 7-47. Select the Permissions properties (left pane), then click the Search button.

5. Select the Permissions item in the left pane, click the Search button in the right pane, then enter **QC** as the partial name you want to search on (as shown in Figure 7-48). This will bring up the list of your three QC test users.

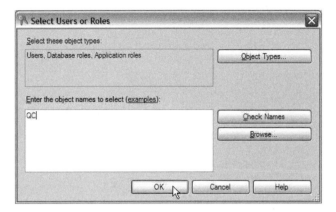

Figure 7-48. Preparing to search on QC user names

6. Select each of the three user names, as shown in Figure 7-49, so that the green check mark appears to the left of the user name, then click the OK button.

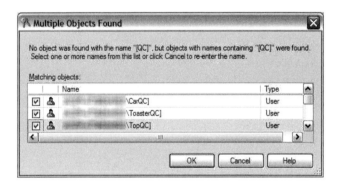

Figure 7-49. Selecting the test-users to modify permissions

7. For each of the three test users, check the Grant selection box for the **Select** permission, then click the OK button (shown in Figure 7-50).

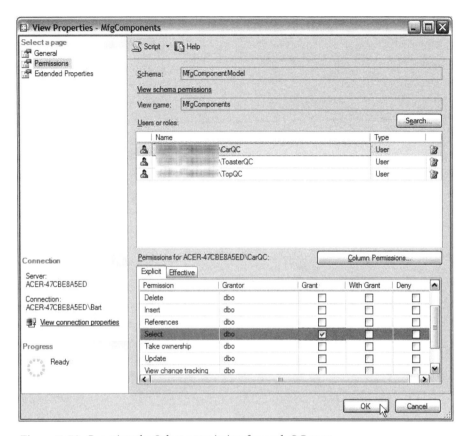

Figure 7-50. Granting the Select permission for each QC user

Testing

Now you should be in a position to test what data is exposed to each user. You can do this in the SQL Server Modeling Command Prompt window by impersonating a user with the **runas** command. Bring up the SQL Server Command Prompt window, and execute the following code:

```
runas /user:CarQC "sqlcmd.exe /y25"
```

The /y25 switch on the sqlcmd.exe command is required, and sets the display width for the SQLCMD prompt window. The system will prompt for the CarQC user's password, which should be the same as the user name (see Figure 7-51). After that is accepted, a separate SQLCMD window will appear, where you can run SQL queries as the CarQC user against the MfgComponents view.

Figure 7-51. *Using the runas command to impersonate the CarQC user opening a SQLCMD window*

In the SQLCMD window that comes up, you're now running as the CarQC user. Enter the following SQL code (see Figure 7-52):

```
use Repository
go
```

The system should present the following message: `Changed database context to 'Repository'`. Next, enter the following SQL commands:

```
select Name, Level, Folder from [MfgComponentModel].[MfgComponents]
go
```

Now you might expect to see a listing of only the Car line components, since it is the CarQC user who entered the query. But instead, you get this: `The SELECT permission was denied on the object 'ReadableFoldersView', database ' Repository', schema 'Repository.Item'.` (shown in Figure 7-52).

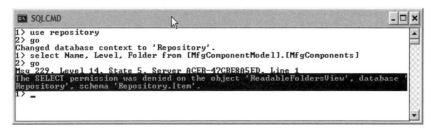

Figure 7-52. *Permission denied to ReadableFoldersView*

I forgot (intentionally) to set up user access to **ReadableFoldersView**. I wanted you to see the type of error message that occurs in this situation. SQL Server gives detailed error messages when a permissions error occurs, so instead of seeing something like "Access denied – error code 229," you see exactly what permission is being denied, and what object, database, and schema are involved. Detailed error messages can be helpful in diagnosing and fixing these kinds of problems, so it's always good to take a close look. (If you're an experienced programmer, this hardly needs to be said.)

In this case, the user needs **SELECT** access to **ReadableFoldersView** because the code that defines the **MfgComponents** updatable view used the system-provided **ReadableFoldersView** (refer to Figure 7-3, line 20) to determine which rows of the view can be exposed to the user.

Let's return to SSMS to fix this problem. In the Views section of the Repository database, right-click on Repository/Views/Repository.Item.ReadableFoldersView and select the Properties option (see Figure 7-53).

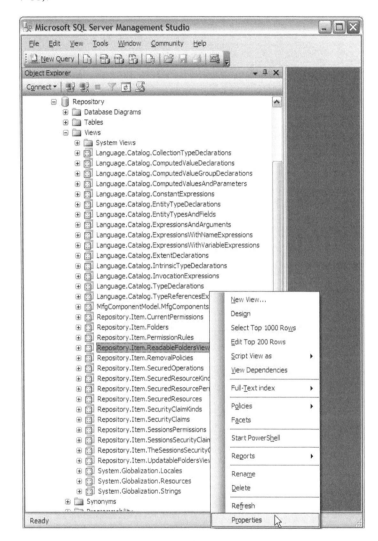

Figure 7-53. *Setting up to grant the QC users SELECT access to ReadableFoldersView*

Use the same procedure you used previously (refer to Figure 7-50) to grant **SELECT** access to **ReadableFoldersView** for the three QC users. Return to the SQLCMD window and hit the Up arrow twice to bring back the SQL **SELECT** statement, and press Enter, then enter the **go** command. This time you should see the data that's available to the CarQC user (shown in Figure 7-54).

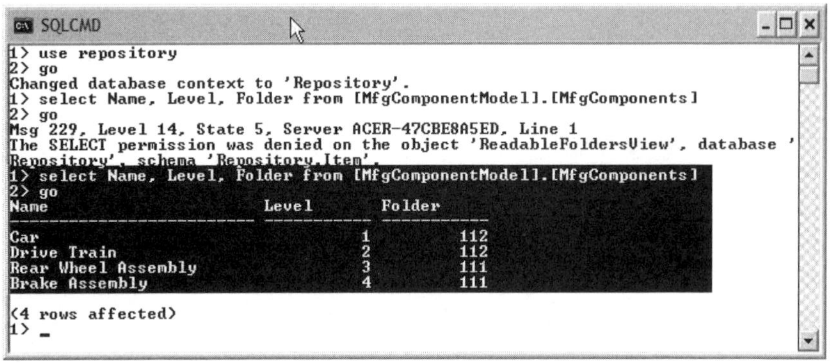

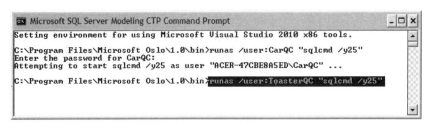

Figure 7-54. *Data returned by the SELECT query entered by the CarQC user*

The data returned is as you would expect, so let's test to see if the permissions for the other two users, ToasterQC and TopQC, are working. Close the SQLCMD window (since that window is running as CarQC) and return to the SQL Command Prompt window. Press the Up arrow twice to return to the previously entered **runas** command and change **CarQC** to **ToasterQC**, then press Enter to execute the command (see Figure 7-55).

Figure 7-55. *Setting up to run a SQLCMD window as theToasterQC user*

When prompted for the password, enter **ToasterQC** (or whatever password you used for setting up the ToasterQC login). In the new SQLCMD window, enter the usual preliminary lines to switch to the Repository database, then the same query you used as the CarQC user (see Figure 7-56). This time, running as the ToasterQC user, you should see only the MfgComponent entities for the Toaster manufacturing line.

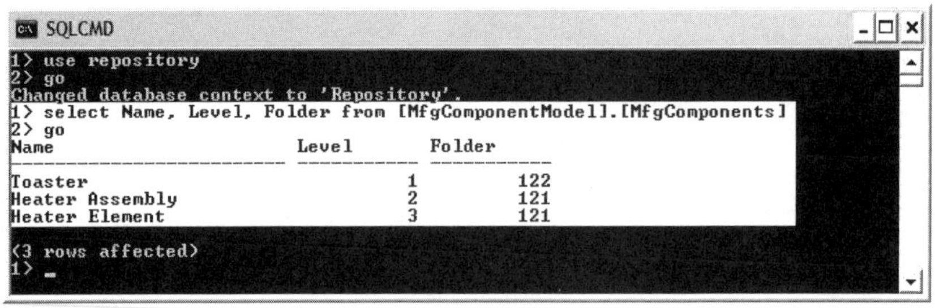

Figure 7-56. *Data returned for theToasterQC user*

Finally, go through the same procedure for the TopQC user. Running as the TopQC user, you should see the data for both the Car and the Toaster manufacturing lines (shown in Figure 7-57).

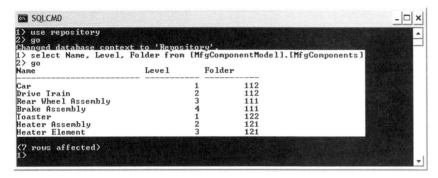

Figure 7-57. Data returned when running as theTopQC user

Summary

In this chapter, I've presented an exercise to illustrate how SQL Server Modeling Services provided by the Repository and the BDL can be applied to provide fine-grained (row-level) security features in the context of the SQL Server Modeling framework. One intent of this particular example was to show how security services, using the folder pattern, could be used to constrain the visibility of certain data sets to certain users. I also wanted to familiarize you with a range of tools (SSMS, several facets of Visual Studio, Quadrant, the command prompt), services, and patterns that are available for building an application.

I applied several patterns, provided by the framework, to set up security features needed for a hypothetical QC application. I used the folder pattern (introduced in Chapter 6) to partition the data among a hierarchical set of folders according to manufacturing line and QC attributes, and then restricted the exposure of this data to three test QC manager users in accordance with their respective roles.

Besides the folder pattern, several other patterns were used in the course of implementing this example:

- **AddViewsInsteadOfTriggers**: This pattern applies system-provided **INSTEAD OF** triggers to intercept certain actions in a way that enforces constraints on what a particular user can see or do.

- **AddFolderForeignKey**: This pattern facilitates the use of folders in types and extents, and defines the foreign key of the folder attribute used in the **MfgComponent** type.

- **HasFolderAndAutoId**: The **MfgComponentsTable** extent was redefined as a mix-in of the system-defined **HasFolderAndAutoId** type and the **MfgComponent** domain type. I also used **HasFolderAndAutoId** to help set up the use of folders in defining the **MfgComponent** type and the **MfgComponents** updatable view.

The **PatternApplication** code was installed and used to set up the hooks enabling the use of these patterns.

APPENDIX A

■ ■ ■

Intellipad Primer

Intellipad is a text editor created to support, in particular, developers writing models and languages using Microsoft Oslo's M, and it's great for other text as well. It includes language services for M, including syntax highlighting, error checking, semantic completions, and project compilation.

Intellipad is also designed to be customized by users and extended by developers. Extensibility is achieved using named components. Features can easily be added or modified, giving an editing experience that ranges from the simplicity of notepad to the power of rich language support. Intellipad uses components defined in declarative markup to customize the user experience.

Intellipad contains a built-in Python interpreter. Users can customize, extend, and automate the editor by writing Python scripts.

Intellipad Basics

This section covers the basic components and design features of Intellipad: buffers, views, modes, and the mini-buffer. Understanding these aspects will make it easier to customize Intellipad or invoke features that make it easier to perform certain tasks.

Buffers

Fundamentally, Intellipad is an editor for Unicode text. A buffer represents the data model for the text being edited. Multiple buffers can be open in Intellipad simultaneously. Buffers can come from different sources (such as a file system, debugger, the Web, and so on). The source of the buffer determines some of the editing capabilities available. For example, some parts of a buffer may be read-only, preventing the user from editing text in that location. Some buffers might be auto-generated, like a buffer containing a list of compilation errors or a buffer reporting the results of a command.

Intellipad buffers can represent Unicode text from any source. Each buffer in Intellipad is identified by its URI (Universal Resource Identified). When Intellipad is opening a buffer, it uses the URI scheme (`file://`, `transient://`, etc.) to locate the appropriate buffer source to open the buffer and initialize its data. To load Unicode text from a new URI scheme (e.g., `http://` or `ftp://`), a developer would write a buffer source component that provides support for that URI scheme.

Intellipad also provides buffer transforms that take as input a source buffer and render the output in a different way. For example, if you opened this document in Intellipad using the Help menu, you will see that the URI is `IntellipadPrimer.ipadhelp | Rich Text`. This indicates that a Rich Text transform was applied to the source buffer, `IntellipadPrimer.ipadhelp`. This transform processes the text markup and displays the text using different font faces, sizes, and weights. Note that the original buffer, `IntellipadPrimer.ipadhelp`, is also open and displays the text in its raw form. Closing the source of a transform closes the transform buffer as well.

Views

Intellipad supports splitting the editor window into multiple views to display multiple buffers at the same time. Each view is capable of displaying any of the currently available buffers through a menu at the top left of the view. Different views can also show the same buffer in different modes. The view that is active determines which set of menu options appear at the top of Intellipad; different modes often have different menu options.

You can create additional views by activating the view to be split, then choosing Split Vertically or Split Horizontally from the View menu. You can also use CTRL+W,\ to create the vertical split and CTRL+W,- to create the horizontal split. Some Intellipad commands also create new views.

Pull-down menus in the upper-left and upper-right corners of each view allow you to set the active buffer and mode, respectively. If you have multiple views, changing the mode or the buffer of one view does not affect the other views.

Modes

Intellipad enables language-specific support for buffers through modes. *Modes* isolate extension components, allowing different behaviors when editing buffers that have different content types.

When a buffer is opened, Intellipad attempts to associate the file with a mode to provide features like syntax highlighting, additional menu items, semantic completion, and other features. The way this default mode is determined depends on the buffer and its source. For example, when loading file buffers, the file extension is used. An http buffer source might use the mime type to determine the mode.

A pull-down menu in the upper-right corner of each buffer view indicates the current mode and can be used to change the mode.

The same buffer can be opened in different views and have different modes applied in each view. However, not all modes will be meaningful in every context.

The Mini-Buffer

Intellipad provides a way to execute quick, one-line functions through a special buffer called the *mini-buffer*. It can be accessed by pressing CTRL+/ or choosing Toggle Mini-Buffer on the View menu. The mini-buffer opens in a new split, in MiniBuffer Interactive mode. You can type Intellipad commands in this editor, which stays open until you dismiss it. Use function key F1 or the Commands item on the Help menu to view a list of the available mini-buffer commands.

Text typed into the mini-buffer is executed in the context of the Python script engine after first loading a setup script that makes various Intellipad-related variables and modules available. The mini-buffer setup script is located at

```
Components\Microsoft.Intellipad.Scripting\PrivateScripts\MiniBufferCommandSetup.py.
```

The script is executed automatically when Intellipad initializes the mini-buffer.

A user could type the following into the mini-buffer:

```
for x in range(1, 10): Test('')
```

This would run all unit tests 10 times (see Settings\CommandTests.py).

Some commands, such as Zoom and Find, operate on the view that was active prior to clicking in the mini-buffer view. The active view is indicated by a blue highlight outline.

The mini-buffer can also be used to batch commands and issue them. These commands are currently stored only for the Intellipad session; they will not be reloaded the next time Intellipad starts. Take the following for example:

```
>>> def MyNewCommand():
...   Open('c:/foo.txt')
...   Zoom(2.0)
...   Find('<summary>')
...
>>> MyNewCommand()
>>>
```

Working with M in Intellipad

Intellipad has two major features that can help you develop M code: SQL Preview and the domain-specific language (DSL) authoring configuration.

SQL Preview

Intellipad's SQL Preview allows you to easily see the SQL equivalent of M code as you create the code. To access the SQL Preview feature, change the active view to M mode, click the M Mode menu entry, and select T-SQL Preview. SQL Preview splits your active view into two views. The left view contains your M code, while the right view displays the equivalent SQL.

Basic DSL Authoring Configuration

Intellipad's basic DSL authoring configuration allows you to create test input and see the output for a domain-specific language grammar that you are developing, as you develop it. To create the basic DSL authoring configuration, change your active view to DSL Grammar mode, click the DSL menu entry, and select Split New Input and Output Views. Intellipad splits your active view vertically into three views. The left view displays a new buffer whose mode is set to the name of your original DSL grammar buffer. The middle view displays your DSL grammar. The right view displays the same buffer as the left view, but its mode is set to M Graph mode. The left view acts as input data; you can edit text in the left view, and its contents will be parsed in real time according to the grammar rules specified by your DSL grammar. The results of the parsing are displayed in the right view. The displayed output is a textual representation of an in-memory .NET Framework object model.

Customizing Intellipad

This section covers how Intellipad can be customized by changing or adding menus, colors, modes, and commands.

Changing the Menus

Intellipad is designed so that you can add or remove menu options from the menu bar, as well as add or remove items within each option. The file that controls Intellipad's menu settings is MenuBar.xcml, installed in Microsoft Oslo\1.0\bin\Settings\VisualStudio. The top-level MenuItem Headers set the options on the menu bar, while the children MenuItem Headers set the commands within each menu option. The list of available commands can be found by pressing F1.

For example, to add the Zoom Down and Zoom Up commands to the menu under their own menu option, you would add the following XML to MenuBar.xcml.

```
<MenuItem Header= '_Zoom Options'>
  <MenuItem Header= 'Zoom _In' Command='{mis:NamedCommand Name =
      Microsoft.Intellipad.ZoomUp}' />
  <MenuItem Header= 'Zoom _Out' Command='{mis:NamedCommand Name =
      Microsoft.Intellipad.ZoomDown}' />
</MenuItem>
```

Changing the Colors

The color scheme that Intellipad uses to display text can be customized as well. The file that controls how Intellipad displays text is ClassificationFormats.xcml file, installed in Microsoft Oslo\1.0\bin\Settings. Each ClassificationFormat controls the appearance of a different text type. The text type's color is set by the Foreground attribute and is written in hexadecimal ARGB (Alpha-Red-Green-Blue) notation. Not all color entries have an Alpha component; they are not required. To change the color, change the RGB values that the text type uses.

For example, if you wanted to make all keywords appear in purple, you would change the Keyword entry so it looks like this:

```
<act:Export Name='{}Microsoft.Intellipad.ClassificationFormat'>
  <ls:ClassificationFormat Name='Keyword'
    FontFamily='Consolas'
    FontWeight='Bold'
    Foreground='#FF800080' />
</act:Export>
```

Adding New Modes

You can create language modes for your custom DSL by compiling the grammars and placing the MX files in the Intellipad Settings directory (installed in Microsoft Oslo\1.0\bin). To compile your grammar, run the following from a command window:

```
<path to>\Microsoft Oslo\1.0\bin\m.exe <path to .mg file> [/o:<path to .mx output file>]
```

When you restart Intellipad, your new modes will appear in the mode selection drop-down list. To automatically associate your mode with a file extension, add it to FileExtensions.xcml in the Settings directory.

Customizing Commands

Almost all commands available in Intellipad have been written in Python using the object model exposed by the application. The Python files are installed in the Settings directory.

Commands.py contains most of the commands for Intellipad. Configuration-specific commands can be placed in configuration-specific subdirectories (e.g., VisualStudio).

A command definition consists of the following:

- An Executed function definition, which acts as the command handler and provides the logic for the command.

- An optional CanExecute function definition, which determines when the command is enabled (use if you are making your command available using menu items).

To reload the Settings and have changes take effect, you must restart Intellipad.

Intellipad Components

The Intellipad customization and extensibility model is based on named components. Some components are just data, providing configuration information like what color and font to use when displaying keywords, mapping file extensions to modes, and the contents of the menu bar. Most components of that nature are expressed declaratively. Other components provide more complex functionality like commands, buffer modes, or editor behaviors. These components are either exposed in script or compiled .NET assemblies.

Intellipad uses a catalog for locating and activating components. A *catalog* is a list of components and associated metadata. Components can be located in compiled assemblies, Python scripts, and declarative markup files.

At startup, a configuration file with a list of catalog sources is loaded and used to build the catalog. By default, Intellipad looks for a file called ipad.m in the same directory as ipad.exe. See the "Command-Line Options" section later in this Appendix for information on how to specify an alternative startup configuration file. After it is first built, the catalog is cached to speed startup time and is updated when sources change.

Commands are one of the most widely used components in Intellipad. Intellipad uses an input system based on Windows Presentation Foundation (WPF) Commanding. Commands are delegates exported as components that can then be executed when a menu item is selected or a key sequence is pressed. Commands can also be run from script. Metadata attached to command components provides information to the command system like the command's name, its default keystroke, and the editor component the command is targeting (such as buffer, view, window, and so forth).

Compiled Components

Some Intellipad components are complex and benefit from being implemented in a .NET programming language like C# or VB.NET. Classes, properties, and methods in an assembly are marked with custom attributes to indicate what components they are exporting and also what components they depend on (imports).

Declarative Components

XCML files provide a way of defining components declaratively using XAML markup. Some example uses of XCML components are

- Define additional keyboard bindings and the command that they execute.

- Define the Intellipad menu bar and the command that each menu item invokes.

- Define syntax coloring and fonts for various text classifications.

- Define the set of text classifications and inheritance relationships.

- Map file extensions to Intellipad modes.

Script Components

The following code is an example of a command written in Python for copying the path of the current file to the clipboard:

```
@Metadata.CommandExecuted('Microsoft.Intellipad.BufferView',
        'Microsoft.Intellipad.CopyCurrentPathToClipboard', 'Ctrl+Shift+C')
def CopyCurrentPathToClipboard(target, sender, args):
  path = sender.Buffer.Uri
  data = path
  if path.IsFile:
      data = path.LocalPath
  System.Windows.Clipboard.SetData(System.Windows.DataFormats.Text, data)
```

The preceding function has a Python decorator applied to it that exports it as a command component. The parameters to the decorator define it to be a command called `'Microsoft.Intellipad.CopyCurrentPathToClipboard'`, targeting the currently active view, with `'Ctrl+Shift+C'` as its shortcut key binding.

List of Available Modes

Each pane in Intellipad runs in a given mode. The default mode is called the standard mode, and works more or less as a standard text editor. The other modes are specializations or enhancements built on top of the standard mode to support a particular purpose or task, and are listed here:

- *DSL Grammar mode:* Provides support for authoring MGrammar. This includes colorization, error marks for syntactically incorrect MGrammar, and the ability to see how your grammar parses sample input.

- *List mode:* Used internally by certain Intellipad features to create a buffer showing a list of items that can be clicked to navigate to the destination buffer.

- *M mode:* Provides support for developing M code. This includes colorization, error marks for syntactically incorrect M, and the SQL Preview feature.

- *Output mode:* Used in conjunction with the DSL Grammar mode. It shows the textual representation of a .NET Framework object model that is created when a DSL grammar is used to parse sample input.

- *Project mode:* Provides support for project development and configuration. This includes displaying errors in the error list if the content is not a syntactically valid MSBuild file. A project can be displayed in its text (XML) form or in an overview list. You can use the Project → Toggle Project View menu item to switch back and forth (or choose the desired buffer in the buffer list drop-down).

- *Python mode:* Provides support for Python development. This includes colorization and error marks for syntactically incorrect Python. Code coverage is also available if Intellipad is launched with the /coverage option.

- *Rich Text mode:* Used to display Intellipad help and the Intellipad primer. It is a read-only mode that allows markup to drive classifications rather than language services.

- *SQL mode:* Used in conjunction with M mode. It allows you to see the SQL generated by M code.

- *Standard mode:* Enables basic text editing features. All other modes add to and extend Standard mode capabilities.

Command-Line Options

The Intellipad executable (`ipad.exe`) can be invoked from the command prompt with a number of optional command switches or flags. These are enumerated in the following list. Each switch is designated with a forward slash (/) followed immediately by the name of the switch. The vertical bar (|) or pipe symbol should be treated as an OR operator, so [/help|h|?] means that /help, /h, and /? will all work for displaying the command line help text. In those cases where the flag is followed by a postfix + or –, + turns the feature on, and – turns the feature off. Defaults are indicated for these switches in the list.

Usage:
```
ipad.exe [@argfile] [/help|h|?] [/script:value] [file] [/configuration|config|c:value]
         [/buildcache[+|-]] [/coverage:[+|-]] [/crashrecovery[+|-]]
```

- `@argfile`: Instructs Intellipad to read command line arguments from the given file. When used, it must be the first argument and subsequent arguments are ignored.

- `/help[+|-]`: Displays a message box with Intellipad's command line help text. Default: False.

- `/script:<filename>`: Launches the specified script file after startup.

- `file(s)`: Opens the listed file(s) when Intellipad launches. Filenames are not prefixed with a forward slash (/).

- `/configuration:file` (or `/config:` or `/c:`): Specifies the startup configuration, controlling which controls are loaded into Intellipad. Default: ipad.m.

- /buildcache[+|-]: Creates Intellipad cache files and exits. Adding, changing, or removing component files invalidates the cache. Subsequent launches of Intellipad are faster if the cache is still valid. Default: False.

- /coverage[+|-]: Enables the collection of statistics on what functions are called during the execution of scripts in Intellipad. Default: False.

- /crashrecovery[+|-]: Attempts to allow user to save changed buffers when Intellipad crashes. Default: True.

■ ■ ■

Intellipad Mini-Buffer Commands

To use the mini-buffer commands, you must first open up the mini-buffer. Use View → Minibuffer (or Ctrl+/).

- `Call(commandName, arguments=None)`: Executes an Intellipad command by name.

- `ClearMru()`: Clears the list of most recently used files.

- `CloseBuffer(bufferIndex)`: Closes an open buffer.

- `Exit()`: Exits Intellipad.

- `Find(pattern)`: Find a string.

- `FindInBuffers(pattern)`: Find a string in all open buffers.

- `Goto(lineNumber)`: Goes to a line in the currently active buffer.

- `Open(fileName)`: Opens a buffer in the active view.

- `Replace(searchPattern, replacePattern)`: Replaces text in the active buffer.

- `SetEncoding(encoding)`: Sets the encoding.

- `SetMode(modeName)`: Changes the mode of the active view.

- `SetTransform(transformName, parameters=None)`: Sets the transform for the active view.

- `Test(testName, repeat_count=1, fail_fast=False)`: Runs all tests with names that start with the given test name.

- `Zoom(scale)`: Changes the zoom level of the active view.

APPENDIX C

∎∎∎

Intellipad Commands and Gestures

Command	Key Combination	Description
Microsoft.Intellipad.ActivateErrorListBuffer	Ctrl+Shift+E	Shows the error list buffer.
Microsoft.Intellipad.ActivateMiniBuffer	None	Shows the mini-buffer and makes it active.
Microsoft.Intellipad.ActivateOrOpenBuffer	None	If the buffer is visible in a view, this command makes the view active. Otherwise, it opens the buffer in the currently active view.
Microsoft.Intellipad.Backspace	Shift+Backspace | Backspace	
Microsoft.Intellipad.BuildProject	Ctrl+Shift+B	Builds the current project.
Microsoft.Intellipad.CallTestCommand WithArg	None	Test command
Microsoft.Intellipad.CallTestCommand WithoutArg	None	Test command
Microsoft.Intellipad.CloseBuffer	Ctrl+F4	Closes a buffer.
Microsoft.Intellipad.CloseBufferView	Ctrl+Shift+W	Closes a view. The buffer remains open.
Microsoft.Intellipad.CopySelection	Ctrl+C | Ctrl+Insert	
Microsoft.Intellipad.CutSelection	Ctrl+X | Shift+Delete	
Microsoft.Intellipad.DebuggerContinue	Ctrl+F5	
Microsoft.Intellipad.DebuggerStart	F5	

Command	Key Combination	Description
Microsoft.Intellipad.DebuggerStepToken	F10	
Microsoft.Intellipad.DebuggerStop	Shift+F5	
Microsoft.Intellipad.DebuggerToggleInput Breakpoint	F9	
Microsoft.Intellipad.Delete	Delete	
Microsoft.Intellipad.DeleteWordToLeft	Ctrl+Backspace	
Microsoft.Intellipad.DeleteWordToRight	Ctrl+Delete	
Microsoft.Intellipad.DragDrop	None	Handles files dragged into Intellipad.
Microsoft.Intellipad.Escape	Shift+Esc | Esc	
Microsoft.Intellipad.Exit	Alt+F4	Exits Intellipad.
Microsoft.Intellipad.ExpandBufferView Horizontal	Ctrl+.	Expands the width of the active view.
Microsoft.Intellipad.ExpandBufferView Vertical	Ctrl+Shift+.	Expands the height of the active view.
Microsoft.Intellipad.Find	Ctrl+F	Opens the mini-buffer and calls the Find function.
Microsoft.Intellipad.FindInBuffers	Ctrl+Shift+F	Find in all open buffers
Microsoft.Intellipad.FindNext	F3	Finds the next instance of a string.
Microsoft.Intellipad.FindPrevious	Shift+F3	Finds the previous instance of a string.
Microsoft.Intellipad.FindSelectedNext	Ctrl+F3	Finds the next instance of the selected string.
Microsoft.Intellipad.FindSelectedPrevious	Ctrl+Shift+F3	Finds the previous instance of the selected string.

Command	Key Combination	Description
Microsoft.Intellipad.FocusBufferMenu	Ctrl+Alt+B	Sets keyboard focus on the active view's Open Buffers drop-down menu.
Microsoft.Intellipad.FocusBufferViewDown	Alt+Down	Moves the view focus down.
Microsoft.Intellipad.FocusBufferViewLeft	Alt+Left	Moves the view focus to the left.
Microsoft.Intellipad.FocusBufferViewNext	F6	Moves the view focus to the next view in the list of open views (regardless of position on screen).
Microsoft.Intellipad.FocusBufferViewPrevious	Shift+F6	Moves the view focus to the prior view in the list of open views (regardless of position on screen).
Microsoft.Intellipad.FocusBufferViewRight	Alt+Right	Moves the view focus to the right.
Microsoft.Intellipad.FocusBufferViewUp	Alt+Up	Moves the view focus up.
Microsoft.Intellipad.FocusModeMenu	Ctrl+Alt+M	Sets keyboard focus on the active view's Modes drop-down menu.
Microsoft.Intellipad.Goto	Ctrl+G	Opens the mini-buffer and calls the Goto function.
Microsoft.Intellipad.GrammarEditing Environment	Ctrl+Shift+T	Opens a MG file in the basic DSL authoring configuration.
Microsoft.Intellipad.HelpCommands	F1	Displays Intellipad help.
Microsoft.Intellipad.Indent	Tab	
Microsoft.Intellipad.InsertNewline	Shift+Enter	Enter	
Microsoft.Intellipad.MakeLowercase	Ctrl+U	
Microsoft.Intellipad.MakeUppercase	Ctrl+Shift+U	

Command	Key Combination	Description
Microsoft.Intellipad.MoveCurrentLineTo BottomOfView	Alt+Home	
Microsoft.Intellipad.MoveLineDown	Down	
Microsoft.Intellipad.MoveLineUp	Up	
Microsoft.Intellipad.MoveToEndOfDocument	Ctrl+End	
Microsoft.Intellipad.MoveToEndOfLine	End	
Microsoft.Intellipad.MoveToNextCharacter	Right	
Microsoft.Intellipad.MoveToNextWord	Ctrl+Right	
Microsoft.Intellipad.MoveToPreviousCharacter	Left	
Microsoft.Intellipad.MoveToPreviousWord	Ctrl+Left	
Microsoft.Intellipad.MoveToStartOfDocument	Ctrl+Home	
Microsoft.Intellipad.MoveToStartOfLine	Home	
Microsoft.Intellipad.NavigateToUri	None	Opens the Uri given in args, leaving the current buffer visible.
Microsoft.Intellipad.New	Ctrl+N	Opens a new untitled buffer in the active view.
Microsoft.Intellipad.NewGrammarEditing Environment	None	Opens a new MG file in the basic DSL authoring configuration.
Microsoft.Intellipad.NewProject	Ctrl+Shift+N	Create a new CSharp modeling project.
Microsoft.Intellipad.Open	Ctrl+O	Opens a file in the active view.
Microsoft.Intellipad.OpenMru	None	Opens a buffer listed in the most recently used list.
Microsoft.Intellipad.OpenStartFiles	None	Opens buffers specified on the command line.

Command	Key Combination	Description
Microsoft.Intellipad.PageDown	Page Down	
Microsoft.Intellipad.PageUp	Page Up	
Microsoft.Intellipad.Paste	Ctrl+V | Shift+Insert	
Microsoft.Intellipad.Primer	None	Opens the Intellipad primer.
Microsoft.Intellipad.Redo	Ctrl+Y | Alt+Shift+Backspace	
Microsoft.Intellipad.ReformatDocument	Ctrl+E,D	Reformats the document by changing the indentation of each line.
Microsoft.Intellipad.ReloadSettings	Ctrl+Alt+F5	Reload the configuration settings of Intellipad.
Microsoft.Intellipad.Replace	Ctrl+H	Opens the mini-buffer and calls the Replace function.
Microsoft.Intellipad.ReplaceNext	F4	Finds and replaces the next instance of a string with another string.
Microsoft.Intellipad.ReplacePrevious	Shift+F4	Finds and replaces the previous instance of a string with another string.
Microsoft.Intellipad.ResetSelection	Esc	
Microsoft.Intellipad.RunTests	Ctrl+R,A	Runs Intellipad's built-in self tests.
Microsoft.Intellipad.Save	Ctrl+S	Saves the contents of the buffer in the active view to their current file location.
Microsoft.Intellipad.SaveACopy	None	Saves a copy of the buffer in the active view to the specified file location.
Microsoft.Intellipad.SaveAll	Ctrl+Shift+S	Saves the contents of all buffers currently opened by Intellipad.

Command	Key Combination	Description
Microsoft.Intellipad.SaveAs	None	Saves the contents of the buffer in the active view to the specified file location. The original buffer is closed, discarding any changes.
Microsoft.Intellipad.ScrollDownAndMove CaretIfNecessary	Ctrl+Down	
Microsoft.Intellipad.ScrollUpAndMove CaretIfNecessary	Ctrl+Up	
Microsoft.Intellipad.SelectAll	Ctrl+A	
Microsoft.Intellipad.SelectCurrentWord	None	
Microsoft.Intellipad.SelectEnclosing	None	
Microsoft.Intellipad.SelectFirstChild	None	
Microsoft.Intellipad.SelectLineDown	Shift+Down	
Microsoft.Intellipad.SelectLineUp	Shift+Up	
Microsoft.Intellipad.SelectNextSibling	None	
Microsoft.Intellipad.SelectNextSiblingExtend Selection	Alt+Shift+Down	
Microsoft.Intellipad.SelectPageDown	Shift+Page Down	
Microsoft.Intellipad.SelectPageUp	Shift+Page Up	
Microsoft.Intellipad.SelectPreviousSibling	None	
Microsoft.Intellipad.SelectPreviousSiblingExtend Selection	Alt+Shift+Up	
Microsoft.Intellipad.SelectToEndOfDocument	Ctrl+Shift+End	
Microsoft.Intellipad.SelectToEndOfLine	Shift+End	
Microsoft.Intellipad.SelectToNextCharacter	Shift+Right	
Microsoft.Intellipad.SelectToNextWord	Ctrl+Shift+Right	

Command	Key Combination	Description
Microsoft.Intellipad.SelectToPreviousCharacter	Shift+Left	
Microsoft.Intellipad.SelectToPreviousWord	Ctrl+Shift+Left	
Microsoft.Intellipad.SelectToStartOfDocument	Ctrl+Shift+Home	
Microsoft.Intellipad.SelectToStartOfLine	Shift+Home	
Microsoft.Intellipad.SetEncoding	None	Sets the file encoding of the buffer in the view.
Microsoft.Intellipad.ShowCompletions	Ctrl+Space	Shows possible completions of a token.
Microsoft.Intellipad.ShowDefinitionList	F12	Shows a list of definitions.
Microsoft.Intellipad.ShowNotifications	None	Shows the notification buffer.
Microsoft.Intellipad.ShowReferencesList	Shift+F12	Shows a list of all things that reference the highlighted item.
Microsoft.Intellipad.ShowScriptBuffer	None	Opens the interactive Python script buffer in the current view.
Microsoft.Intellipad.ShowSqlBuffer	None	Opens the interactive SQL buffer in the current view.
Microsoft.Intellipad.ShrinkBufferViewHorizontal	Ctrl+,	Shrinks the width of the active view.
Microsoft.Intellipad.ShrinkBufferViewVertical	Ctrl+Shift+,	Shrinks the height of the active view.
Microsoft.Intellipad.Space	Space	
Microsoft.Intellipad.SplitHorizontal	Ctrl+W,-	Splits the active view into two views, one above the other.
Microsoft.Intellipad.SplitVertical	Ctrl+W,\	Splits the active view into two views, side by side.
Microsoft.Intellipad.ToggleBehavior	None	Toggles the specified behavior on or off.

Command	Key Combination	Description
Microsoft.Intellipad.ToggleFileChanges Notification	Ctrl+W,N	Toggles if you want notification that an open file is changed outside of Intellipad.
Microsoft.Intellipad.ToggleFullScreen	Alt+Shift+Enter	Toggles full-screen operation of Intellipad on or off.
Microsoft.Intellipad.ToggleLineNumber	Ctrl+Shift+L	
Microsoft.Intellipad.ToggleMiniBuffer	Ctrl+Shift+D I Ctrl+/	Toggles the mini-buffer view on or off.
Microsoft.Intellipad.ToggleOverwriteMode	Insert	
Microsoft.Intellipad.ToggleWordWrap	Ctrl+W,W	
Microsoft.Intellipad.TransposeCharacter	Ctrl+T	
Microsoft.Intellipad.TransposeLine	Alt+Shift+T	
Microsoft.Intellipad.Undo	Ctrl+Z I Alt+Backspace	
Microsoft.Intellipad.Unindent	Shift+Tab	
Microsoft.Intellipad.YankLine	Ctrl+L	Copies the line(s) where the cursor is.
Microsoft.Intellipad.ZoomCommand	Ctrl+W,Z	Opens the mini-buffer and calls the Zoom function.
Microsoft.Intellipad.ZoomDown	Ctrl+-	
Microsoft.Intellipad.ZoomUp	Ctrl+=	

APPENDIX D

■ ■ ■

The Quadrant Menu Tree

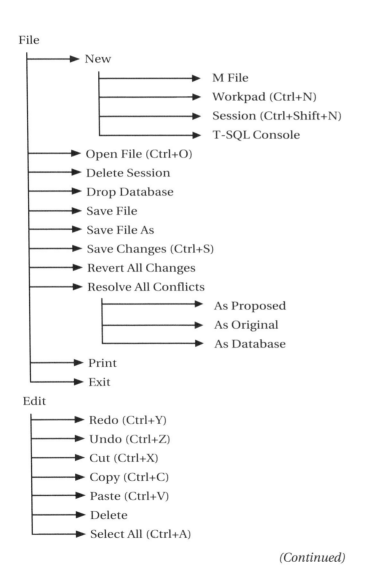

File
- New
  - M File
  - Workpad (Ctrl+N)
  - Session (Ctrl+Shift+N)
  - T-SQL Console
- Open File (Ctrl+O)
- Delete Session
- Drop Database
- Save File
- Save File As
- Save Changes (Ctrl+S)
- Revert All Changes
- Resolve All Conflicts
  - As Proposed
  - As Original
  - As Database
- Print
- Exit

Edit
- Redo (Ctrl+Y)
- Undo (Ctrl+Z)
- Cut (Ctrl+X)
- Copy (Ctrl+C)
- Paste (Ctrl+V)
- Delete
- Select All (Ctrl+A)

(Continued)

View

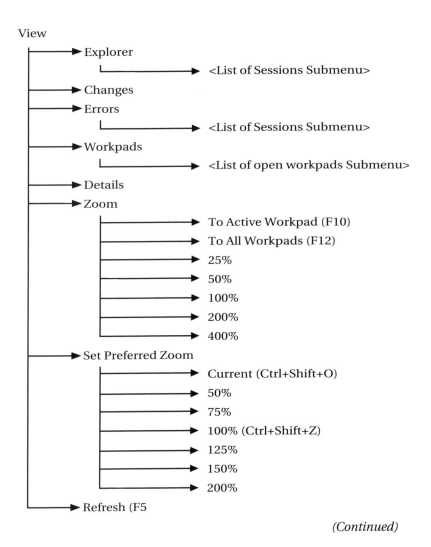

- Explorer
  - \<List of Sessions Submenu\>
- Changes
- Errors
  - \<List of Sessions Submenu\>
- Workpads
  - \<List of open workpads Submenu\>
- Details
- Zoom
  - To Active Workpad (F10)
  - To All Workpads (F12)
  - 25%
  - 50%
  - 100%
  - 200%
  - 400%
- Set Preferred Zoom
  - Current (Ctrl+Shift+O)
  - 50%
  - 75%
  - 100% (Ctrl+Shift+Z)
  - 125%
  - 150%
  - 200%
- Refresh (F5

(Continued)

Workpad

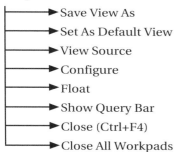

- Save View As
- Set As Default View
- View Source
- Configure
- Float
- Show Query Bar
- Close (Ctrl+F4)
- Close All Workpads

Data

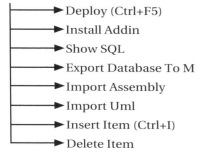

- Deploy (Ctrl+F5)
- Install Addin
- Show SQL
- Export Database To M
- Import Assembly
- Import Uml
- Insert Item (Ctrl+I)
- Delete Item

Help

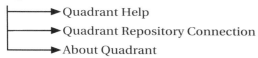

- Quadrant Help
- Quadrant Repository Connection
- About Quadrant

APPENDIX E

■ ■ ■

Generated T-SQL
for the Car Model Example

The following listing is the generated T-SQL code for the CarTypeExample M code shown in Figure 5-10 in Chapter 5.

```
set xact_abort on;
go

begin transaction;
go

set ansi_nulls on;
go

if not exists
(
    select *
    from [sys].[schemas]
    where [name] = N'CarTypeExample'
)
    execute [sp_executesql] N'create schema [CarTypeExample]';
go

if not exists
(
    select *
    from [sys].[schemas]
    where [name] = N'EngineModule'
)
    execute [sp_executesql] N'create schema [EngineModule]';
go

if not exists
(
    select *
    from [sys].[schemas]
    where [name] = N'$MRuntime.CarTypeExample'
)
```

```
        execute [sp_executesql] N'create schema [$MRuntime.CarTypeExample]';
    go

    if not exists
    (
        select *
        from [sys].[schemas]
        where [name] = N'$MRuntime.EngineModule'
    )
        execute [sp_executesql] N'create schema [$MRuntime.EngineModule]';
    go

    create function [CarTypeExample].[Check_Cars_Func]
    (
        @Year as int
    )
    returns bit
    as
        begin
            return case
                when @Year >= 1769
                then 1
                else 0
            end
        end;
    go

    create function [CarTypeExample].[Check_Cars_Func1]
    (
        @Year as int
    )
    returns bit
    as
        begin
            return case
                when @Year <= 2020
                then 1
                else 0
            end
        end;
    go

    create function [EngineModule].[HorsepowerPerCylinder]
    (
        @Eng as xml
    )
    returns decimal(19,6)
    as
        begin
            return convert(decimal(19,6),
            (
                select (@Eng).value(N'(/entity/Horsepower)[1]', N'int') as [Item]
```

```
        )) / convert(decimal(19,6),
        (
            select (@Eng).value(N'(/entity/Cylinders)[1]', N'tinyint') as [Item]
        ))
    end;
go

create function [EngineModule].[Check_Engines_Func]
(
    @Cylinders as tinyint
)
returns bit
as
    begin
        return case
            when @Cylinders >= 1
            then 1
            else 0
        end
    end;
go

create function [EngineModule].[Check_Engines_Func1]
(
    @Cylinders as tinyint
)
returns bit
as
    begin
        return case
            when @Cylinders <= 12
            then 1
            else 0
        end
    end;
go

create function [EngineModule].[Check_Engines_Func2]
(
    @Horsepower as int
)
returns bit
as
    begin
        return case
            when @Horsepower < 1000
            then 1
            else 0
        end
    end;
go
```

```
create function [EngineModule].[Check_Engines_Func3]
(
    @Fuel as nvarchar(max)
)
returns bit
as
    begin
        return case
            when @Fuel in
            (
                N'gas',
                N'diesel',
                N'propane'
            )
            then 1
            else 0
        end
    end;
go

create table [EngineModule].[Engines]
(
    [Id] int not null identity,
    [Cylinders] tinyint not null,
    [Horsepower] int not null,
    [Fuel] nvarchar(max) not null,
    [Description] nvarchar(max) not null,
    constraint [PK_Engines] primary key clustered ([Id]),
    check ([Horsepower] between 0 and 65535),
    constraint [Check_Engines] check ([EngineModule].[Check_Engines_Func]([Cylinders]) = 1),
    constraint [Check_Engines1] check ([EngineModule].[Check_Engines_Func1]([Cylinders])↵
  = 1),
    constraint [Check_Engines2] check ([EngineModule].[Check_Engines_Func2]([Horsepower])↵
  = 1),
    constraint [Check_Engines3] check ([EngineModule].[Check_Engines_Func3]([Fuel]) = 1)
);
go

create table [CarTypeExample].[Cars]
(
    [Id] bigint not null identity,
    [Mfr] nvarchar(max) not null,
    [Model] nvarchar(max) not null,
    [Year] int not null,
    [Engine] int not null,
    constraint [PK_Cars] primary key clustered ([Id]),
    check ([Year] between 0 and 65535),
    constraint [FK_Cars_Engine_EngineModule_Engines] foreign key ([Engine]) references↵
 [EngineModule].[Engines] ([Id]),
    constraint [Check_Cars] check ([CarTypeExample].[Check_Cars_Func]([Year]) = 1),
    constraint [Check_Cars1] check ([CarTypeExample].[Check_Cars_Func1]([Year]) = 1)
);
```

```
go

create table [$MRuntime.EngineModule].[Engines_Labels]
(
    [Label] nvarchar(444) not null,
    [Value] int not null,
    constraint [PK_Engines_Labels] primary key clustered ([Label]),
    constraint [FK_Engines_Labels_Value_EngineModule_Engines] foreign key ([Value])↵
 references [EngineModule].[Engines] ([Id]) on delete cascade
);
go

create index [IR_Engine] on [CarTypeExample].[Cars] ([Engine]);
go

create table [$MRuntime.CarTypeExample].[Cars_Labels]
(
    [Label] nvarchar(444) not null,
    [Value] bigint not null,
    constraint [PK_Cars_Labels] primary key clustered ([Label]),
    constraint [FK_Cars_Labels_Value_CarTypeExample_Cars] foreign key ([Value]) references↵
 [CarTypeExample].[Cars] ([Id]) on delete cascade
);
go

create index [IR_Value] on [$MRuntime.EngineModule].[Engines_Labels] ([Value]);
go

create function [$MRuntime.EngineModule].[LookupInEngines_Labels]
(
    @name as nvarchar(max)
)
returns table
as
    return
        select top (1)
            [t3].[Id] as [Id],
            [t3].[Cylinders] as [Cylinders],
            [t3].[Horsepower] as [Horsepower],
            [t3].[Fuel] as [Fuel],
            [t3].[Description] as [Description]
        from [$MRuntime.EngineModule].[Engines_Labels] as [p]
        cross apply
        (
            select [$Engines3].[Id] as [Id],
                [$Engines3].[Cylinders] as [Cylinders],
                [$Engines3].[Horsepower] as [Horsepower],
                [$Engines3].[Fuel] as [Fuel],
                [$Engines3].[Description] as [Description]
            from [EngineModule].[Engines] as [$Engines3]
            where [$Engines3].[Id] = [p].[Value]
        ) as [t3]
```

```
            where [p].[Label] = @name;
    go

    create index [IR_Value] on [$MRuntime.CarTypeExample].[Cars_Labels] ([Value]);
    go

    create function [$MRuntime.CarTypeExample].[LookupInCars_Labels]
    (
        @name as nvarchar(max)
    )
    returns table
    as
        return
            select top (1)
                [t3].[Id] as [Id],
                [t3].[Mfr] as [Mfr],
                [t3].[Model] as [Model],
                [t3].[Year] as [Year],
                [t3].[Engine] as [Engine]
            from [$MRuntime.CarTypeExample].[Cars_Labels] as [p]
            cross apply
            (
                select [$Cars2].[Id] as [Id],
                    [$Cars2].[Mfr] as [Mfr],
                    [$Cars2].[Model] as [Model],
                    [$Cars2].[Year] as [Year],
                    [$Cars2].[Engine] as [Engine]
                from [CarTypeExample].[Cars] as [$Cars2]
                where [$Cars2].[Id] = [p].[Value]
            ) as [t3]
            where [p].[Label] = @name;
    go

    commit transaction;
    go
```

Index

Symbols

! exclamation point, indicating conflict, 97, 101
% binary infix modulo operator, 125
>>> Find('|') Intellipad mini-buffer command prompt, 17
* asterisk
    indicating data changed but not saved, 91, 97, 101
    as Kleene operator, 43, 84
    next to buffer name, 14
    with slash (/*...*/), indicating block comments, 82
. dot operator, 127
/ forward slash, 82, 213
// double slashes, 82, 116
? question mark
    indicating stale data, 97, 102
    as Kleene operator, 43, 84
: ascription operator, 118, 122
[ ] brackets, 123
{ } curly braces, 36, 122
| pipe, 42, 213
+ plus sign, 42, 84

A

abstract syntax trees (ASTs), vs. M Graph, 53
alpha characters, 42
ascription operator (:), 118, 122
asterisk (*)
    indicating data changed but not saved, 91, 97, 101
    as Kleene operator, 43, 84
    next to buffer name, 14
    with slash (/*...*/), indicating block comments, 82
ASTs (abstract syntax trees), vs. M Graph, 53

B

BDL (Base Domain Library), 173, 176
Behaviors option (Intellipad Edit menu), 19
block (multi-line) comments (/*... */), 82
brackets ([ ]), indicating lists, 123
buffer transforms, 207
buffer view, 14
buffers, 14, 207

C

Call() command (Intellipad mini-buffer), 25, 215
CarComponents (sample) model, 81–113
    CarModel file and, 85–89
    CarTypeExample module and, 118, 128–133, 229–234
    deploying, 85–87
    derived types and, 118
    Drive Train subsystem and, 91
    editing in SQL Server, 95
    extents for, 129
    MfgComponentModel and. *See* MfgComponentModel
    My Car sample record and, 90
    quality control system for, 139–161
    Suspension subsystem and, 92
    T-SQL code for, generating, 131
    viewing/adding data to, 87–93
catalogs (list of components), 211
claims-based security, 163
ClearMru() command (Intellipad mini-buffer), 25, 215
CloseBuffer() command (Intellipad mini-buffer), 25, 215
collection operators, 123
collection type (M language construct), 120, 122–125

You Need the Companion eBook

Your purchase of this book entitles you to buy the companion PDF-version eBook for only $10. Take the weightless companion with you anywhere.

We believe this Apress title will prove so indispensable that you'll want to carry it with you everywhere, which is why we are offering the companion eBook (in PDF format) for $10 to customers who purchase this book now. Convenient and fully searchable, the PDF version of any content-rich, page-heavy Apress book makes a valuable addition to your programming library. You can easily find and copy code—or perform examples by quickly toggling between instructions and the application. Even simultaneously tackling a donut, diet soda, and complex code becomes simplified with hands-free eBooks!

Once you purchase your book, getting the $10 companion eBook is simple:

❶ Visit **www.apress.com/promo/tendollars/**.

❷ Complete a basic registration form to receive a randomly generated question about this title.

❸ Answer the question correctly in 60 seconds, and you will receive a promotional code to redeem for the $10.00 eBook.

233 Spring Street, New York, NY 10013

Offer valid through 11/10.